Freedom and Constraint

H. M. Gluckman, 1911 - 1975

Freedom and Constraint

A Memorial Tribute to Max Gluckman

Edited by Myron J. Aronoff

1976
Van Gorcum, Assen/Amsterdam, The Netherlands

© 1976 Van Gorcum & Comp. B.V., Assen, The Netherlands

No parts of this book may be reproduced in any form, by print, photoprint, microfilm or any other means without written permission from the publisher.

ISBN 90 232 1392 0

Printed in the Netherlands by Van Gorcum, Assen

Table of Contents

Myron J. Aronoff, Freedom and Constraint: A Memorial Tribute to Max Gluckman 1

Don Handelman, Some Contributions of Max Gluckman to Anthropological Thought 7

Elizabeth Colson, From Chief's Court to Local Court 15

Joyce Pettigrew, Conflict Escalation in the Punjab 30

Bruce Kapferer, Conflict and Process in a Zambian Mine Community 50

Sholomo Deshen, Of Sign and Symbols: The Transformation of Designations in Israeli Electioneering 83

Moshe Shokeid, Conviviality Versus Strife 101

A. J. F. Köbben, The Periphery of a Political System 122

Myron J. Aronoff, Ritual Rebellion and Assertion in the Israel Labor Party 132

Max Gluckman. Summarised Curriculum Vitae (30-9-1974) . . . 165

Biography and Publications, Education and Posts 169

Freedom and constraint:
A memorial tribute to Max Gluckman

Editorial Introduction

The shocking news of the death of Max Gluckman produced not only a void in anthropology, but also produced a deep sense of personal grief and loss for all who knew him well. Many of us felt impelled as immediately as possible to register our respect and affection for the memory of this great man in some tangible way. This memorial volume is the manifestation of the fulfillment of this desire. The fact that so many scholars amidst their many commitments were not only willing, but were anxious to give top priority to writing original essays dedicated to Max's memory within 3 months is surely an impressive testimony to the respect and affection which he inspired in his colleagues and friends.

I was warned by isolated skeptics that it was impossible to produce articles of scholarly merit within such a short time of sufficient number to fill one issue of our journal. The results of my solicitation of contributions necessitated the joint publication of this double issue. And I am proud to announce that the articles in this volume were given the regular process of evaluation received by all articles published in POLITICAL ANTHROPOLOGY. This is a testimony to the dedication of the contrubuting authors, the members of the editorial board of PA, and the experts who aid them in making their evaluations. I am grateful to all of these people and to our publishers for making this publication possible.

It is true that major essays comprehensively evaluating Max Gluckman's contributions to political anthropology could not be completed in time for this volume. This would have required more time than we had in order to meet our publication deadline. Such evaluative essays will no doubt appear in the several memorial volumes presently being prepared which will appear in the more distant future. However, Don Handelman's essay provides the most brilliant concise summary of Gluckman's contributions which could have possibly been written on such short notice (it was originally read at an 'in memoriam' colloquium in honor of Max held at the Hebrew University of Jerusalem on April 24, 1975). Handelman outlines with great insight and originality Gluckman's contributions relating them to fields of research which, to the best of my knowledge, have thus far not been publically recognized. I am convinced that Handelman's essay will be a major reference for all future evaluations of Gluckman's contributions to the field. This essay highlights and introduces the major concepts which are elaborated through the analysis of diverse ethnographic studies by the other contributors.

Each author elaborates a theme or themes which was either central to or was stimulated by the teaching interests and writings of Gluckman. All of the contributors, except Colson and Köbben, were former students of Gluckman. All had been closely associated with Gluckman as colleagues and/or friends for many years, starting with Elizabeth Colson's close association with Max which dates back to 1946 to some of the younger contributors who were among Gluckman's last doctoral students and who have been closely associated with him for the past ten years.

The contributing scholars represent a variety of nationalities as is befitting an international journal, including the U.S.A., the United Kingdom, Australia, Holland and Israel. The essays deal with a rich variety of socio-cultural settings including Surinam, Africa, India and Israel which reflects the wide diversity of Gluckman's own interests. If the ethnographic coverage of Israeli society appears to be somewhat over-represented, this does not only reflect the bias of the editor's personal networks, since from 1963 until his death in Jerusalem Max had devoted his major efforts towards organizing and supervising the most comprehensive anthropological research scheme that has ever been conducted in Israel. This research, which involved over a dozen scholars and has already resulted in several major publications (cf. the Manchester University Press series on Israeli society), occupied the major part of Max's time and efforts during the last 12 years. Max Gluckman had both strong intellectual and emotional interest in Israel, and I am therefore convinced that he would not have objected to having an ample representation of the fruits of his impressive scientific investment in the anthropological investigation of Israeli society represented in the first major tribute to his memory.

With considerable insight Handelman identifies as the main theme running through almost all of Gluckman's writings 'the relationship between institutional constraint and individual choice in social systems'. His abiding interest in the problem of 'order and social control in society', his perceived dialectic between social cohesion and social conflict, and the many other themes on which he wrote so extensively are united in their relationship to this central interest. This theme also runs throughout and unites all of the essays in this volume.

Elizabeth Colson's analysis of the evolution of local courts in Southern Zambia is compared and contrasted with Gluckman's work among neighboring peoples. In comparing her analysis of the development of Tonga courts with Gluckman's work on the Barotse, Colson follows Gluckman's main focus. As she states, 'he (Gluckman) stressed that the courts could not be understood divorced from the society that created them and of which they formed a part. He urged that one must examine how the courts expressed and acted upon the kinds of interests held by those the courts served, both over whom the court had jurisdiction and those dominant in the larger political and economic universes to which the local people ultimately related'. She shows that the Lozi and Tonga 'viewed their courts in different fashions and tried to use them in rather different ways', and in so doing provides, within a truly comparative perspective, a fascinating account of continuity and change in a local judicial system within the context of wider societal and political changes. In addition she gives us greater insight into the fascinating process of how people attempt to use and manipulate the social institutions which order and constrain their behavior.

Joyce Pettigrew deals with the spread of conflict from the village level through the state political system and analyses the features of rural Punjab society which facilitate and structure the expansion of such socio-political strife. As she points out 'The spread of conflict from a small unit into the wider system is a recurring theme in Gluckman's writing'; and following Gluckman, Pettigrew argues for the need to analyse village disputes within the context of a single system comprised of both local and state arenas. Pettigrew makes an important original contribution to the definition and analysis of factions as a means of settling disputes, of resolving conflict, and of structuring protest by integrating different levels of the political system. In addition to presenting, through an excellant example of the use of extended case analysis, an engrossing account of Jat social structure and political process Pettigrew makes an important theoretical point in arguing that the multiple affiliations incorporated into the factional structure lead to factional cohesion, but through the polarization of the factions prevent the wider integration of rural society.

A strikingly similar theme is developed by Kapferer in his richly detailed account of conflict in a Zambian mine community, which follows the basic framework of Gluckman's analysis of conflict. However, Kapferer, like the other contributors to this volume, is not uncritical of certain aspects of Gluckman's concepts which he adapts and develops. He is particularly critical of some of the functions which Gluckman attributed to conflict and of the processes which lead to their resolution. Kapferer stresses that 'the extent to which loyalties of a more inclusive nature 'unifying' individuals and groups at one level necessarily suppress the operation of more exclusive loyalties and interests at another'. The fact that Kapferer and Pettigrew, working independently with very different ethnographic material, have come to almost identical theoretical conclusions tends to give added weight to the importance of their contributions to, and adaptation of Gluckman's writing on social conflict and its relation to societal integration and cohesion.

Max and I had many long conversations, even friendly arguments, and extensive conversations about my application and adaptation of his concept of 'rituals of rebellion' to a 'modern' political party in a contemporary 'complex' society. Although sensitive to, and respectful of the specific definitions Max used in analysing 'traditional' societies, I have long been convinced that his concepts could profitably be adapted and applied to similar phenomina in contemporary society. Max was not at first convinced and insisted that I use quotation marks to qualify my use of such terms as 'taboo' and 'ritual' in contemporary contexts. Although he was not a man who was easily convinced to do so, he eventually changed his position to the extent that he finally agreed that the events I analyse in my contribution on the Standing Committee of the Israel Labor Party could be legitimately labeled ritual (without quotation marks) and that indeed the application of the concept ritual of rebellion was appropriate in that it provided an important dimension in understanding the behavior of the actors in question. The unforgetably stimulating discussions at the Burg Wartenstein Symposium no. 64 on Secular Ritual were important factors which influenced both Gluckman's change of position and my analysis of the 'assertive' aspects of the ritual proceedings I report here. Significantly my analysis owes a great debt to the original contributions of Gluckman, Victor Turner who was in turn influenced by his teacher Gluckman, Terrence Turner, who was influenced by Victor Turner... in a chain of intellectual kinship of which I am convinced Max would have whole-heartedly approved. My analysis ties in with the 'grand theme' in the sense that I deal with the attempts of political actors to assert spheres of freedom through symbolic action within an essentially highly constraining, if not oppressively rigid, political structure.

Still within the sphere of symbolic activity, Shlomo Deshen's stimulating analysis of the dynamic processes through which signs and symbols change their character and mutate is an original anthropological contribution to the study of electioneering in particular and of culture change in general. Deshen's main premise is 'that symbols (and designations generally) are the elemental components of culture, and the study of culture change demands precise study of the dynamic processes pertaining to symbols'. In his analysis of the electioneering activities of politicians and supporters of religions parties among North African immigrants in Israel, Deshen documents the manipulation of religious symbols in secular political contexts which lead to the 'activation and transformation of political signs and symbols'. He also provides us with a case study of the process whereby cultural inovation is brought about through the activities of individuals who exercise choice and initiative in an attempt to make political gains (whether they be of a personal or collective, material or normative nature).

While most of the essays in this volume deal with standardized forms of conflict resolution, Moshe Shokeid discusses more spontaneous gatherings of political opponents in impromptu leisure activities. Shokeid argues, rightly in my opinion, that in contrast to 'man in strife' who has been given considerable attention in the literature, 'the convivial man' who is guided by an etiquette of sociability and polite behavior has been neglected. I have argued elsewhere that, 'There is a danger when one focuses analysis primarily on political relationships in a community that one may over-emphasize incidents of social strife and neglect or undervalue the importance of incidents of social cooperation and feelings of general consensus'; and I give several explanations why I think this happens (Aronoff, 1974:48-9). Shokeid vividly describes the interaction of persons normally in strife with one another, in jocular and friendly social festivities. He argues that by introducing these types of informal encounters into the analysis of the dynamics of social relationships in rural and other 'face-to-face' societies, social mechanisms can be discovered which help to explain how such societies do not disintegrate in the face of endemic oppositions and strife. Shokeid points out that although explanations why I think this happens (Aronoff, 1974:48-9). Shokeid vividly the hostile attitudes and relationships did not change significantly as a result of the friendly interactions at such parties, they provided temporary relief from the ongoing hostility and dispute. He argues that these sudden and temporary changes of heart 'prompted the belief and fostered the illusion that the prevailing conflict might one day vanish forever'. I would add that both phenomina, i.e. the respite from conflict and the hope this fostered that some day such amicable relationships would prevail, are respectively tangible and symbolic acts of men asserting themselves against the web of institutionalized relationships of strife in which they are immeshed within the limited sphere of freedom available to them in such social contexts.

We return to a similar theme in a very different cultural environment with André Köbben's vivid account of how the Djuka of Surinam attempt to manipulate the will of the Paramount Chief (*Granman*) (and the gods) to their own advantage, and yet are seriously constrained in the degree of freedom in which they can do so by their deeply held reverance for his authority and their fear of the mystical sanctions which they believe he can invoke. Köbben gives a sensitive portrayal and analysis of how men bound to their belief in ideological norms attempt to interpret, assert, and use aspects of these norms to their own advantage, but succeed in doing so only within clearly bounded limits. Köbben's account is reminiscent in this respect of Gluckman's analysis of the 'reasonable man' among the Barotse, in which, as Handelman perceptively states, Max developed a 'morphology of ideation, embedded in social contexts, and rooted in the problematics of inter-subjective communication'. I can only enthusiastically agree with Handelman's statement that, 'His 'reasonable man' is one of the finest arguments in anthropology against 'normative idealization' '.

A significant testimony to Max Gluckman – the teacher, represented in this volume is the obvious fact that he did not produce uncritical disciples. Max's students, while tremendously stimulated by his ideas, criticised and adapted them to meet the contengencies of new field situations which differed significantly in most cases from those studied by Max. It is a tribute to his great scholarly achievements that his original contributions are fruitfully applied to such a wide diversity of socio-cultural contexts in rapidly changing conditions, and to his greatness as a teacher that his former students retain not only great respect and affection for him, but have felt free to criticize, adapt, or even reject the original ideas of their teacher. Max Gluckman not only gave his students intellectual tools and set a high standard (through his personal example) of intellectual honesty and personal and professional integrity, he also strongly stressed his own deeply felt humanitarian values. As Joyce Pettigrew wrote (in personal correspondence), 'It was central to our teaching that a concern solely with culture, as a system of subjective value, would parochialize any effort towards understanding human society'. It is for all of these reasons and many more too numerous (and in some cases too peronal) to mention, that Gluckman's former students, in Handelman's words, 'With all their diverse interests and variant career lines, ... continue to acknowledge their common ancestor; and so their diverging approaches are often reconciled beneath a common and valued rubric – a heritage I think Max would approve of'.

Myron J. Aronoff

Some Contributions of Max Gluckman to Anthropological Thought*

DON HANDELMAN
The Hebrew University of Jerusalem

When Max came to anthropology, during the late 1920's, it was an infant discipline, still suckling on the remnants of unilinear evolutionism, and diffusionism – although our subject had begun to evolve in directions we recognize today, through Boasian ethnography, the functionalist formulations.
of Radcliffe-Brown, and the revolution in fieldwork stimulated by Malinowski. Max's leave-taking finds anthropology a healthy, diverse and burgeoning discipline – firmly grounded in the comparative study of man's works – his cultural forms, social institutions, and human relationships. Max's contributions to the emergence of anthropology have been profound – to the signal extent that many of the ideas he stimulated and developed are so much a part of anthropological parlance, that we often forget with whom they originated. For four decades this creative and synthetic mind provided anthropology with many of the foundations upon which we rest today. In this sense, my personal image of Max is that of a bridge spanning the growth and florescence of anthropology – but a bridge which continues to extend to the horizon as we tread its path.
He told me on a number of occasions that, when compared with his generation of anthropologists, our's had much more difficulty in making contributions to our subject – since everything that his generation wrote was new at the time. While this may have been so, only a few of his generation will be remembered as long, and as well, as Max will be, for his manifold accomplishments. Tonight I can mention only a few of these – part of his thinking on the problem of social order, an aspect of his work on law, and his effect on certain methodological advances in social anthropology.
Max had an abiding interest in the problem of order and social control in society. One great theme which reverberates throughout his work is that of the relationship between institutional constraint and individual choice in so-

---

* Read to an 'in memoriam' colloquium in honor of Max Gluckman, held at the Hebrew University of Jerusalem, April 24, 1975. Other participants were S. N. Eisenstadt and Moshe Shokeid.

cial systems. While he never resolved the nature of this balance, its on-going dialogue stimulated advances in both spheres. Early on he recognized, in contrast to the functionalism of Radcliffe-Brown, that social systems were integrated through different modes in time and space; and that these domains were interdependent – yet often discrepant, and sometimes contradictory. In turn, this led him to search for conceptions which could explain continuity and discontinuity in social order; and, more significantly, how continuities generated discontinuities, and how the latter in turn contributed to social cohesion.

In part, this thinking led him to historical analysis, in 'real' time, on the assumption that only a diachronic perspective provided a spectrum of data through which the forms of custom could be delineated, and which would provide evidence of the morphology of institutions in which they were embedded. In addition, his concern with social relationships led him to recognize the centrality of social conflict in human affairs – and the need to reconcile the problem of conflict with that of order. In regard to this problem he worked on materials from segmentary, or 'stateless', systems that lacked the formal apparatus of social control familiar to students of more complex societies, and also on materials from rudimentary East African kingdoms.

From these materials he developed his ideas about 'cross-cutting ties', where similar interests between kinds of persons cut across oppositions to bring about a reconciliation in those nodes of social structure which generated the greatest frequency of conflict. In 'The Peace and the Feud', a re-analysis of the Nuer, he demonstrated how exogamy and co-residence with non-kinsmen balanced the divisive effects of segmentary opposition, to prevent feuds and maintain social order. Here he wrote, I think profoundly:

> The smaller the area involved, the more numerous the social ties. But as the area narrows, the occasions which breed quarrels between men multiply; and here it is that their conflicting ties both draw them apart, and bring them into relationship with other people who see that settlement is achieved. In this way custom unites where it divides, co-operation and conflict balancing each other. (Gluckman 1956:23).

His concern with the divisiveness within cohesion led Max to re-examine certain first-fruits ceremonies among the South-Eastern Bantu; and to recognize that these were, in his terms, 'rituals of rebellion.' Such rituals openly expressed social cleavages and social tensions; where, for example, women asserted their dominance over men – in contrast to their usual subordination – and princes behaved as if they coveted the throne, while commoners openly derided established authority (Gluckman 1963:112). But such rituals were legitimated and validated by a social order which went unquestioned. Therefore these rituals emphasized that conflict between role categories existed within the valued confines of that order, and were not attempts to alter its morphology.

As was frequently the case with ideas that Max formulated, his students were able to carry them further. Thus Turner later demonstrated that such rituals stressed cohesiveness because the sacred order represented the highest plane of symbolic valuation and integration – therefore the sacred was simultaneously the strongest societal vessel within which to stress, and within which to contain social conflicts. The highest affirmation of social order thus encouraged and contained the most basic expressions of its dissolution; thereby re-affirming once again the ordering of the system.

Max then applied the formulation of 'rituals of rebellion' to the place of periodic civil wars in the kingdoms of South-East Africa, as cyclical or 'repetitive' mechanisms through which pursuit of the kingship canalized local territorial segments away from the tendency to split off from a kingdom, and so become independent. In this way, the conflicts of such wars of succession strengthened the over-riding value of the kingship itself, and thus the unity of the system, at the expense of the actual persons who filled the role of king.

In his initial formulation of 'rituals of rebellion' (the Frazer Lecture of 1952), Max still held to a central tenet of 'organic functionalism' – that the components, or institutions, of the system were *necessary* for its maintenance. However, in his introduction to 'Order and Rebellion in Tribal Africa', published in 1963, he wrote:

> I was still thinking in crude functional terms of institutions ... contributing to the maintenance of a rather rigidly conceived social structure (p. 20) ... I now *abandon altogether* the type of organic analogy for a social system with which Radcliffe-Brown worked and which led me to speak of civil war as being necessary to maintain the system. Social systems are not nearly as integrated as organic systems, and the processes working within them are not as cyclical or repetitive as are those in organic systems ... I think therefore much more in terms of series of social processes ... These are never perfectly adjusted; and hence processes do not cancel themselves out as in organic systems' (1963:38-39).

In reviewing 'Order and Rebellion', the American africanist, Ronald Cohen, wrote: 'This amazing recant, of which there are very few in anthropology, brings Gluckman much closer to contemporary social scientific thinking outside British anthropology' (1965:56).

While I think that the seeds of this shift in position are evident as early as 1940 (in his 'Analysis of a Social Situation ...'), I have dwelt on it at length because – criticisms to the contrary – Max's 'institutionalist' position was not a static one. In contrast to Radcliffe-Brown, who saw social process as simply the functioning of structure, his conception of 'the peace in the feud' and of 'rituals of rebellion' stressed a self-perpetuating and a self-integrating *dialectic* between cohesion and conflict which energized the political systems he studied. But, in terms of the shift in position quoted above, such systems did not exist in a perfect state of institutional integration. Therefore the contradictions in interests and values among institutions could again provide a basis for a dialectic with *directional thrust*.

Max was always eminently sensible in maintaining that if we had to comprehend opposition and conflict in order to analyze cohesion and social order, then we also had to comprehend social stability if we were to recognize 'true' social change. In shifting well away from 'organic functionalism', he cleared the decks for a re-consideration of social change, in his plenary address to the American Anthropological Association in 1966, which was entitled, 'The Utility of the Equilibrium Model in the Study of Social Change.'

Here Max maintained that a culture pattern, or an institution, had its own built-in 'time scale'. Further, that each institution in a society had a particular time-scale built into its structure – so that we could not analyze an institution unless we recounted its operation in terms of its particular time-scale, which he called its 'structural duration'. He defined the 'structural duration' of an institution as: '... that period of time required to work out the implications of its rules and customs within the biological, ecological, and social environment" (1968:221). An institution, then, followed through the phases and alterations *coded* within its structure, in a cyclical or oscillating fashion, until it presented the same form it had started from.

Three analytic problems then arose: (a) building a 'model' of an institution that accounted for its structural alterations in structural time; (b) connecting the interdependencies, and discontinuities, among the different structural durations of institutions within a social system; and (c) then 'throwing' these configurations of 'structural duration' into 'real time' or 'historical time' to account for two kinds of processes: (i) change resulting from the interplay of discontinuities in the external environment – (ecological changes, wars of conquest, culture contact, and so forth) – as they affected the institutional configurations of structural durations (process in structural time); and (ii) change resulting from the imperfect integration within the structural duration of an institution, and between the structural durations of complexes of institutions. Thus, under the most stable of circumstances, institutions oscillated through their different structural durations, generating an accumulation of small changes which resulted in what Max termed 'limited structural change.' These could culminate in 'radical structural change' – which, of course, could also result from major alterations in the societal environment.

In this work Max moved from the idea of a 'dialectic of balanced opposition' which maintained a system through time, to a conception of system which continuously generated internal change through discontinuities in its structural durations. In this conception, the 'relative stability' of institutions was maintained by their structural oscillations through historical time – a kind of fly-wheel or balance-wheel through history, in which lengthy durations of 'real time' had to pass before many of the discrepancies and discontinuities between structural durations, and within a structural duration, would become felt.

My own feeling is that this is a seminal work on social order – and I would essay a guess that if we are able to map the structual durations of institutions, and connect their unfolding through structural time to symbolic oppositions and transformations uncovered by the structuralists, we may begin to attain a goal which enchants many anthropologists – a developmental or generative 'code' to particular cultures.

Max is recognized as a pioneer of the anthropology of law, along with Hoebel and Schapera. His 'Judicial Process Among the Barotse', published in 1955, (Gluckman 1955), and 'The Ideas in Barotse Jurisprudence', published in 1963 (Gluckman 1963), provided a substantial forum for the development of ideas on, and methods of description of, social control in a tribal society. Yet I would like to touch on an aspect of this corpus which has not received sufficient attention.

Max considered himself an 'institutionalist' concerned, above all, with the normative applications of Barotse law. But I think his Barotse materials differ significantly from his other work, in presenting something of a 'phenomenological' position, at a time when this was quite unknown in British or American anthropology.

Perhaps this is most evident in his conception of the 'reasonable man' among the Barotse. He notes that '... in litigation these general rules (of law) have to cover a great variety of actual situations in life. They can only do so if the general moral ideas involved can be brought to bear on the particularities of a perhaps unique situation' (1963:191). Thus a process of intersubjective cultural understandings must mediate between formal norms and human actions – and Max set out to delineate this process through the conception of the 'reasonable man', '... by which abstract legal rules are focused on to the varied circumstances of life' (1963:199). Thus the 'reasonable man' enabled Barotse judges to interpret and evaluate litigants against culturally acceptable, but uncoded, standards, by bringing ' ... into their definitions many facets of Barotse life which are not ostensibly part of the law' (1963:180).

Using these folk precepts, Barotse judges evaluated litigants accooding to whether they behaved as would the 'reasonable incumbents of a particular role' – whether they behaved according to standards which a typical Barotse would find acceptable; or whether their behavior contained mitigating circumstances – I might note that 15 years later, American sociologists were defining the perception of 'deviance' according to whether 'conditions of failure' were present or not. In other words, whether a 'reasonable onlooker' could interpret an action as containing circumstances that explained or excused this behavior (McHugh 1970).

The folk ideas of the reasonable man thus mediated between formal norms and the vagaries of particular life-circumstances. While formal norms were limited in number, the potential number of particularistic life-situations which might require legal intervention were manifold. Hence the idea of the reasonable man contained a structure of accordian-like expansion – reasonable husbands, wives, landlords, tenants, princes, and reasonable times for reasonable things – all could be accomodated to match law and case.

Max's final point is a functional one – that this process of ideation enables the law, as an institution, to adapt, to cope with changes, and so to survive. However, to arrive at this conclusion he had to develop a morphology of ideation, embedded in social contexts, and rooted in the problematics of inter-subjective communication. His 'reasonable man' is one of the finest arguments in anthropology against 'normative idealization'. Outside of the anthropology of law it did not receive just recognition, possibly because Max came to be so closely identified – and incorrectly so – with the epithet of static structural-functionalism.

That this label was so ill-deserved is further demonstrated by Max's influence on methods that helped to delineate the situational selection of roles and identities in social life. Here most of the work was carried out by his students and close colleagues, after he had supplied the initial stimulus.

In 1940 Max first published an 'Analysis of a Social Situation in Modern Zululand', (Gluckman 1958), in which he analyzed a series of interrelated events to demonstrate how Zulus and Whites were intimately involved in a single social system. By the late 1950's, analyzing a social situation required taking a 'series of specific incidents affecting the same persons or groups through a period of time, and showing how these incidents ... are related to the development and changes of social relations among these persons and groups . . .' (1967:xv) – this was the extended case method.

Through this approach the dialectic between data and analysis intensified – for the anthropologist who presented extended cases could carve – or mutilate – his data in more limited ways. If his case included conflict, as well as cooperation, then he was bound to explain these phenomena in relation to one another, since his cast of characters would remain relatively constant. As the anthropologist was drawn closer to his data, he was made more aware of *variation,* for his actors appeared to exercise considerable choice in deciding to whom, and in what measure, they would relate in differing circumstances. Thus anthropologists became sensitive to the mediation of norms by situation and context. Norms were no longer seen as simply directing social life – but they were made relevant and applicable to situations through the interests and decisions of the cast of characters who inter-related with one another. While the study of morphology then became more complex, it was also drawn closer to, and derived from, the complexity of social life in different cultural contexts.

These developments continue to affect anthropological thought. In current political anthropology, the social situation has become transformed into concepts of 'social field' and 'arena', following the works of Turner and Bailey, students of Gluckman; while in the study of social relationships, the method of network analysis had its genesis in the works of Barnes and Clyde Mitchell, again students of Gluckman. In turn, Kapferer, a student of Mitchell and a younger colleague of Gluckman, has integrated network analysis with transactional theory.

Put simply, Max was a great educator, who trained two generations of students to respect data and the richness of cultures other than their own; and who imbued his students with a basic sets of assumptions about the nature and method of social analysis. With all their diverse interests and variant career-lines, most of them continue to acknowledge their common ancestor; and so their diverging approaches are often reconciled beneath a common and valued rubric – a heritage I think Max would approve of. And *we* pay tribute to a master craftsman whose artifice and artifacts will be well worth the attention and respect of generations of anthropologists to come.

LITERATURE CITED

COHEN, RONALD. 1965. Review Article. *American Anthropologist,* 67: 950-957.
GLUCKMAN, MAX. 1955. *The Judical Process Among the Barotse.* Manchester: Manchester University Press.
–. 1956. *Custom and Conflict in Africa.* Oxford: Basil Blackwell.

–. 1958. *Analysis of a Social Situation in Modern Zululand* (The Rhodes-Livingstone Papers, No. 28). Manchester: Manchester University Press.
–. 1963. *Order and Rebellion in Tribal Africa.* New York: The Free Press.
–. 1963a. *The Ideas in Barotse Jurisprudence.* New Haven: Yale University Press.
–. 1967. Introduction. In *The Craft of Social Anthropology.* Edited by A. L. Epstein pp. XI-XX. London: Social Science Paperbacks.
–. 1968. The Utility of the Equilibrium Model in the Study of Social Change. *American Anthropologist,* 70: 219-237.
McHugh, Peter, 1970. A Common-Sense Perception of Deviance. In *Recent Sociology,* No. 2. Edited by Hans Peter Dreitzel, pp. 152-180. New York: MacMillan.

From Chief's Court to Local Court*

The Evolution of Local Courts in Southern Zambia

ELIZABETH COLSON
University of California, Berkeley

Introduction: This article contrasts the working of 'native' or chiefs' courts, in colonial Northern Rhodesia, with that of their descendants, 'local' courts of independent Zambia, which are constituted under Local Courts Act No. 20, 1966, as revised in Local Courts Act No. 54, 1972.
Zambia is one of the few African countries which still maintain courts staffed by local men appointed to administer the customary law of their people. Although I am concerned only with the courts of the Plateau and Gwembe Tonga of Mazabuka and Gwembe Districts, comparable changes have gone on elsewhere in Zambia, including Barotseland about whose legal system Max Gluckman wrote so much and so cogently.

* This article is based on field research in Mazabuka District (including the area later gazetted as Choma District), August 1946-September 1947, June 1948-August 1950, September 1968; and in Gwembe District July 1949, September 1956-September 1957, January 1960, September 1962-September 1963, July-August 1965, September 1968 (3 days), July-December 1972, June-August 1973. Field work through 1963 was supported by the Rhodes-Livingstone Institute, now the Institute for African Studies in the University of Zambia. The Institute also provided logistic support and hospitality on all futher visits. The 1965 visit was supported by the African Studies Committee of the Social Science Research Council and American Council of Learned Societies; the 1968 visit by the Kafue Basin Study Team of the Zambian Government; the 1972 and 1973 visits by Grant GS-3295 of the National Science Foundation held jointly with Professor Thayer Scudder of the California Institute of Technology. The research Committee, University of California, Berkeley, has provided funds to assist the analysis of some of the data. I am much indebted to my colleague, Thayer Scudder, who has shared the long-term study of Gwembe District since 1956 and has made his field notes available to me. Benjamin Shipopa served as my clerk/interpreter in Mazabuka District and on the first visits to Gwembe District. I am grateful to the many chiefs and cousellors, court clerks and messengers, and parties to disputes, who discussed cases with me over the years, but owe a special debt of gratitude to Chiefs Chona and Chipepo and their courts. James Chinjavata, Local Courts Advisor for Zambia, discussed with me the evolution of the local court system. I must also thank the Anthropological Colloquium of the University of Virginia for an opportunity to present an earlier version of this paper in November 1973.

In a collection of essays devoted to his memory, it seems appropriate to turn to the body of data on Tonga courts which has accumulated over many visits to Zambia. Gluckman had a special interest in the Tonga among whom he had worked in 1945 as a member of a team examining land-holding. I began my own observation of Tonga courts in 1946-47 as an officer of the Rhodes-Livingstone Institute under Gluckman's direction. Over the years we had many discussions on the Tonga material and the contrasts with the Barotse system and on changes in the court system of Zambia. Our last discussion, in August 1974, was evidence of his continued interest in having more published on the Tonga courts. We talked then about procedures, rather than about the illumination that can come from the analysis of a particular case (Gluckman, 1973). He was perhaps most interested in my report that the courts still retained much of their old character as of 1973 and that they had not yet been replaced by magistrates courts as planned at the time of his last visit to Barotseland in 1966 (Gluckman, 1967, pp. 427-428).

Gluckman's own contribution to comparative jurisprudence and the anthropology of law was firmly based on his own field work among Zulu and the people of Barotseland, including the dominant Lozi. He had therefore worked in communities characterized by close-knit social networks whose members perforce played many roles as they interacted with each other. Such communities Gluckman called 'multiplex'. He stressed the inherently moral quality of the activities in which members of such communities could engage themselves, since each action could have repercussions over the whole field of social life. He saw the judicial process as firmly embedded in the on-going life of active people who tried to cope with the inevitable clash of personal and group interests by using a great number of devices for avoiding, damping down, mediating, adjudicating, or attempting to transcend anger, jealousy, envy, cupidity and arrogance. The court was only one device and usually it was only one stage in an on-going process of social relationships. On his 1966 visit to Barotseland, when he tried to trace the subsequent careers of the disputes he had recorded in the 1940s, he found that 'in the type of relationships under examination, a case in court is a climax to one set of events, and sets in train other events (Gluckman, 1967, p. 437).'

Unfortunately THE ROLE OF THE COURTS IN BAROTSE LIFE was never finished to stand beside the two books which were to have been part of the same trilogy: THE JUDICIAL PROCESS AMONG THE BAROTSE OF NORTHERN RHODESIA (1955 and 1967) and THE IDEAS IN BAROTSE JURISPRUDENCE (1965). But in these volumes and in the many essays he wrote on the subject of law, he stressed that the courts could not be understood divorced from the society that created them and of which they formed a part. He urged that one must examine how the courts expressed and acted upon the kinds of interests held by those the courts served, both those over whom the court had jurisdiction and those dominant in the larger political and economic universes to which the local people ultimately related.

Tonga Courts in the 1940s: The judicial systems of Barotseland and the Tonga districts of Southern Province had certain fundamental differences in the 1940s, which stemmed from the very different natures of their political and social orders. The Lozi and other people of Barotseland were heirs of an ancient kingdom and knew a hierarchy of officials and courts, with the king's court the apex of the system to which all appeal ultimately flowed. A Barotse citizen was a subject of the king and had the right to justice from the king, either directly or through his subordinates. The Northern Rhodesia Native Courts Act of 1929 only recognized what was already a very effective set of judicial institutions and formalized the means whereby appeal could go from the king's court to the territorial judiciary.

The Tonga had been raided by Lozi, and Ndebele, and had sometimes sent tribute to the Lozi to buy themselves free from attack, but they settled their own disputes in local moots which were face to face confrontations of kin groups, with their supporters, or they used mediators who negotiated with each other and their own principals to avoid confrontation. Though in one or two portions of their territory chieftainship was recognized, for the most part they had neither courts nor chiefs nor any willingness to recognize the right of others to come to decisions that would determine their lives. A hierarchy of authority came to them with the colonial regime. They first knew courts either as captives among Lozi or Ndebele or in the person of early officials of the British South Africa Company who regarded themselves as judges because they were administrators. The Company appointed local men as chiefs and these in turn were given the duty of hearing cases brought before them by the people they were said to represent. The 1929 Native Authority act served to formalize the judicial authority of these appointed representatives of the administration. It also consolidated the many small chieftaincies into larger units under the few chiefs who survived the winnowing process and gave larger areas of jurisdiction to their courts. The courts then handled not only the affairs of a few neighbourhoods whose people were in close association with the chief, but could also claim the right to hear cases of people who lived miles from court, were strangers to the chief and his associates, and regarded the chief as a usurper. Nevertheless, in 1946 the courts were the most popular aspect of the native authority system and adjudication of disputes the most important function of the system.

Different as the social orders of Barotseland and Tonga country may have seemed, the courts were enmeshed in the same larger system. The colonial government was attempting to mold the judical procedures of native courts throughout the territory to a common pattern, even though the courts were expected to administer different bodies of customary law. But the resemblance between Tonga and Barotse courts was also based on another historical factor. When the courts were first established in Tonga country, the chiefs looked to Barotseland for a model and in many instances appointed Lozi residents in their villages as assessors or court clerks on the theory that Lozi knew how courts should be held. By 1946 all counsellors and court clerks were Tonga, but the first appointees had left their imprint on the system. That Tonga courts used 'the reasonable man' as a key concept in their cross-examination and summing up may be a legacy of that period.

Nevertheless, Lozi and Tonga viewed their courts in different fashions and tried to use them in rather different ways. In Barotseland the courts derived much of their dignity from the respect owed to the king and his officials as representatives of the power and tradition of the Barotse nation. The Tonga have the maxim, 'Any man may call himself a chief (*mwaami*, which once was used for any rich man or man with followers), but that does not mean that we will follow him.' Here it was the award of a court by the administration that gave each chief his legitimacy in the eyes of most of his people. In a sense the court was his office. But the Tonga did not regard their chief as their superior, nor did they rank courts in any hierarchy of authority and appeal. They saw no reason why they should take their cases to one chief rather than another or why they should accept the verdict of any court if it did not suit their convenience. A case considered settled in one court could turn up a few months later in another, be carried to a third, perhaps then to appear in the Appeal Court (held four times a year when chiefs with their counsellors sat both as the Native Authority and the Native Appeal Court for the district). The loser at that point might take the case back to some chief's court and so on and on (Colson, 1948, pp. 11-12).

In this the Tonga behaved much like the Tiv of Nigeria, another egalitarian people, of whom Bohannan (1957, p. 64) reports, 'Tiv litigants would seem to believe that the proper and correct solution of a dispute 'exists'. It 'is'. The task of the judges is to find it. In the old days the principal litigants would go from one elder of the community to another until they discovered one who could penetrate the details of the case and emerge with this 'correct' solution . . . It is obvious to the Tiv that when a right decision has been reached, both litigants will concur in it . . .' The Tonga do not seem to have shared this conviction that there must be a right solution, but they were not deterred from seeking a decision in their favour by a fear that a court would fine the persistant suitor for contempt of court. Most used a court to attempt to find a solution, but this did not mean that they would follow the words of the court. Others used the court as one more arena in which to continue confrontations with rivals or enemies and wanted to score points or win a victory rather than find a solution. In this they carried forward the tactics of the moot into the new arena (Epstein, 1973, p. 661).

If the Tonga ranked courts it was in terms of the wisdom and influence of their members and the convenience of location and day of hearing. Ranking was situational and varied through time and in respect to different cases. They chose to summon each other in the court that momentarily served their interests best. Courts competed with each other for popularity since a full case book was regarded by the court and the district office as evidence of the importance of the chief and his popularity among his followers. Chiefs and counsellors, even court clerks who were more likely to be sticklers about procedure, were prepared to accept all comers, although even in 1946 they might take the precaution to direct immediate kinsmen to the court of another chief to avoid the charge of favouritism.

The elaborate political structure of Barotseland found its echo in the Barotse courts where court officials had their appropriate functions and spoke in due term. The Tonga, who dealt with each other in simpler terms, viewed their courts as functionally undifferentiated although they knew that chiefs, counsellors, court clerks, and messengers had different titles, insignia and salaries. Usually the court messengers stood, the chief sometimes sat in a room behind the bench talking with visitors, and the counsellors and clerk sat on the bench with the clerk writing the brief record; but any one of the court members might cross-examine, take notes, and go into the huddle from which the verdict was announced. If the chief was not present, they announced the verdict as his and told him about it afterwards. Officially the chief controlled the court, but court clerks, who more frequently met with district officers and were expected to be able to explain what had been done and why, sometimes tried to usurp the chief's authority and run the court on lines they thought the district officers would approve. A case heard in the Chipepo Court, Gwembe District, in July 1949, illustrates something of the tensions existing within a court whose members did not see their roles as clearly differentiated.

Case I

The case involved the citing of the men of a nearby village who had failed to turn out to build the camp for the District Commissioner and other chiefs summoned to attend a meeting of the Native Authority to be held at Chipepo. The men were also alleged to have spoken abusively to the district messenger who had summoned them to work. Some of the defendants had been fined and told to leave the court for a short time. The chief had been counting the money they had paid in fines which he then handed to the clerk.

Clerk: Before the district messenger left, he said we must charge each of them £ 6.

Counsellor: What can we do? They have paid. We are not sure that they did use abuse (*kutukila*) to the messenger. We only heard this from the messenger. Perhaps we will get £ 6 from all of them together.

The clerk insists that they ought to pay more.

Chief: No, they will pay only £ 1 each. We have been charging them only 10 shillings for running away from public work and now we have fined them £ 1.

Clerk: All right. It is up to the chief. If he doesn't want them to pay £ 6, they must pay a fine of 5 shillings.

Chief: Why do you say this about 5 shillings? Don't say that. It looks as though you are now showing contempt (*kutukila*) to me.

Clerk: They should pay. It is not all right to use abuse.

Counsellor: It is up to the chief.

Chief: I wonder! You never agree with the way I settle a case. When I say it, you ought to agree. When are you going to agree with me?

The clerk continued to grumble about the fines and the next defendant in the case was fined £ 2.

The clerks were the forerunners of the more professional courts which were to emerge later. But in the 1940s the courts maintained their close links with the local communities they served and reflected this both in their procedures and in their judgments. Spectators, including those involved in other cases, were very much part of the court. The court building stood in the chief's village, and men, women, and children wandered by, stood in the windows, and provided an appreciative audience for the drama of the court. Spectators could be converted into witnesses or assessors at a moment's notice. Points of custom were referred to older people sitting against the walls and anyone might be asked what he or she thought of particular behavior. The hum of approval or note of dissent, that underrode the presentation of the case and the process of cross-examination, guided the case, somewhat in the same way as the reaction of consultants guides the course of a divination, or, as Epstein reports, the progress of a Tolai moot (Epstein, 1973, pp. 660-661).

The authority of the court, such as it was beyond that given to it by the colonial administration, derived largely from this involvement of the general public in a forum in which contenders faced an emerging consensus backed by public opinion. If contenders refused to accept the collective wisdom, their penalty lay in the discomforts attendent on the continuance of their dispute or the nuisance of walking the miles to some other court which might or might not be in session and have time to give them a hearing. Since most cases involved disputes between neighbours or kinsmen, disputants either had strong motives for accepting a verdict which would allow them to continue to live on terms, or they were involved in long-term enmities which meant that they used the courts as arenas in which to carry on their confrontations rather than as a means of adjudication.

The court usually knew something of the background from which a case emerged. It might give a verdict on a particular point at issue and then explore the various stages which had led to this particular confrontation. It might decide that no case could be made which required a verdict but still probe the relationships and urge behavior appropriate to generous and upright men and women and attempt to show the contenders how they had departed from this standard and so involved themselves in dispute. The court might also decide that the original complaint was of little importance and devote itself to what it regarded as an actionable issue that had emerged through the process of the case. It would then give a verdict on that issue. In the course of the hearing it might transform plaintiff into defendant and vice versa or decide that the real case lay between the plaintiff and some one else in the court room who was then thrust into the defendant's position. Since it probed all aspects of a dispute, it recognized no statute of limitations: old quarrels, old debts, old claims to inheritance or bridewealths, and the action of kin now dead might be regarded as relevant. In this respect it behaved like the village moot, which still existed and still exists, though more and more it tries to model itself upon the court in its own procedures.

Tonga courts, and the local people served by the courts, held by the principle which Gluckman claimed was characteristic of the courts of multiplex societies, including the Barotse: *'ubi jus, ibi remedium.'* Unlike Lozi judges, Tonga chiefs and counsellors might declare themselves uncertain of what law might apply or how legal principles could be stretched to cover a case, but in 1946 this rarely troubled them unless they dealt with a case sent to them by administrative or technical officers since they sought a remedy for whatever it was that had led people to come before them (Gluckman, 1965, p. 1, 177). In Barotseland a powerful kingship exercised its authority 'through a hierarchy of councils which acted as parliaments, executives, and courts of justice: yet their proceedings in court, while highly marked by a distinctive etiquette, had no special procedures to restrict the search for redress by the allegedly aggrieved. Anyone could plead any suit in whatever words he himself pleased' (Gluckman, 1965, p. 4). As Gluckman said, 'One went to court and reported one's distress.' (Gluckman, 1965, p. 3). The etiquette of Tonga courts was of a simpler nature and such as it was it derived largely from Lozi appointed to the first native courts or from the district office, but otherwise the formulation stands. The court not only explored the issues and gave judgment: it also tried to convince those who heard the verdict that justice had been done. Those who left the court disconsolate or indignant might be called back with the comment, 'He (or she) doesn't understand. We must explain to him where he was wrong. He can't be happy about this decision until he understands where he was wrong.' The court was anxious that plaintiff, defendant, and witnesses concur in the verdict.

The informality of the court and the degree to which it reflected local opinion were linked to the composition of the court. None of its positions were full-time jobs. The court usually met for one day during the week and during the period of hard agriculture work might suspend operation altogether. Most of the time chief, counsellors, court clerks, and messengers busied themselves in the same occupations as other villagers, whose style of life they shared. They depended upon cultivation for their subsistence and were subject to the same rights and obligations as other men. When they left the court building they left behind them most of the trappings of authority associated with it and became more or less equals with their fellows. Unfortunately this also made them vulnerable to their fellows who might still hold them responsible for decisions they had made in the court. It was not uncommon for court messengers especially to be beaten if they encountered angry litigants at beer drinks in other villages before memories of court room humiliation had had a chance to fade. Chiefs and counsellors therefore attempted to find solutions that would keep the peace: court clerks who came more fully under the influence of the district office and legal concepts stemming from the magistracy, and who as men of some years of schooling saw themselves as members of an educated elite, were more inclined to stress simple solutions derived from legal principles.

The Reform of the Courts: Under the colonial system, one of the duties of the district office was the review of the case books from the native courts; decisions could be queried, courts required to rehear cases, and chiefs and counsellors reprimanded. Litigants indignant at a decision might report the court to the district office as unjust or corrupt. In a sense, the district officer sat in every court, influencing its judgements and procedures. But Tonga courts were particularly vulnerable to this influence, since Tonga chiefs and counsellors also depended upon the district office to underwrite their own authority. All knew that it was the administration that had created both chiefs and courts and those who flouted them also challenged the district administration. Frequently the court tried to obtain compliance with its decisions by urging, 'This is the law of the government (*mulao wa flumende*)'. and it maintained, 'We get the law from the government.' To the district office, chiefs and counsellors might plead the validity of custom, but in their own courts they stressed that they operated with a law derived from the European officials (Colson, 1948, pp. 10-11).

In the years after World War II, the courts came under closer scrutiny as the district staff increased, district officers had more time for touring, and colonial policy began to stress the importance of political and economic development rather than the maintenance of law and order. Whereas in the earlier years administrators were required to respect customary usages, they were now called upon to urge native authorities to legislate for 'development'. Courts increasingly became devices through which the new legislation was to be implemented. Since uniformity in organization and procedures was now policy, territorial wide training centers could be established to which chiefs, counsellors, and court clerks were sent to be taught their jobs. These jobs began to be defined as full-time occupations. Salaries were increased and a pension scheme came into existence. The administration encouraged the use of Native Authority funds to provide improved housing for chiefs and court clerks. All this meant that those in the system had more to lose if they antagonized district officers and others in the administration. The Tonga courts began to be staffed by semi-professional bureaucrats rather than by villagers with an understanding of local predicaments and a knowledge of the limits of customary behavior.

The courts also had to cope with the fact that they had jurisdiction over an increasingly differentiated population, whose members differed in education, occupation, wealth, religion, and style of life. Since Mazabuka District is an area with a large immigrant population from other districts and other regions of central Africa, the Tonga courts also had to contend with litigants who might appeal to different bodies of customary law as well as with educated men who argued that they should be subject to none. Many of the latter regarded the customary courts as one more instance of the inferior institutions provided for Africans in a multi-racial country and wished to be judged by 'European' law just as they wished to have the same education, living standards, jobs and political status as the Europeans. Gwembe District had a more homogeneous population until the early 1960s and until then its courts had less to contend with than those of Mazabuka District. They continued to draw largely upon local custom in their hearings. Yet even they began to adopt more formal procedures and to observe the hierarchy of appeals laid down by the Native Courts Advisor for the territory.

These reforms made the courts more vulnerable to the colonial administration. It also politicised the courts in a new fashion in the later days of the colonial period when those involved in political protest were cited before the courts and the courts were expected to uphold the power and legitimacy of the colonial regime through their decisions. Chiefs and counsellors were subject to dismissal if they refused or openly backed the new African political leaders who first contested the formation of the Federation of the Rhodesias and Nyasaland and then fought for an independent Zambia. Although the stated aim of the reforms of the court system was the development of a system in which the judiciary had neither an administrative nor a legislative role, the events of this period led to a blatant disregard of the principle. As members of the Native Authority, chiefs and counsellors were expected to pass legislation banning political party activity in their areas; then as administrators they were expected to arrest those who refused to obey the order; and finally as judges they were expected to sentence those who appeared before them. The Federal and Territorial governments tried to disguise the increasingly arbitrary nature of their rule by emphasizing that the chiefs were traditional leaders who spoke for the majority of their people against a lunatic fringe of political agitators. They continued to speak of traditional and customary law and confused this with justice and the popular will. They assumed they had all three at their disposal. By emphasizing custom, it was also possible for the administration to deny legal representation to those who appeared before the chiefs' courts, for lawyers trained in English law by definition knew nothing of the procedures or principles that governed local tribunals.

In Zambia, as elsewhere in Africa, the coming of independence found chiefs and their customary courts largely discredited among the political leaders and liable to challenge even among villagers who found the formality of court procedures more and more alien to them and who resented being called to account by the courts for offenses against one or other of the numerous technical regulations now on the books. The United National Independence Party pledged itself to the swift abolition of customary courts, except perhaps for land law, and to the introduction of a unified system of law for all of Zambia, to be administered through a single system of courts under trained magistrates (Gluckman, 1967, pp. 427-428). Villagers by then, at least in Tonga-speaking areas, found this prospect less appealing than some years before, as during the period of transfer of power they had found it possible to use the political party as a control on both chiefs and district administrators. In 1963 and 1965 they regarded the local court as the appropriate place to settle their own disputes if the court was conveniently located and had little fear that the court would attempt to impose unpopular technical rules upon them (Colson, 1971, pp. 198-199). The elite, however, continued to press for a unitary system.

The shortage of trained personnel and the expense of funding a more highly trained judiciary throughout the country led the government to settle for a more gradual phasing out of customary courts. In the interim period it has settled for removing the courts from the aegis of the chiefs, who are no longer permitted to preside or to participate officially in hearings. They have lost their judicial function, save as informal arbitrators and mediators, just as they have lost their administrative functions. They remain as a salaried corps of 'traditional leaders'. The courts have been placed directly under the Ministry of Justice, which seeks to bring the customary courts into close conformity with the standards of the legal profession through various training programs for personnel and close supervision of the work of the courts by Local Courts Advisors stationed in the various provinces. All this is in line with the slogan, 'One nation, one judiciary' (Spalding, Hoover, and Piper, 1969).

A. L. Epstein, in a brief discussion of the trend in post-independence Africa towards the abolition of customary law, points to the impact of an influential body of professional lawyers many of whom 'received their training overseas and returning home to take up practice, found themselves barred from appearing in the customary courts. Furthermore, given their own professional training, they tended to despise the non-technical rules and procedures of the customary law, and to express contempt for those who were able to administer it without the benefit of formal study in a law school.' (Epstein, 1974, pp. 38-39).

There were few trained African lawyers in Zambia at the time of independence, but the number has increased steadily since that time. They are likely to have an ideal of law and the judicial process based on training in Europe or America or in the new Law School of the University of Zambia. Their influence should continue the trend towards a single unitary legal system controlled by statute, precedent, and a body of technical rules which are uniform throughout the country.

Local Courts in 1972-73: By 1972 the local courts of Tonga country no longer seemed integral parts of the local scene. The chiefs had vanished from the court room and with them had gone the office of counsellor. Court buildings usually stood somewhat apart from villages, which meant that only those with business at court were likely to listen to cases and they were not encouraged to participate as chorus and spokesmen for public opinion. Adjudication was now the business solely of two robed justices (some of whom might have formerly served as counsellors). The justices composed the court, although the court clerk might still have a major influence on their decisions and the conduct of a case as the spokesman for the technicalities of the law. The reduction in size of the court was in line with national policy, developed by legal advisors in the Ministry of Justice who held that hearings were speeded up and cases settled more expeditiously with fewer justices. The Ministry of Justice was considering a policy of appointing only one justice who could then be given a higher salary and also required to have more legal training. One court clerk might serve two or more courts, alternating between them on some fixed schedule linked to days set for the hearing of cases and days set aside when he would be available to write out summons and other forms.

Justices were full-time employees, as were court clerks and messengers, and when not hearing cases they were expected to be available to consult with those who might need advice. Much sifting of cases therefore went on outside the court room, and the justices could hardly come to the hearing without some preconceived ideas about the case derived from the earlier encounter with plaintiff and plaintiff's supporters, and sometimes with the defendant as well if both had appeared at the same time to take out a summons and the justices had had to decide which should have the role of plaintiff. Often, of course, the justices had preconceived ideas based on earlier encounters with the litigants in other cases heard in the court. They dealt with known quantities, but the formality of the court procedure sought to deny this and assimilate the court to a system which maintains judicial ignorance.

The courts now concerned themselves with particular issues rather than with a generalized dispute, or sought to do so in line with the understanding of justices and court clerks that this was the appropriate procedure in adjudication. Justices made no pretense of an ignorance of the background of a case, but they refused to permit litigants to introduce what they now called irrelevant detail. Litigants might try to proceed in the old fashion, but the justices

From Chief's Court to Local Court

interrupted to tell them to stick to facts, not to digress, and that only the issues cited in the summons might be raised. If no legal issues were at stake, potential litigants were told not to bother the court with nonsense cases. Witnesses too were restrained from enlarging on what they knew and were told to answer specific questions and to avoid hearsay evidence.

The greatest continuity with the courts of the 1940s lay in the continued moral stance of the court itself. Justices lectured litigants and witnesses, much in the old manner, appealing to codes of honourable behavior as well as to points of law; and they continued to urge litigants to admit to their mistakes and to accept a verdict as just. They had no qualms about berating those in the court for their short-comings and passing moral judgments even when they felt inhibited from a legal verdict. Such procedures, however, seemed less effective than they had been, given the absence of a general audience representing the public and the refusal of the justices to explore the ramifications of a dispute and thereby seek a solution to its many discontents.

On the other hand, there was frequently less reason for the court to explore in depth given the fact that litigants belonged now to a differentiated society and frequently enough were no longer involved in the old multiplex sets of relationships. The court still handled divorce, adultery, elopement, impregnation and other cases of what could be called family law, but fewer such cases were on the docket. Villagers frequently preferred to settle their disputes through moots or mediators and used the threat of a court summons as a means to force an opponent to pay damages or rectify a wrong. If school teachers or other elite were involved in such cases, they usually tried to have them transferred to a magistrate's court where they could rely upon a lawyer to befuddle their village opponents. The local courts handled cases arising from crop-destruction by unherded livestock, where the issues were clearcut and there was no need to invoke the reasonable man. They also handled cases of assault, many of which involved chance-met strangers who got into an argument at one of the many beer halls that had sprung up in rural areas or at one of the village beers catering to all-comers. Even if the quarrel was between neighbours, it was recognized that in beer people fought and that it was the physical damage that had to be assessed rather than long-term discontents. Assault cases might also be taken to the police now stationed in rural areas and then before the magistrate, who could be summoned for a hearing, but the magistrate was likely to handle the case only as a criminal matter to be settled with a fine or prison sentence. Most victims preferred to bring a civil suit in the local court which would award them damages. Given the circumstances under which the assault usually took place, the court was the only means a victim had to force settlement since in cases between strangers the village or neighbourhood moot is useless.

Finally the courts scheduled many cases involving debt. A few were cases of disguised theft brought as civil suits because the plaintiffs were interested in compensation and the restoration of stolen property rather than the punishment of the offender, which would be the result if they laid a charge of theft before the police. Other debt cases, however, and these were the majority, were brought by shopkeepers trying to recover from customers who had been given credit. As small claims courts in the United States tend to be monopolized by corporations trying to collect rents and other debts (Nader, n.d.), so Tonga courts are more and more the locus of claims arising from the spread of businesses throughout the rural areas and the growth of impersonal relationships based on contract. The court may adjust the schedule of repayment to the debtor's financial circumstances, but it has no need to probe the overall relationship of creditor and debtor.

Legal advisors in the Ministry of Justice, seeing the declining number of cases adjudicated in some of the local courts, have pondered the advisability of reducing the number of courts in the interest of economy and efficiency. The reduction would make it more difficult for people to appeal to the courts since courts would become more widely spaced and difficult of access. The arguments for minimizing the number of courts ignores the continued importance of the local courts as an ultimate sanction that people use to bring their fellows to accept settlement of disputes through moots or mediators. Today the threat to take a recalcitrant opponent to court is still a very real one, as witness the nember of instances where a case is scheduled and then withdrawn from the docket because a defendant has agreed to settle after receiving a court summons. The further villagers must travel to reach a court, the less likely they are to be able to use it as an effective sanction.

The work of the local court cannot be understood apart from the larger social matrix, as Gluckman insisted. The local court forms an essential element in the total range of judicial resources available to villagers and others now working and living in the rural areas. The court's own procedures may make it less congenial to villagers than it once was, though more congenial to others who may use it, but the very unwillingness of villagers to become subject to its procedures has given it a new role in local litigation. The court is also evolving as the place where disputes can be settled that arise between those in a contractual relationship or between those who find themselves among strangers as they take advantage of the right to geographical and social mobility that citizenship in a modern state confers. They have no possibility of using the moot or the other devices open to those who count on continuity and the multiplexity of their relationships and so come more and more to depend upon the ability of the court to defend them.

LITERATURE CITED

BOHANNAN, PAUL, 1957. *Justice and Judgement Among the Tiv*. Oxford: Oxford University Press.
COLSON, ELIZABETH, 1948. Modern Political Organization of the Plateau Tonga, African Studies 7 (2-3): 1-14.
–. 1958, *Marriage and the Family Among the Plateau Tonga of Northern Rhodesia*. Manchester: Manchester University Press.
–. 1960, *The Social Organization of the Gwembe Tonga*. Manchester: Manchester University Press.
–. 1962, *The Plateau Tonga*. Manchester: Manchester University Press.
–. 1971, *The Social Consequences of Resettlemen*t. Manchester: Manchester University Press.
–. 1974, *Tradition and Contract*: The Problem of Order. Chicago: Aldine Press.
Epstein, A. L. 1954, Juridical Techniques and the Judicial Process: A Study in African Customary Law, *Rhodes-Livingstone Paper* No. 23. Manchester: Manchester University Press.
–. 1973, The Reasonable Man Revisited: Some Problems in the Anthropology of Law, *Law and Society Review*, Vol. 7, No. 4: 643-666.
–. 1974, Introduction, pp. 1-39 in A. L. Epstein, ed., *Contention and Dispute: Aspects of Law and Social Control in Melanesia*. Canberra: Australian National University Press.
GLUCKMAN, M. 1955. *The Juridicial Process Among the Barotse of Northern Rhodesia*. Manchester: Manchester University Press.
–. 1965, *The Ideas in Barotse Jurisprudence*. New Haven: Yale University Press.
–. 1967, *The Judicial Process Among the Barotse of Northern Rhodesia* (revised edition with two additional chapters). Manchester: Manchester University Press.
–. 1973, 'Limitations of the Case-Method in the Study of Tribal Law', *Law and Society Review*, Vol. 7, No. 4: 611-642.
NADER, L. In press 'Powerlessness in Zapotec and United States Society', in R. Adams and R. Fogelson, *The Anthropology of Power*. New York and London: Seminar Press.
SCUDDER, T. 1962, *The Ecology of the Gwembe Tonga*. Manchester: Manchester University Press.
SPALDING, FRANCIS O., EARL L. HOOVER and JOHN C. PIPER. 1970, 'One Nation, One Judiciary': The Lower Courts of Zambia, *Zambia Law Journal* Vol. 2, Nos. 1 & 2: V-XIV, 1-289.

Conflict Escalation in the Punjab[1]

JOYCE PETTIGREW
The Queen's University of Belfast

In this paper I will consider the spread of conflict from a small village into the state political system and the organisational features of rural Punjab society that facilitate such expansion. In this connection I will describe a series of incidents that occurred between 1940 and 1965. The spread of conflict from a small unit into the wider system is a recurring theme in Gluckman's writing. The data presented here will bear on another of his interests, namely that of delimiting suitable arenas for study in complex societies. The expansion of conflict is of interest in the context of three problems.

Firstly, it has certain methodological implications for traditional anthropological studies in India which usually have considered a village their main observation centre and, *a priori*, regarded it to be a unit of analysis. This tradition has continued despite the appropriate comments of Dumont and Pocock, many years ago, in an article entitled 'Village Studies' that

> 'The influence of anthropological methods elsewhere ... have created the fundamental supposition that the clue to an understanding of Indian society lies in the village.' (1957:26)

My data will indicate the usefulness of treating village, local area and state in a manner which portrays them to be one system. Village quarrels and local disputes frequently become state issues because of an already existing set of oppositions at state level and to which the respective disputants in these smaller units can align and with whom they find common cause by stressing the mutually beneficial aspects of an alliance. Village and local area disputes are thus so in name only as their political repercussions are rarely confined to the unit in which the incident first occurred. It is particularly factional loyalties and also ties of friendship and patronage and in some instances affinal links that establish connexions between the various parties to a dispute and which do not allow its containment in any one unit. Thus, secondly, in the Punjab rural areas, neither divisiveness nor cooperation is confined to small units. The wide ranging networks of co-operative ties characteristic of the Punjab rural scene seem neither to have been noted nor incorporated in the literature on development in rural India. This literature portrays India as consisting of innumerable isolated village societies. To take an example, the theme, of a very influential article 'Traditional Social Structures as Barriers to Social Change' in *Agricultural Development and Economic Growth* (ed. Southworth and Johnston, 1967) is the absence of a web of interpersonal allegiances. However, patterns of social organisation in the Punjab rural areas as evidenced in the particular conflict situation discussed in this paper will be seen to extend co-operation beyond the boundaries of small units and to mobilize a large number of people for collective action. Conflicts in a village, local area, and in the State as such, lead to the personnel involved extending their links outwards. The conflict can thus be considered as contributory to extensive co-operation. Thirdly, the data I present on Punjab rural society and on its major community – the Sikh Jats (landowners) – indicate those of its features that would reduce the capability of the social system to act cohesively and this necessarily has implications for the Sikh separatist movement. These are the other problems to which the data can be directed but which I cannot consider at this stage.

In the Punjab the means of settling disputes, of resolving conflict, and of structuring protest, of whatever kind and at whatever level, is by joining a faction (*paarti*)[2]. A faction is a state-wide political alignment. It is composed of a combination of persons at different levels of the political system. These individuals are usually political leaders at state level who are linked to influential persons in the local areas who, in turn, are able to commit a following in the villages of those areas. But factional linkages are not only vertical. They are also horizontal; for the various local area leaders in the Punjab belonging to the same faction know of each other and unite when required. The external unity of the faction is secured by opposition to a unit of like nature and its internal unity by patronage.

According to Punjabis members of the same faction are recruited in terms of their enmities and friendships. As members of the same faction they share loyalty to each other's interests. Patronage relationships also usually operate *within* the faction connecting people who in fact regard themselves as equals. They are exchange relationships characterised by reciprocity. Reciprocity is not only the value base but it is also the economic and political base of social relationships. It is when the opposing faction – similarly organised and not in any way different as a social unit – does not share in as much of the distribution of benefits as it considers legitimate that it puts into operation certain mechanisms of redress and protest whereby it gains power to reciprocate to its own members more fully.

Factions are non-local and hence there are no mechanisms for containing conflict within the unit within which it initially occurs. This form of organisation does not assist the cohesion of village, local area or state because the conflicts occurring in smaller units are not absorbed by the wider social system but find support from it. That is, the same type of conflict prevails in the wider social system. Co-operative ties are also encapsulated within the faction. Because of both these structural features, paradoxically, division does create solidarity within significant sections of the wider system – namely within each faction. Gluckman's model in *An Analysis of a Social Situation in Modern Zululand* (1958:63-64) is of considerable explanatory value in this respect, when he states:

> 'In any social system there is a dominant cleavage into groups which runs through all social relationships in the system. This dominant cleavage is rooted in the fundamental conflict of the system ... In any part of the system there may be subsidiary cleavage, operating similarly in that part of the system to the dominant cleavage in the whole system, but the subsidiary cleavages will be affected by the dominant cleavage.'

Cleavages in various types of local units coincide and one type of cleavage – a factional one – assumes overwhelming salience[3].

Wide-ranging ties of co-operation are established not only through factional linkages but also through kin and affinal ties. The partrilineal-extended family, like the faction, is non-local (See figures I and II). These two types of solidarity operate in the absence of: an urban rural cleavage, attachment to the village, class or caste loyalties[4]. All or any of these, were they to exist, would locate allegiances and divisions in distinct and relatively permanent units. The absence of these other forms of solidarity explains the range of possible co-operation and the scale of likely unification. The structure is, thus, conducive to the presence and continuance of non-local units and this explains why the eruption of conflict in any arena can create societal schism.

I *Relevant Notes on the Social Structure*

Ramifying connections among the Jats are a consequence of wide-ranging exogamy. Jats marry out of the clan of their father and mother and out of the village of both. The internal composition of Jat families also encourages extensive contact with others. Family members are frequently diverse in terms of their occupation, activities, place of residence, and in the different networks to which they belong. Industrialists, film producers, landlords, professional persons and smugglers are among those that may be included in

Figures I and II. Examples of jat patrilineal extended families illustrating their non-local nature.

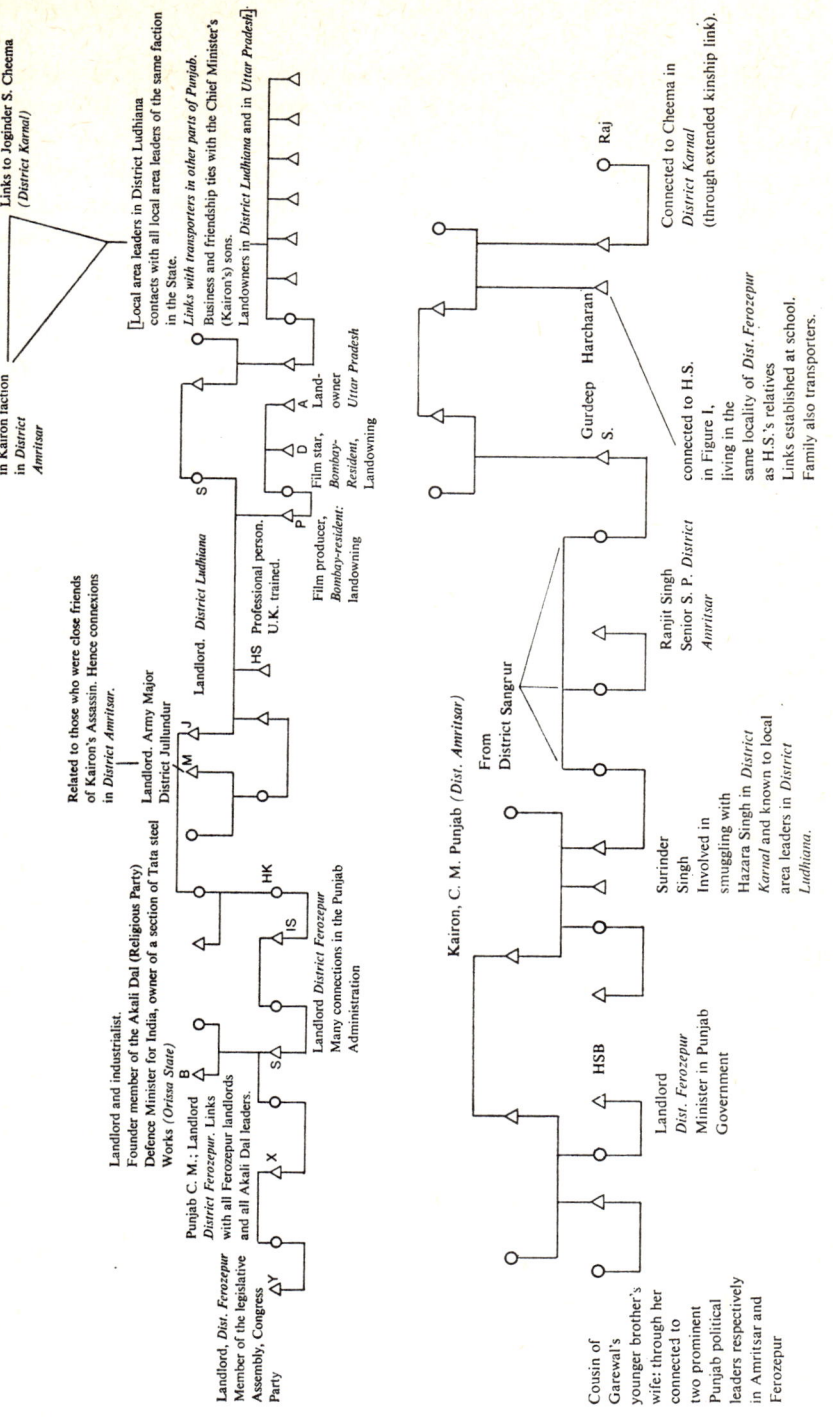

any one family. Each family has thus multiple connections of the most diverse kind. (See figures I and II). Those who are professional persons may use the links of their relatives in smuggling to set themselves up in business and those who are film producers in Bombay may have pretensions for politics and eventually use the acquaintances of those of their relatives in Punjab operating in the political arena. The development of relationships with a wide range of persons is facilitated by varied family connections.

The recruitment of the Jats into certain activities similarly contributes to the situation where co-operative ties operate in an extremely wide arena. Some of these activities are not only organised on a State-wide basis but they are also India-wide, e.g., transporting and smuggling. Jats participate in state institutions such as the central body controlling the Sikh temples (which has its own separate system of electoral constituencies and employs innumerable personnel), the regional assembly, and in the army, the civil and police administration. The institutions in which they participate and the activities in which they engage, have very rarely merely a village or local reference.

The rural areas are accessible and the villages are not isolated. Very many important political leaders, administrative officers occupying senior government positions and innumerable army officers come from villages. They rarely lose contact with their relatives or with the connections of those relatives, paying lengthy visits at harvest time and returning to their ancestral lands and homes to retire. By virtue of the activities and connections of these persons, villages are involved not only in the life of the province but also in that of the nation. The situation bears some resemblance to that described by Friedl (1959) for North Eastern Greece.

The existence of this complicated web of ties spanning rural society implies an attitude towards communicability: remoteness is not respected; approachability is emphasised. And, in fact, the rural areas are criss-crossed by a network of roads and there is an efficient transport system. The political manifestation of this is visible in the attitude to and the reality of power. Power belongs to a faction and its members. It is the outcome of a bargain between those controlling separate spheres of influence (in the police and civil administration, in the villages and local areas) to rule the State together. A leader attains his position with the help of factional supporters in the local areas and their village followers; they engage in the reciprocal protection of each other's sphere of influence. The nature of a political leader's power thus extends co-operative networks into the local areas and villages. Power has no legitimacy unless it is shared and seen to be shared. The tradition and right of complaint whereby a villager with a grievance can go and personally protest to the State Minister concerned is an action consequent on this notion of power and primarily effective because of it. Whichever faction is in power controls the resources of the political party as such and becomes an agency for the retention and distribution of benefits to followers. The apparatus of the political party, thus enters small village arenas and the allegiances and the divisions of those arenas are exploited to the maximum and have political reverberations throughout the State. Issues at state-level become issues in the local areas and in the villages of those areas. In turn village conflicts and allegiances show some degree of correspondence to those at state-level. Reciprocation is one reason why leaders involve themselves in local quarrels and why their followers in a local area may offer support in state-level matters. Patronage dispensed by a political patron within the faction creates rural solidarity and sometimes urban-rural solidarity, because of the non-local nature of the faction: followers come not only from his own local area but from all local areas. Faction members are thus united in the State as such by their friendships, their mutually beneficial co-operation, as well as by their shared enmity; sometimes by all three.

The web of ties (see figures I and II) created by factional loyalties, friendships, affinal ties, and connections formed on the basis of participation together in certain activities that have a non-local reference, keep those in the rural areas in touch with each other. Had there been an attachment to locality among the Jats they would have been masters only of the countryside[5]. Their participation in state affairs resulted in political alliances including not only individuals from differing localities in the rural areas, but also urbanites. In the dispute described in the following pages there were, at least, two prominent urbanites, (in the sense of 'of non-landowning origin') involved. Factional polarisation is, in fact, facilitated by the lack of the containing mechanism of an urban rural divide for both co-operation and conflict. The organisational patterns of the social structure extend rather than limit co-operation but the co-operation is contained in and by the factional divide.

In a conflict situation such as I will shortly describe, the units that are mobilised have no reference to locality. (It hence may be said that one reason why village studies are irrelevant in the Punjab lies in the nature of conflict). What is most noticeable in this situation is the progressive expansion of the area affected by the dispute and the involvement of an increasing number of institutions and their personnel.

The following description is constructed from data gained from court records, through observation and in unstructured interviews both in the State capital and in District Karnal. This district was not the area in which I did most of my fieldwork and the information I am now using was gathered for purposes of cross-checking whether or not the faction could be taken to be a representative unit of the political system.

II *Background to the Dispute (Participants and their linkages)*[6] (see figure III)

Figure III.

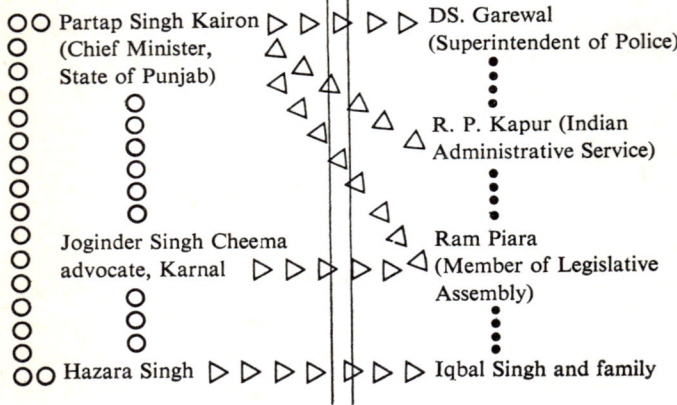

Diagrammatic representation of the pattern of alliances
in District Karnal subsequent to 1975

Specific antagonisms ▷ ▷ ▷
Specific linkages ○○○○○○
Cleavage ═══════
Co-operative relationships not based
on personal ties. ● ● ● ● ●

The setting for most of the following events is District Karnal of the East Punjab. Many participants in the conflict had known each other independently in United Punjab, i.e., prior to the partition of the Indian sub-continent. Their respective activities at that time form the context for the linkages subsequently established in District Karnal. In the early 1940's two brothers, by the names of Hazara Singh and Piara Singh gained considerable prominence in three districts of West Punjab as *rassagirs* – those who organise cattle stealing on an extensive scale. Such people do not, themselves, engage in the stealing. This is done by gangs under their command. They are persons of considerable power and their present position of importance in what is now Pakistan is noted by Alavi (1971)[7]. The Muslim Superintendent of Police (SP) of Hazara Singh's home district had taken Hazara Singh's help on account of his own personal rivalry with his Additional District Magistrate and it was under his patronage that Hazara Singh was able to enlarge his field of operations to three districts. Eventually the two officers were transferred, being replaced by a Scot and an Irishman. Hazara Singh and his brother were arraigned for theft, robbery and murder. More than thirty cases were brought against them and they were given a prison sentence of fifty-two years. They happened to be in jail at the time of the Quit India movement against the British and to be in the same jail as Partap Singh Kairon, subsequently to become Chief Minister (CM) of the Punjab in 1956. Kairon was a political prisoner but he and Hazara Singh became acquainted when Hazara Singh was attached to Kairon as an attendant. The future CM was impressed by the way Hazara Singh organised resistance among the convicts to the jail administration and it seems made a mental note of this.

Another character subsequently involved in activities in District Karnal was one Ram Piara, a Hindu, who was President of one of West Punjab's District Congress Committees. He had been imprisoned also in 1942 for participating in the Quit India movement. Subsequent to Independence he continued his activities in the Congress Party, becoming Chairman of the Karnal District Congress Urban Rehabilitation Committee at a time when Kairon was Rehabilitation Minister, Punjab. He became acquainted with a lawyer in Karnal city – Joginder Singh Cheema. Cheema was also from West Punjab and was known to Hazara Singh and his brother. He came in contact with Kairon while the latter was Punjab Development Minister. Cheema, Hazara Singh and Ram Piara had in common that they were from adjoining areas in West Punjab; in fact, Cheema and Hazara Singh were from neighbouring villages. They were all refugees and they sought to get a refugee elected from the Karnal city constituency to the Punjab State Assembly. Since the Sikh campaign for a Punjabi-speaking province then being conducted was arousing much Hindu resentment in the State, Cheema decided to put forward a refugee Hindu as candidate, choosing Ram Piara. And, in 1957, the latter took his seat in the State Assembly.

Refugees from West Punjab were a minority in the Karnal area and they (Jat Sikhs, urbanite Sikhs, and Hindus Alike) demonstrated an initial cohesion in matters relating to land and positions of local influence. The circumstances that allowed such cohesion among ruralite (principally Sikh) refugees were, firstly, that many villages at partition had migrated as collectivities. Secondly, in accordance with Punjab Government policy, groups of refugees from the different districts of West Punjab were assigned to specific districts in East Punjab[8]. This arrangement tended to preserve the character and identity of West Punjab settlements in a different setting. It was, indeed, the existence of his continuing set of social relationships that in many ways enabled Hazara Singh and his brother to re-establish their position of prominence.

Certain conditions of the post-partition situation were also conducive to this. Firstly, East Punjab is smaller in area than West Punjab and accordingly, when the province was divided, the Punjab government put into operation with respect to landholdings a system of graded cuts whereby each refugee landowner autmatically suffered a reduction in his size of landholding. For larger landowners this meant a loss of ninety-five per cent of their land. Then, in the years following partition, in accordance with central government policy, a land ceiling was imposed of thirty standard acres. Refugee landholders, therefore, suffered twice.

There thus exist objective factors which explain the dominance of Hazara Singh and Cheema in District Karnal. (I say this because participants themselves emphasize their friendships and their enmities.) Their domination was related to the interests of Sikh landholders to obtain the best land at the time of land consolidation and to increase their landholdings as such. The situation in undivided Punjab had been different. There, a number of links operated independently in what were then separate arenas. Thus, Kairon and Ram Piara were connected by their participation in the Congress movement; Kairon and Hazara Singh were linked by being in the same jail; while Cheema and Hazara Singh came from neighbouring villages and were friends. Kairon's connection with Cheema was consolidated by the latter's control of District Karnal[9]. In the situation created by socialist government policies on land in post-partition India and the communal distribution of population in which refugees, predominantly Sikh, were in a minority in a Hindu area which had an acute land shortage, these linkages lost their specific transactional character becoming part of the wider system of linkages which the objective requirements of the new situation created.

Many of those who settled in District Karnal had been employed by Hazara Singh as cattle lifters. As a person with legal training, Cheema gained considerable popularity by guiding them and others in land disputes and in defending them on obtaining his law degree in 1961. While Hazara Singh arranged the actual appropriation of land, Cheema arranged that its control be legalised. Friends from the same area, they were now together refugees as well as partners in helping their community. Their relationship was confirmed by the objective situation – that Sikhs needed local influence, it being a predominantly Hindu area. It may be said Cheema needed no special prestige or legal skill to regularise land adjustments, transfers and seizures. People knew he was acquainted with Hazara Singh and knew the character of Hazara Singh. Hence, although many cases were brought before the courts, these failed due to lack of evidence. In addition, the association of both with Kairon as a Minister was known. This further enhanced Cheema's position. In discretionary cases the police and the magistrates would take his position into account. It must be said that Kairon, indeed any Sikh Minister, was likely to have favoured the results of these activities, if not the means. Indeed it was Kairon, as Rehabilitation Minister, who had demanded that there be a Central Government contribution to any schemes for refugees[10].

The local influence of both Hazara Singh and Cheema was used to benefit the Kairon faction of the Congress Party. Landlords, people of reputation such as the *sarpancs* (headmen of villages), were approached to influence those dependent on them, e.g., tenants, labourers, those in receipt of loans and obliged to return favours. They secured District Karnal for the Kairon faction of the Congress Party. Cheema also seemed to look after the social welfare of Kairon's supporters in the national arena too. One such person was the Premier of Kashmir, for whose friends and relatives Cheema would arrange hunting facilities. Kairon, in turn, would oblige Cheema. When Cheema went to Delhi, for example, he would stay with friends of Kairon's Assistant Inspector General of Police, Punjab. One set of links led to another. For example, Cheema's Delhi acquaintances requested the help of Hazara Singh in the eviction of their tenants. Although the expansion of these links is interesting in itself, I cannot go into this here.

Into this local Karnal situation Garewal was posted as SP for the tighter reinforcement of law and order. He was a distant relative of Kairon's[11]. Formerly he had been head of Police Training HQ and prior to that had been in the army where he had risen to the rank of Major. He had a reputation for bravery and ruthlessness, and subsequently became one of Punjab's most senior police officers. His appointment had a state as well as a local reference. It had a state reference in so far as it was influenced by the policy of the Punjab government to post as SP those both capable of independent action but also susceptible to political control and willing to curb the brutal zeal with which lower ranks normally carried out their task. This was state policy which, in turn, had a national reference, in that Kairon was favoured by the Centre as a leader precisely because of his ability to hold the Punjab for the Congress Party and to keep in check Sikh separatist demands. For this reason, energetic personalities, personally loyal, were usually selected to head the various sections of the administration in the districts[12].

Before the dispute, Garewal and Cheema were not on bad terms. However, their respective roles and differing positions *vis-a-vis* the refugees from West

Punjab settled in District Karnal automatically implied opposition – one enforced the law against them and the other was their supporter irrespective of law. Hazara Singh had extremely good relations with certain police officials due to his having obliged them with small favours. Garewal's power was hence undermined by both Cheema and Hazara Singh. The conflict which provoked explicit opposition, however, began two years before he took over control of the district. To this I now turn.

III *The Dispute*

In a particular village of District Karnal a quarrel developed. It was between Hazara Singh who had been released from prison in 1952 following on an exchange of prisoners between India and Pakistan, and the family of one, Iqbal Singh. Village disputes are invariably over land and positions of local influence; and this one was no different. Up until 1952 Hazara Singh and Iqbal Singh had been friends. But, at consolidation, Hazara Singh asserted he was not given enough of the best land. In 1953, when Hazara Singh's brother Piara Singh won the election for *sarpanc* (headmanship) of the village against Iqbal Singh, the latter and his brother, who was a retired military officer and was from a family which commanded local respect, challenged his election and registered a complaint that no bad character would occupy any office. In retaliation, in 1955, Hazara Singh arranged a murderous raid on Iqbal Singh's house. All but Iqbal Singh himself were killed, including his pregnant wife and his brother. A case was registered in the local police station against Hazara Singh and his brother under the relevant section of the penal code but shortly after being arrested they were released on bail since, at the time of the murder, they had taken care to get involved in a petty case in a different district and hence were in police custody when the murder took place. In 1957, they were still free and had committed another murder and theft about the time Garewal was appointed as SP Karnal. They represented a challenge to his power since they were virtually competing with him for control of the district.

On July 15th, Hazara Singh was due to appear before the magistrate in Karnal yet again on the charge of murdering Iqbal Singh's family. He was again going to escape conviction because no prosecution witnesses were likely to come forward and it is alleged he was planning to murder those who had been summoned to appear in court. Since they could not be convicted legally, Garewal and nine other police officers entered into a conspiracy to kill them and make it appear that they had met their death in an armed encounter with the police during which, in the course of self-defence, the police had

had to fire in them. On July 14th, Hazara Singh went to the State capital to see the CM and complained to him that his life was in danger from the Karnal police. The CM directed his private secretary to telephone the SP Karnal to give both brothers legal protection. Garewal received the message but interpreted it as ministerial interference in his administrative job as police officer. When Hazara Singh and his brother were returning from the State capital the same evening Garewal, with a party of nine other police officers, murdered them. The subsequent police report contained the story of an armed encounter, in the course of which Hazara Singh fired at the police and was fired at in return. For defiance of orders Kairon demoted Garewal to the rank of Assistant Sub-Inspector of Police, transferred him, and placed him under an officer who was still in police training at the very college where Garewal had once been Vice-Principal. Subsequently, he was again transferred. Simultaneously, a Superintendent in the CID was sent to Garewal's previous place of posting to investigate any malpractices and irregularities committed by him during his period of service there. It was the CM's intention to get the matter tackled by departmental enquiry, i.e., to discipline Garewal internally. The factional cleavage in the society, as such, prevented this.

IV *The Escalation of Conflict*[13] *(Alliances subsequent to the Dispute)*

The first section of this paper presented the facets of the structure that facilitate the development of co-operative ties in the Punjab rural areas. I then discussed the content of the linkages of personnel involved in a particular conflict. I next consider the pattern these linkages formed subsequent to the dispute.
Grounds for the possible expansion of the dispute lay not only in the function of each linkage for individual participants but also in how these were structured by the dominant cleavage and how that cleavage rendered, of societal significance, innumerable private ties of co-operation and conflict. The expansion has to do with such factors as how people get things done, what they expect to get done for themselves and the social consequences of these acts and expectancies on faction formation. I will argue that factional cleavage is certainly not a cleavage based on the values sustaining Punjabi culture, that is, in the friendships and enmities that Punjabis would themselves stress.
The divisivences that split the village in which Hazara Singh and Iqbal Singh had quarreled was due to the fact that Hazara Singh was known to have links outside the village while the very fact that Iqbal Singh was able to

make persistent attempts over a two-year period to rally prosecution witnesses against Hazara Singh indicates that he had links in the local area too. Subsequently, in 1957, Hazara Singh and Garewal were competing for the loyalty of the area's police and for control of the area as such, and it was this situation in the district that led Garewal to murder Hazara Singh – this, and the fact that Hazara Singh had previously approached the Chief Minister for protection to counteract the SP's undermining of his influence in Karnal. Garewal's action altered the balance of power, and thus Cheema initiated a magisterial enquiry at which those favoured by Hazara Singh in the past gave evidence to the effect that the encounter version was false. The Additional District Magistrate pronounced it a case of murder and 10 officers, including the SP, were arrested and the bail of all was cancelled by the High Court. Before the magesterial enquiry Cheema had gone to Delhi taking with him a deputation of his *'paarti'*. Hazara Singh's mother had also gone to Delhi to meet Nehru. She complained to the Prime Minister that the forces of law and order in the Punjab were themselves an agency of murder. Nehru is reported to have then insisted that there should be a court case because it was bad for the democratic reputation of the country if its police were known to be gangsters. This sequence of events emanating from a village and then from a local area spread into the State towards the end of 1957. It was Garewal's activities that ensured that the conflict could not remain one localised to District Karnal. He fabricated evidence against the CM accusing the CM of being personally responsible for the humiliation and harassment he suffered subsequent to his demotion. He alleged that the CM had intimate acquaintanceship with Hazara Singh and his brother, thereby implying not only that the CM patronised lawlessness but also that the protection which he requested for Hazara Singh and his brother was due to his friendship with them. To that extent he had diverted the course of justice. The allegations were publicly made, Garewal seeking the support of all those disaffected with the CM in the State of Punjab as such as allies in his insubordination. On the pretext that he could not get a fair trial in the Punjab due to the CM's personal animosity to him, the case was transferred to Delhi to be heard by a judge from a different province. After his acquittal, when he applied for reinstatement, he asked for transfer to the administrative cadre of another state. These actions widened not only the area of conflict but also the numbers of persons involved.

Similarly, Iqbal Singh, since his whole family had been murdered by what were subsequently categorised as the CM's men, joined the opposing faction in the State. The murder of his family was useful to the opposition to prove the CM's association with bad characters. All those who were in any way intimidated by Hazara Singh, or who were resentful of Cheema for one reason or another became part of the opposing faction's structure of links.

Iqbal Singh's opposition derived from a village conflict. That of Ram Piara MLA emanated from the local situation in Karnal in which he had been elected to the state legislature with the help of the Kairon faction. As a result of antipathy to Kairon's supporters in the local area he aligned himself with the opposition to Kairon in the Assembly. His antagonisms thus did not arise out of the situation surrounding the murder of Hazara Singh but were related to his attempt to establish local independence of the Kairon faction. He raised the issue of Garewal in the Assembly at a meeting of Congress Members of the Legislative Assembly (MLAs) from the entire Punjab. With this action, the conflict was extended into the state legislature. He did not confine his opposition to one issue but lodged a complaint to the All-India Congress Committee that, at the Chief Minister's instance, a certain amount of hostility was being directed at him from unofficial quarters; he complained, too, about the irregular purchases of land by the CM's sons. His opposition on these varied bases implied linkages with those of the CM's opponents involved in these other concerns and thus further extended the range of alignments on both sides. Also, that opposition was not restricted to a specific period of time. He subsequently participated in no-confidence motions against the CM in the Assembly and, in the judicial commission of enquiry into Kairon's rule of the State, he aligned not only with dissidents in the Congress Party but also with prominent Sikh separatists to bring about the downfall of Kairon. The origin of these antagonisms was in the local area, yet they had such far-reaching repercussions in the State and an impact on the state political process. It again became a local area matter when those known to the CM's supporters in Karnal beat up Ram Piara in 1963. This was yet another evidence of the interdependence of village, local area and state affairs in Punjab.

The dispute also divided the police administration where internal rivalries resulted in the falsification and fabrication of evidence as an indication of factional position[14]. Some officers gave evidence against Garewal in the court case either for ambition or out of dislike. The CM had a personal interest in proving Garewal's guilt and used these rivalries. If, under pressure, a police officer refused to give evidence against Garewal, a son or other family member would be arrested on a false charge. The investigating officer is described as 'moving heaven and earth to get the accused convicted' and had personal access to the CM. It was a police officer especially trusted for his loyalty to the CM who conducted the enquiry into Garewal's activities during his previous posting. Kairon thus organised his support in a similar fashion to that of the opposing faction as a precondition for its effective persistence in its competition against a like unit.

Cheema for example acted as a prosecution witness against Garewal. The social consequence of his act was that it solidified his support in the district on a factional basis – all opposed to Garewal and all those who were beneficiaries of Hazara Singh's rule in the countryside aligned together, locally behind Cheema and provincially behind the CM. It was because of this that in later years Cheema is said to have had 'The DC (Deputy Commissioner) and SP in his pocket'.

The administration always sensitive to political pressure resented the interference so visible in the Garewal case[15]. The divisions within both the police and civil administration were exacerbated by the judicial harassment of the Commissioner for Ambala division (R. P. Kapur), of which District Karnal is a part, who happened to be Punjab's most senior administrative officer. Eight cases were started against him and his relatives upon his failure to comply with a request to give evidence for the prosecution.

The way in which relationships developed in the course of the dispute was such as to cement ties within the '*paarti*' and exacerbate those between the two '*paartis*'. Before the murder of Hazara Singh, when Cheema was on friendly terms with Garewal, he was not at all concerned that the latter was a murderer. (Garewal had murdered a servant on his father's estate when he was $13^{1}/_{2}$)[16]. He became concerned when Garewal socially manifested his antagonism, first in the local area by murdering Hazara Singh, and then made the matter a state affair by accusing the CM of acquaintanceship with bad characters. Only when that social situation arose did the Kairon faction comment on what they had so far significantly failed to mention, namely, that the SP himself had a past criminal record. As Cheema put it 'Both Hazara Singh and Garewal were dacoits. The only difference was that one became an SP.'

The width of the cleavage at any time could be measured by the intensity of the slander. Kairon was slandered with reference to various forms of illegality. For example, Iqbal Singh gave an affidavit in court stating that the CM came to his village to personally put pressure on him not to act as a prosecution witness, and that the CM threatened him that dire consequences would ensue should he not to do so. Likewise, Ram Piara alleged that there was a specific political motive behind his attack. Garewal after his acquittal in March 1960 continued opposing Kairon and spoke publicly of there being 'a reign of terror in the Punjab' as a result of which he claimed no one would dare to come forward to support him in the departmental inquiry which he still had to face.

Punjabi explanations for these alignments, the existence of which is indicative of the expansion of conflict, were in terms of the friendship and enmity of the actors involved. Certainly, friendship and enmity do explain, on one level, the wide sets of linkages that were mobilized and which, in turn, resulted in conflicts in the administration, legislature, village, and local area such as I described. But a cultural explanation of the expansion of conflict by reference to the extremism of the Punjabis, their aggressive individualism and the totality of their loyalties to their friends is incomplete. For, friendships developed and enmities were formed under the impact of the dominant societal cleavage. Ram Piara, for example, took the side of Garewal and aligned with him in the same faction even when he had no personal liking for him. Likewise, Kapur's antagonism, which was personal – to the CM and had arisen in another context, was structured by the factional cleavage which was societal. It was expressed in the socially institutionalized manner, i.e. by joining the opposing faction. Similarly, too, Cheema's action as a prosecution witness against Garewal is an indication of *paarti* loyalty; it stated his position as a member of the CM's faction. Likewise, although one reference for Kairon's action may have been his concern as CM with legality, and yet another (by all accounts) his developing personal antipathy to Garewal, the political reference of his action was his unwillingness to antagonise his local support. In these circumstances whether or not he was friends with Hazara Singh and Piara Singh was irrelevant for the functioning of the structure. The slander that accompanied the dispute in all its phases took place in the context of the society's principal cleavage and was itself the indication of factional opposition. The cleavage intensified opposition and strengthened alignments, and actions displaying friendship and animosity were structured by it even though they might have been conceived by participants to have had a personal basis. It is hence not relevant to explain friendship and enmity in a cultural idiom. Friendship and enmity are stated structurally and their significance as social acts is derived from the fact that they take place in a structure in which there is a pre-existing factional cleavage. The fact, then, that there is a polarization of relationships on a friendship/enmity basis over the entire Punjab area is not what is significant. What *is* significant is that this division thereafter governs the development of all relationships – with whom one shall co-operate and with whom one shall conflict. Shared friendships and shared enmities create a situation of polarization, but the mechanisms by which friendships and enmities come to be shared is explained by the factional structure.

It remains a problem to explain why the various linkages connecting participants create no more than factional cohesion, and do not integrate rural society, given that the various heads of families do occupy a variety of roles and have affiliations with various groups. Nadel (1957:71) has argued that

> 'the advantages of role summation lie in the strengthening of social integration and of social control. For the more roles an individual combines in his person the more is he linked by relationships with persons in other roles and in diverse areas of social life'.

In Punjab the multiple ties and diverse roles occupied by family members does not prevent rural society crystallizing into two opposing blocks each of which forms a cohesive set of allegiances. Despite differing allegiances there is one type of conflict and all conflicts involve the same type of split. The data shows multiple affiliations to be incorporated within the factional structure. This, in turn, implies that a man's very different pursuits are conducted with the help of the same set of links – factional links. This undoubtedly aids ease of operation in innumerable varied activities. That there is no incompatibility between a man's differing roles and associated sets of connections could, of course, be explained with reference to Jat Siks's perceptions that differences do not represent contradictions but are complementary. But it would seem that most of this empirical data can be comprehended by Firth's characterisation of the faction as 'structurally diverse' (1957). Three attributes of the faction are important in the spread of conflict: its varied membership; the co-operative manner of interrelation of its personnel; and that it is non-local. It is because of the structure of the faction as a communicating network of linkages on a non-local basis that lines of cleavage in all units coincide. Hence conflicts are cumulative and reinforce each other.

NOTES

1 An earlier version of this paper was read at a departmental seminar in the Department of Social Anthropology University of Tel Aviv in April 1974 and I thank the participants in the seminar for their comments, particularly Dr. Emanuel Marx. For his help in suggesting a number of minor revisions at a much later date I thank my colleague Dr. Ladislav Holy.
2 A fuller discussion of factions, their structure and mode of recruitment, is present in chapter six of my book, *Robber Noblemen*.
3 The vertical cleavage characteristic of rural Punjabi society, may be contrasted with Andalucian social structure (as described by Pitt Rivers) where cohesiveness in pueblos would appear to complement the wider societal class cleavage. In neither the Punjab nor in Andalucia can cleavage be adequately explained by reference to the social systems of small communities. However, given the nature of Pitts Rivers' data he can more readily treat the world outside the pueblo as intrusive.

4 See chapters four and five of Robber Noblemen. With respect to the question of caste, Alavi (1972) states that
   'In the Muslim rural society of West Punjab it is the kinship system rather than caste which embodies the primordial loyalties which structure its social organisation'.
Regarding my own data on the Jat Sikhs of East Punjab, I would substantially agree with him but only add that other allegiances are as equally important as kin ties namely ties of affinity, patronage, friendship, and factional loyalties, as this paper shows. In any situation, all these allegiances are manipulable. The manipulability of all allegiances is the fundamental characteristic of the structure.

5 As was the case for example with the Morelos revolutionaries led by Emiliano Zapata described by John Womack (1969: 216)
   'It was as if their very concern for the local cause inhibited them from involving it seriously in national affairs. Having become national figures, they had incurred the obligation of acting nationally, but not, they feared, the capacity for it'.

6 The material in the remaining part of this paper was gathered with the aid of S. Joginder Singh Cheema, advocate, Karnal, and his family. His friends in New Delhi – Om and Lily Malhotra, as well as Mir Nasrullah, Minister in the Government of Kashmir, and now Divisional Commissioner, Jammu, were also extremely helpful at all times. I thank them all for their hospitality and co-operation. I had also a number of meetings with D. S. Garewal, then Deputy Inspector General, Punjab Armed Police, Jullundur Range, (subsequently Assistant Inspector General of Police Punjab, and now Inspector-General of Police, Punjab,) and Ram Piara, member of the Punjab Legislative Assembly, for Karnal city constituency.

7 'The Politics of Dependence in a West Punjab Village", *South Asian Review*, vol 4, no. 5.

8 Those in District Karnal were predominantly from Districts Gujranwala and Sheikhupura.

9 It was remarked 'he could get anyone elected'. He still had considerable local influence even after the death of Kairon and was capable of offering protection to those whom the police illegally entangled in court cases.

10 Spokesman, 4 February 1953.

11 So also was Cheema. Kairon had two sisters and a daughter; one of these sisters was married to Cheema's brother-in-law's brother.

12 Further illustrative examples of this pattern may be noted: Chaudhri Subha Singh, D. C. Ludhiana, S. Mohinder Singh Bedi, former D. C. Sangrur and then D. C. Karnal. Commenting on this pattern a senior administrative officer affiliated to the Kairon faction, said of the CM
   'Either he had a loyal DC or an SP who could be trusted. Or sometimes the favourite and loyal DCs were moved around at the right moment'.
Jai Inder Singh, one time President of Amritsar District Congress Committee (Urban) remarked that the DC and SP tended to have more power when district politicians where insubordinate and weak, while in the absence of strong administrative officials in the district, the CM tended to rule through the Congress Party machine as for example in both the urban and rural areas of District Amritsar. That this situation should have existed at all was due to the fact that the offices in the district administration were not important in themselves but

rather the factional personnel who occupied them. With the separation of the judiciary from the executive in 1964, after the resignation of Kairon as Chief Minister, the DCs were deprived of the last of their remaining significant functions, namely, control over the district magistrates.

13 By using the term escalation I do not commit myself to the viewpoint that the origins of conflict are in the village: I begin my description of conflict in a village for purely procedural reasons since I fundamentally agree with the position taken by Swartz (1970: 66)

'...unit guides are used only to indicate the starting place of the study and not to set down its boundaries.'

14 One important fact in the spread of polarization in the administration was the transfer of officers from one post to another, either in promotion, or in demotion. Nearly all the officers accused in the trial by the time of the appeal of the Punjab government in 1960 against the acquittal of D. S. Garewal, had been posted to other districts. In their distribution they were spread over the entire Punjab. This aided the circulation of news about the dispute and rendered available for interested parties a body of comparative data which undoubtedly would exacerbate a variety of disputes in other areas and at all levels of the political system.

15 Because recruitment to the administration is on a merit basis, administrative standards are initially at a high level. This was one reason why the administration did not take kindly to political interference.

16 All India Reporter, Nagpur Section, 1937 pp 280-281.

LITERATURE CITED

ALAVI, H. 1971. The Politics of Dependence: A Village in West Punjab, *South Asian Review* 4, 2: 111-128.

–. 1972. Kinship in West Punjab Villages, in *Contributions to India Sociology*. Edited by T. N. Madan, pp. 1-27. Delhi: University of Delhi Press.

COURT OF THE SESSIONS JUDGE OF MEERUT, 1964. Criminal Revision no. 167, S. Nishan Singh and others versus The State through Ram Piara.

CIRCUIT BENCH OF THE PUNJAB/HIGH COURT AT DELHI. Criminal Appeal no. 2-D, State of Punjab versus D. S. Garewal and others.

FIRTH, R. 1957. Editor, Factions in Indian and Overseas Indian Societies *British Journal of Sociology* 8: 291-342.

FRIEDL, E. 1959. The role of kinship in the transmission of national culture to rural villages in mainland Greece, *American Anthropologist* 61: 30-8.

DUMONT, L. AND POCOCK, D. 1957. Villages Studies, *Indian Sociology* 1: 23-41.

GLUCKMAN, M. 1958. *An Analysis of a Social Situation in Modern Zululand*. Rhodes Livingstone Papers no. 28. Manchester: Manchester University Press.

KARNAL MURDER CASE. 1965. D. S. Garewal's memoir of the events leading up to this trial, presented to the President of India in an appeal for reinstatement in The Indian Administrative Service.

NADEL, S. F. 1957. *The Theory of Social Structure*. Melbourne: Melbourne University Press.

PETTIGREffi, J. J. M. 1975. *Robber Noblemen*. London and Boston: Routledge & Kegan Paul.

PITT RIVERS, J. A. 1961. *The People of the Sierra.* University of Chicago Press. Phoenix Edn.
SOUTHWORTH, H. M. and JOHNSTON, B. F. 1967. *Agricultural Development and Economic Growth.* Ithica and London: Cornell University Press.
SWARTZ, M. J. 1970. Area Studies, Theory and Cross Cultural Comparison, *African Studies Review* XIII, 1: 63-7.
WOMACK, J. 1969. *Zapata and the Mexican Revolution.* New York: Alfred Knopf.

Conflict and Process in a Zambian Mine Community

An appreciation of some of Max Gluckman's theories of conflict[1]

BRUCE KAPFERER
University of Adelaide

Among his many contributions to anthropology Max Gluckman is well-known for his emphasis on the study of social conflict. He applied his interest in conflict, which he restricted 'to refer to oppositions compelled by the very structure of social organization' (1965:109), to a wide number of contexts ranging from ritual (1954), the study of small-scale tribal politics (1955) to the colour bar and apartheid in South Africa (1958, 1971) and modern urban industrial environments (1961a, 1965) to name but a few. He criticised the Malinowskian functional view of integrated, harmonious socio-cultural systems (1948) and developed an alternative approach well-exemplified by his advocacy of 'situational analysis' (1961b) and 'the extended-case method' (*see* Van Velsen 1967), which did not make Malinowskian assumptions about societal integration. As Harris has noted Gluckman worked from within a structural-functional anthropological tradition established by Durkheim via Radcliffe-Brown. To quote Harris,

> Although Gluckman and other social anthropologists have written extensively of the matter of conflict, and unresolved tension, they have done so only within the framework of their Durkheimian heritage, in terms of how, despite such conflict, social solidarity is maintained (Harris 1969:560).

Harris' appraisal of Gluckman requires some qualification. Undoubtedly the main thrust of Gluckman's position is conflict as a cohesive force. But Gluckman does not, with his emphasis on the maintenance of order and social solidarity, exclude an interest in conflict as it relates to social process and change. Conflict for Gluckman is often productive of equilibrium (dynamic rather than static) but it is not automatically so. In his analyses we find him constantly searching for the conditions, the processes (which give rise to conflict and alternatively are produced by it), which either lead to an equilibrium or radically transform social and political systems (1958, 1969a). For example, conflict in Gluckman's view becomes potentially transformative when individuals and groups on either side of a dominant social cleavage become unified and oppose each other challenging the fundamental organizing principles of their social system. Conflict is not transformative when it divides and internally differentiates members of a population on one side of a dominant cleavage and at the same time unites them in terms of their interests with individuals and groups on the other side of the dominant cleavage.

Gluckman certainly derives much of his theoretical approach from Durkheim and Radcliffe-Brown. But, particularly in his treatment of conflict, he also owes much to Simmel and Marx. Simmel (1955) is especially relevant and he attaches a similar significance to a variety of conflict processes. But Gluckman's work is also a development on Simmel. Unlike Simmel he anchors his analyses in the intricate fabric of particular social contexts consciously locating them in their proper sequence of historical events. Gluckman also stressed, in contradistinction to the main scholarly emphasis of his colleagues at the time, the need to place the small-scale communities of anthropological study in their wider socio-economic and political arena or field. He argued, for example, that the behaviour of African traditional leaders had to be understood in terms of their position within the broader colonial administrative and political system (1948, 1958, 1969b). His emphasis through the study of conflict of isolating the basic socio-cultural principles and contradictions which structure societies and behaviour in them was a significant contribution to the anthropological tradition from which he emerged and at times severely criticised.

These qualifications aside, the point largely remains that Gluckman's own work concentrates more on conflict as expressive and reflective of underlying social organizational principles rather than upon its transformative aspects. In this analysis I examine a process of local political conflict in a Zambian mining community largely from within Gluckman's theoretical perspective on the study of conflict. I also adopt one of his analytical techniques first applied to a study of Zululand, 'situational analysis'. But at the same time rather than concentrate on conflict in its socially unifying aspect I show how as part of its course social and political relationships are transformed as well as are the issues which generate and structure the conflict. Furthermore, I examine critically some of the functions he attributes to conflict and the processes which lead to its resolution. In particular I consider such issues as how conflicts produce cohesion, the function of cross-cutting ties in the resolution of conflict and the extent to which loyalties of a more inclusive nature 'unifying' individuals and groups at one level necessarily suppres the operation of more exclusive loyalties and interests at another.

The Situation: A Strike

On the 19th February 1964 the local branch of the Northern Rhodesia African Mineworkers Union (now the Zambian Mineworkers Union) at Broken Hill (now Kabwe) lead and zinc mine called its members out on strike. The strike lasted for over five weeks and was the largest industrial disturbance in the history of the mine. Considerable local violence largely directed against members of the African mining community marked both the strike itself and the events leading up to it. Groups of Africans, employees and others not employed by the mine company, roamed the mine African housing areas at night, stoned houses and threatened and attacked leaders of local African associations. During the strike riot police were called, and tear gas used, to quell a demonstration of men and women, some of whom were arrested and charged. Three other salient features of the strike and the events leading up to it are noted. First, leaders of the main employee organizations lost control over their rank and file supporters. Second, the strike involved a virtual stoppage of work across all sections of the African mine labour force. Africans in mine Staff and non-Staff categories were commonly aligned against Management, despite, as I will shortly describe, the deep-rooted historically and socially based antagonisms which divided then. Thirdly, the mineworkers explicitly struck for the removal of an African member of staff from mine employment. This was not the issue which directed the progress of events in the mine community leading up to strike action, although as an issue it contained elements which undoubtedly precipitated the strike. The point here, to be elaborated later, is that the publically expressed issues which aligned and mobilised the African population prior to the strike were largely not those in terms of which the strike was called and eventually resolved.

The following analysis will be mainly directed to an examination of the conflict within the mine community as this relates to the particular characteristics of the strike and the events leading up to it - its violence, the failure of the leaders of the major African organizations to control its course, the development of a common alignment of all workers in opposition to management, and its shift in overtly expressed issues. I begin by broadly sketching in a description of the local mine community and setting it within the wider national political and social context of the time. This latter is an exercise the importance of which Gluckman never tired of stressing, and which he constantly demonstrated in his own work, to colleagues who might otherwise neglect it practicing as they did a profession which emphasised the description of small communities.

The setting

The lead and zinc mine at Broken Hill, located 120 miles south of the Zambian Copperbelt towns and 86 miles north of the national capital at Lusaka, was the first major mining venture in Zambia. Lead and zinc were discovered at Broken Hill in 1902 and it began major production after 1906 when the growing town was linked by rail to the South. By early 1907 some 11,000 tons of calcined zinc ore had been exported through the Mozambique port of Beira to Wales. The mine was continually bedevilled by technical difficulties and it was not until the mid-1930's that these were overcome and the mine was to enter a new productive life. In 1928 a new technical process was pioneered there for the extraction and production of zinc from zinc silicate ores. Problems of flooding were also overcome. This was to prove important as ores above the water level were becoming exhausted, but with the control of the water problem considerable reserves of ore were discovered below the water level. In 1937 the Anglo-American Corporation became managers and consulting engineers to the mine and this corporation today in association with the Zambian Government controls the mine. It is important to note, however, that at the time of fieldwork the mine was completely owned and administered by the Anglo-American Corporation.

In 1963 the Company employed 1,828 Africans and 490 Europeans. Most of its African employees lived in the mine township which in 1963 had a total population of 8,710. But some 300 African mine employees and their families lived in the surrounding Mine Plots or Farms. These Mine Farms were established in 1925 on the initiative of the Mine Company in a bid to stabilise its working population. Miners on these farms are entitled to continue living there after retirement, whereas those living in the main mine township must vacate their houses on completion of service, although, if they so desired, the Company would permit them to live on a Mine Farm or Plot upon retirement. Conditions of mine employment relative to those in other kinds of employment have tended to reduce turnover and migration out of Broken Hill mine employment. This coupled with the long history of the mine, and improvements over the years in mine efficiency and technology have produced a remarkably even age structure for the mine especially when this is compared with the age structure for those resident in the main municipal housing areas (*see* Kapferer 1966). Demographic surveys I conducted in the main Mine and Municipal areas between 1964 and 1966 show the number of adult males in the age categories between 20 and 50 to be approximately equal for the mine. In the Municipal areas the majority, by far, of the resident adult males cluster in the middle age ranges between 25 and 44 years of age.

The Mine has a strictly controlled labour intake, only a limited number of jobs fall vacant and few new jobs are created every year. Thus in 1964, inclusive of both Europeans and Africans, 267 jobs were vacated and 272 new workers were engaged. In previous years more people have left jobs than were replaced. The Mine offers numerous employment benefits not normal in other sectors of employment. Long leave of up to three months was granted those employees who had completed the prescribed number of years of service. Short leave was readily given to those who because, for example, of some family crisis, had to return to their rural home villages. On retirement small pensions were paid. As already stated, the Company actively encouraged its employees to remain in town after the completion of service, as evidenced by the establishment of the Mine Farms and Plots scheme.

Most of the Mine residents had been born in rural areas and had migrated to town. They were drawn from a variety of tribal areas mainly in the Central, Northern and Eastern Provinces of Zambia. Although speaking many different languages the *lingua franca* of the Mine African population was Ci Towne or Ci Copperbelte, which combined elements of the two major language groups, Ci Bemba and Ci Nyanja mingled with many words of English or Afrikaans origin (Epstein 1959).

Of the Africans employed on the Mine, 435 were in Underground jobs and 1,393 were employed in Surface work. The categorical distinction between Underground and Surface work was of some importance for the internal social differentiation of the mine labour force but of greatest significance was the division of the work force into Staff and non-Staff categories. African Staff jobs consisted of all those engaged in the supervision of labour groups and industrial tasks. In addition were included such Management affiliated jobs as those of clerical worker, industrial training assistant, welfare worker and medical assistant. Staff were paid on a monthly basis whereas non-Staff categories were paid according to the number of work days they had completed. There were also wage differentials according to which Mine Plant area a miner worked in and also shift differentials. Staff in general received higher wages than other African employees. The division between Staff and non-Staff was not only reflected in the different nature of their work and higher pay but was also evident in everyday social life outside the Mine Plant. Staff tended to live in the better houses, had other visible signs of status – they wore suits in contrast to the boiler suits of the non-Staff, and often owned cars. They also tended to separate themselves socially. It was a regular pattern for them not to drink in the local mine beer halls but to visit the bars in the town centre. Both Staff and non-Staff belonged to separate labour oganizations, the former to the Mines African Staff Association (often referred to later as the Association) and the latter to the Northern Rhodesian (later the Zambian) African Mineworkers Union (later referred to as the Union or A.M.U.). Both organizations had local branches on the mine but their head offices were on the Copperbelt.

All Mine employees lived on Mine property and were subject to the administration of the Mine Management in most areas of their lives both on and off work. At the time of fieldwork a reorganization of the Mine administrative and industrial structure was in progress. During 1962 major extensions were made to the Plant area. A new Smelting Furnace (the I.S.F. or Imperial Smelting Furnace) was built which enabled the Mine, for the first time, to smelt lead and zinc in the one operation. Prior to this, the solvency of the Mine had been largely dependent on the production of zinc. As with other technological developments on the Mine in the past[2], the Management accorded both prestige and relatively high wages to those employed there. The wages earned were in many instances higher than those gained from work in similar categories of employment in other sectors of the Mine. In some cases these wages approached the salaries received by African Staff.

At this point the dual wage and employment structure of the Mine should be noted whereby Africans were paid at lower rates than their European counterparts (*see* Bates 1971; Berger 1974; Brown Commission 1966). In addition, many jobs were reserved for Europeans and there was little opportunity for African promotion and advancement within the industrial structure. A.M.U. had been pressing for some time for a revision of the dual wage structure and a clearly stated advancement policy. There was considerable feeling among African Staff and non-Staff on the Broken Hill mine that wages should come into line with those for Europeans engaged in similar work and that a new promotion and advancement programme should be worked out. The major effect of the opening of the new Furnace for the mineworkers, therefore, was to increase their consciousness of, and their pressure for, the need for job advancement and higher wages.

In June 1962 the Company announced that it was beginning a job re-evaluation study and that the grievances of the African workers would be met. The results of the study were to be made available by the end of the year but this was not to be until the latter part of 1964, two years after the job re-evaluation study had begun. The delay in the publication of the results of the study was to provide important political ammunition during the events of the Mine in 1963 and early 1964. The delay served to cause and increase widespread discontent among the African work force.

Concurrent with the extensions to the Mine Plant and the growing local pressures for increased salaries and the revision of the system for job advancement various changes also took place in Mine Administration. Before 1963 Africans both on and off work were subject to the control of Management officials in the African Personnel Office. In 1963 an Industrial Relations Department was organized headed by officials who had instituted a similar change at the Copperbelt mine of Nchanga. This Department was made responsible for all activities of European and African employees relevant to their work in the Mine Plant area. Administration of Africans off work and in the township areas came under the office of the Location Superintendent later known as the Community Services Manager. By administratively separating the control of township affairs, covering such aspects as housing and welfare, the Management sought to prevent disputes emergent from the domain of township life feeding into the work context and disrupting production. It also aimed to reduce the racial component in its management of the mine work force, for as with the Industrial Relations Department, the Community Services Department catered for both African and European sectors of the work population.

Earlier, in February 1961, Management instituted a new body known as the Mine Township Council. Managements' stated objective in its formation was 'to create a body whereby African residents could be enabled to take a progressively increasing share in the administration of the Mine African Township (Meeting Minutes, 1960). The Council was divided into a number of sub-committees which dealt with women's activities, sports, recreation and entertainment, education and also with problems concerning the leasing of Mine property to traders. The main function of the Council was to act as an advisory body to the Community Services Manager. Until 1964 the Africans who served as councillors were predominantly Staff.

Management administrative and industrial changes aggravated an already existing discontent among the mine African population. Not only did they increasingly press for a new industrial agreement with the Management for higher wages and advancement but also the establishment of such bodies as the Mine Township Council accentuated divisive forces (between Staff and non-Staff) already present in the community.

The mood of the country at the time was generally one of great change. Northern Rhodesia was on the verge of independence. The two major nationalist parties, the African National Congress and the United National Independence Party, had joined in a coalition government but were engaged in a bitter rivalry in preparation for the 1964 elections to decide which party was to lead the country into independence. There was some uncertainty in the political climate but it was clear to the African miners that many of the racial barriers to their interests would be removed. The changes in the wider social and political environment gave the miners a greater sense of urgency in pressing their claims.

The following analysis is concerned primarily with the events leading up to the February 1964 mineworkers' strike. It is directed by three related central concerns. These are, first, the function of conflict as a cohesive force in the social field constituted out of the arena of the mine community[3]; second, conflict as a major factor in producing a change in the organization of political and social relationships; and, third, conflict as productive of a shift in the overt issues which initially underlined it.

Events on the mine pre-october 1963

I begin with a brief account of the relationship between the principal parties engaged in the mine community preparatory to the foundation of a new African mineworkers' industrial organization, the United Mineworkers Union, in September 1963 and its entry into the mine political arena. The principal bodies concerned are the Mine Management, the African Mineworkers Union, the Mine African Staff Association, the Mine Township Council and the United National Independence Party. Broadly characterized, the situation was composed of a set of cross-cutting interests, loyalties, and social relationships inter-linking individuals and organizations both across the major cleavage between management and worker, and across the mine African population. Management, of course, with its dominant position of power in the mine arena affected in a major way the developing relationships between the various organizations within the African mine community. This being so I start with considering aspects of its position an interests both within the local and wider national context.

As already stated, the Mine Management was operating in a local context where it was subject increasingly to pressure from the general African mine population for a reorganization of the mine wage scheme and a clear statement of policy on, and implementation of, African advancement. Both these issues were fundamental to the industrial and social structure of the mine. The Company had already introduced new elements into the mine industrial structure, occasioned by its opening of the Imperial Smelting Furnace, and also its reorganization of mine administration. Aspects of these developments, particularly of mine administration, were presented by the Company to the African miners as a positive move away from the hitherto racially discriminatory character of mine administration and as a recognition of the need for increased African participation in and control over local community government. Management further declared its recognition of the need for substantial changes in mine organization by commencing a job re-evaluation study. The results of this study were to form the basis for Management proposals for a new wage scheme and general African advancement in the industry. But these moves served only to increase a growing expression of discontent among the African mineworkers. The main complaint voiced by members of the African community, both Staff and non-Staff, concerned the withholding by Management of the results of the job re-evaluation study. Management was seen to be actively reorganizing elements of mine organization which related specifically to its own interests but doing virtually nothing for the interests of its African work force.

A major reason why Management delayed on the publication of its job re-evaluation study is seen in the context of the national political uncertainties of the time. The Central African Federation (comprising Nyasaland, Southern Rhodesia and Northern Rhodesia) officially came to an end in December 1963. But in the latter part of 1962 and throughout 1963, Zambia was governed by a coalition of the two rival African nationalist parties – the African National Congress and the United National Independence Party. Elections were to take place in January 1964. It was evident that U.N.I.P. would emerge victorious at these elections. National leaders of U.N.I.P. declared publicly that they would press for wage increases and the opportunity for Africans to take over jobs until then largely the preserve of Europeans. But, as yet, statements on this subject as they related specifically to the mining industry had not been clearly defined. There was no firm government policy for which the management could frame its actions or, more significantly, a stable government, assured of a relatively lengthy term of office, with which the Mine Company could work a long-term programme. It should also be stressed that Management was concerned to enter the new era of African political independence on favourable terms with the nationalist government and not to be seen as instituting policies completely at variance with national government aims.

The delay in the publication of results of the job re-evaluation study became a central issue for the African mine work force, increased discontent within it and produced division among the executive Union members. Prior to October 1963 the executive of the local Union branch had successfully presented an image as strong defenders of worker interest. This was particularly so in the case of the local branch secretary, a paid Union official. The career of the Union branch secretary, Joy Elijah Kabungo, at Broken Hill, began in early 1962. He arrived from the Copperbelt town of Ndola for a period of three months as a temporary replacement for the then Union secretary who was attending a trade union course in England. During this initial stay he became very popular with the mine population, impressing them as a hard-hitting Union man. In particular, he demonstrated his strength of purpose to the mine workers through his handling of two minor plant stoppages on the Mine. The first stoppage concerned a 9d. wage increment for a section of underground workers. The second stoppage was over a racial incident between a European supervisor and his African subordinate in the Mine Zinc Plant. In both incidents Kabungo successfully negotiated with the Management. The impression he made was so strong that with the return of the permanent Union branch secretary, other local Union officials and members asked the Union Head Office in Kitwe that he be returned on a permanent basis. This demand was acceded to by the Union Head Office and in the ensuing months he consolidated his popularity among the African Union members of the community. Kabungo greatly enhanced his prestige especially in matters involving township administration. He made clear to Management, the Unions' attitude regarding Managements' responsibilities in township maintenance. At the time Management had been pressing for a greater participation on the part of African mineworkers in the repair of lanes and the cleanliness of house surroundings. Kabungo made it clear that as the employer this was clearly the Managements' responsibility, not that of the residents.

At this stage it is pertinent to elaborate on this last aspect of Kabungo's career, for it is important in understanding his and the Union's relationship with other organizations in the mine political arena, the Mine African Staff Association and the Township Council. By its reorganization of the mine administrative structure, specifically its creation of the Mine Township Council, Management provided a base for the expression of increased opposition to it by the Union. Furthermore, it created a condition for the venting of opposition and hostility between members of the African mine population along lines which internally differentiated it. A number of aspects should be noted regarding the formation of the Mine Township Council.

A major ostensible purpose of the Council (established on Managements' initiative) was to give mine Africans a greater and more responsible part in township affairs. But more than this it could have been seen as a move on Managements' part to weaken the Union. It was part of a general administrative reorganization to separate the affairs of the Mine Plant from the affairs of the Township. Management was only too well aware that township housing problems, for example, could be the cause of the disruption of production in the Plant through strike action. There was an acute shortage of housing on the mine. Married miners often had to wait for married quarters and had to live in the cramped single quarters provided for unmarried workers. The Management also made available housing on the Mine Plots and Farms but workers complained about the unhygenic conditions. In any case for many workers, living on the Mine Farms and Plots was felt to separate them from the hub of social activity in the Mine Township and was often considered socially demeaning. Although some miners lived on the Farms, most of the population living there were not mine employees, a considerable number being unemployed, casual labourers, or working for low pay (relative to mine work) in the commercial areas of the town[4]. But even if preferred, the houses in the Mine Township were often old, in a state of disrepair, and inadequately supplied with such basic amenities as running water, washing and cooking facilities. Management had embarked on a programme of building new housing but the few new houses which were then ready went largely to workers in Staff categories. This generated a further source of discontent and hostility among the non-Staff miners to both Management and members of the Staff within the mine community.

I consider it legitimate to argue, therefore, that Management by establishing the Township Council sought to reduce the feedback effect of township-derived complaints into what Management considered to be the separate sphere of Plant/work place relations. In addition, Management attempted to deprive the Union of a considerable source of its influence and power over the mine community: the Union saw the foundation of the Council as a direct threat to the range and strength of its influence. Though approached by Management to participate alongside representatives of other organizations within the mine community, the Union refused to cooperate and especially during Kabungo's term of office actively opposed the work of the Council.

During 1962 and 1963 Kabungo not only attacked the Council – its attempt to influence Management in the allocation of housing, its granting of mine market stall licences to local entrepreneurs and its complicity in causing inflationary prices at the mine market – but also he attacked the social persona of the councillors themselves. More specifically Kabungo and the Union attacked the Council as being predominantly composed of African staff.

Union opposition to the Council almost from the outset[5], combined with Managements' conception as to the type of person most fitted for the duties of councillor mainly restricted the composition to members of the mine African Staff[6]. Managements' view that councillors should ideally have a relatively high educational level and be literate in English in order to participate effectively in the Council, further facilitated this[7]. The Council was easily presented by the Union (and this was accepted by most of its members) as a tool of Management. Here was a body presided over by a Management official, the Community Services Manager, composed of councillors largely nominated by Management and conducting its business in the language of Management – English. Being Staff, the councillors were the very same men who both on and off work acted as the principal agents of Management, controlling and directing the non-Staff employees on behalf of Management interest. The connection between the councillors and Management was perhaps even more self-evident than the connection between the Tribal Representatives and Management which as Epstein (1958) has described was destroyed with the formation of the Union a decade earlier. The Minutes of the Council meetings up to 1964 declare that the councillors dealt with problems more germane to the interests of Staff than to the general mineworking population. Thus, among other things, councillors proposed the building of a golf course and tennis courts – sporting activities in which most of the Union members were uninterested and could not afford. It was the Council which recommended that the usual fare of Westerns shown at the Mine Welfare Hall be discontinued and replaced by improving documentary films – a move far from popular with the general mine public. One councillor, who worked in the mine Industrial Relations Department and who was concerned at the lack of popular interest in Council affairs, suggested at a meeting that prominent members of the mine community be invited to a tea party so that the work of the Council could be explained! An anonymous letter addressed to the Council and written in the Bemba language sums up well the general feelings towards the Council.

> What we are telling you is that you just eat Council money. You do not wish to do what we tell you. We want a night bar here on the mine. If the company refuses, Patel (a local Indian businessman) ought to build it and stock everything. If you do not do this, the Council will die and we will ask the Union to handle this matter for us. Also, do you understand, that if you do not do what we tell you the result will be your own fault. You are dogs and informers and that is the true reason that you do not speak about the things we tell you.

At Union public meetings Kabungo repeatedly attacked the Council and the identity of its members. Not only did he successfully present the councillors as Staff, representative of interests opposed to the interests of the non-Staff workers, and eating out of the hands of Management, but also he drew on deeply rooted historically based memories of the Staff role in mine politics. He pointed to the fact that many of the councillors were either members or leading officials in the local branch of the Mine African Staff Association. Kabungo declared that the current threat of this Council to the Union was but part of an historical precedent established by the Staff when they had, shortly after the establishment of the Union in 1954, broken away to form their own independent organization. Not satisfied with this Kabungo also elaborated on his charges by drawing attention to the fact that some of the councillors, and by extension Staff and Staff Association members, came from tribal areas traditionally associated with the African National Congress, and were members of this political party. Most Union members were also members of the major nationalist party, U.N.I.P., who saw A.N.C. as not simply a major rival to their own party but also opposed to African nationalist ideals and supported by European interests. Kabungo's charge was serious and was specifically levelled at councillors who were at the time leading officials in the Staff Association. It was unfounded but occurred at a period when anyone suspected of A.N.C. leanings in a predominantly U.N.I.P. area could expect acts of personal violence against them. In the words of one Councillor who was also Secretary of the local branch of the Staff Association, 'We (the Staff) became outcast members of the community and it became very difficult to live. At one time his (Kabungo) accusations led to my name being written up all over the place that I was a member of A.N.C. I was almost beaten. It was being said that I was even organizing.' The councillors, the Staff and their Association were labelled as renegades threatening the interests of the bulk of the mine African population and in certain cases opposed to wider nationalist concerns.

I have shown that the growing conflict between sections of the mine African community followed the major lines of social cleavage within the African population and was expressive of basic aspects relating to the social organization of the community. It drove a sharp wedge between Staff and non-Staff members and certainly made everyday life during off-work hours uncomfortable for the former. The major short-term effect of the conflict, as Gluckman and Simmel before him might have argued, was to define clearly the different interests and allegiances which various sections of the population had, and internally unified them behind their respective leaders and, as well, opposed them. Far from promoting the generation of ties cross-cutting these two sections of the community it caused a breaking-off, a suspension and disruption, in such ties of common association as did exist. One additional point I stress is that the conflict was largely occasioned by not just Management's reorganization of its administrative structure but it was also emergent from its relationship of conflict and opposition with the Union. Thus the establishment of the Council, the organization around which the strife initially revolved, can be seen as a move arising out of this relationship whereby Management attempted to reduce, and indeed struck at, the very basis of much of the Union's power and influence.

I now return to certain aspects which began this discussion. Earlier I stated that a major cause of growing discontent through all sections of the mine community was the delay in the publication of the job re-evaluation study and the declaration of the Company's policy for African advancement. During 1963 this caused an increase in demands made by the Union rank and file on its local leaders to place pressure on the Management to divulge its findings. Kabungo and the local Union chairman had their hands tied. The Union Head Office at Kitwe was making preliminary approaches to the Mine Companies to negotiate a new agreement. It urged its local representatives and specifically the Secretary, one of whose major tasks was to liaise between the local branch and the Head Office, to restrain local union members from taking independent action. Towards the latter half of 1963 the union members were becoming increasingly impatient with their leadership. Members of the local union executive began to exploit this dissatisfaction by subjecting both Kabungo and the chairman of the branch to criticism and made bids to wrest control of the Union from the chairman and the secretary. It is possible, although I have no definite evidence, that Kabungo's attacks on the Council and Staff were related to an attempt to divert criticism away from himself and the chairman. (The chairman and Kabungo were close friends.)

This aside, however, it is important to note that the African mine Staff and their Association were also becoming increasingly opposed to the Management, on the basis of its delay. Despite the open conflict between the Union and Staff they were becoming 'united', at least in opposition to Mangement. In this context of wide discontent with Management the rank and file members of the Union were confronted by a leadership which urged them to restraint. But the Union at least had at its disposal the potential use of the 'strike' weapon in a bid to force Management to introduce substantial changes in the mine structure. The Staff, numerically a small proportion of the mine community and less essential to the productive output of the mine, did not have an effective strike weapon. Part of their industrial agreement with Management was that they could not go on strike. Also noted is that some senior Staff, many of whom were militantly for a new wage and advancement scheme, who worked in the Industrial Relations Department as clerical assistants were not permitted by the Management to even join the Staff Association.

The implications of the above considerations for a deepening crisis on the mine in the latter part of 1963 and early 1964 must now be understood in terms of other features of the mine political arena and the wider national context. This period in Zambia's history was fraught with political uncertainty. 1963 was marked by an increase in political rivalry and violence between the two main nationalist political parties as they prepared for the January 1964 elections. Although U.N.I.P. was the dominant political force in most of Zambia's mining towns, its leaders did not see the mine township as areas in which they had close and secure bases of support. It was in the municipal housing area of Broken Hill, for example, and in the Mine Farm and Plot areas, where the bulk of the population were not miners, where U.N.I.P. saw most of its support. There were good reasons for this view. Although most of the miners were at least nominal members of U.N.I.P. and adhered to its nationalist objectives only small numbers of the mine population attended party political meetings. U.N.I.P. meetings in the municipal areas and the town centre were massively and enthusiastically attended mainly by the non-mining population, whereas meetings held on mine property, by way of contrast, were poorly attended. Local and national party organizers were concerned about where the miners' true loyalties lay. This was accentuated by the fact that the Union leadership had not officially thrown their support behind U.N.I.P., as had the other major unions in Zambia's urban areas (*see* Bates 1971). A former Union President (Katilungu) had, before his death in a car crash, become a major organizer for A.N.C. Leaders at all levels of the party structure were deeply suspicious of the role the Union would play in the nationalist struggle.

Given these factors and the impending elections, U.N.I.P. came into sharp opposition to the Union. The organizing activities of Party officials were stepped-up and this converged with certain sectional interests within the mine community. The population living on mine property were not all employed by the mine or related to mineworkers. There were large numbers of unemployed youths eager to secure mine work. But few new jobs were becoming available on the mine and many that did, went to kinsmen of those already in mine employment. Indeed the workers through their Union pressured the Company to this end. With U.N.I.P. assistance many of the unemployed members of the community hoped to exert leverage on the Management to gain work. Indeed, in 1965 and 1966 they achieved some success in this. Most of those who traded in the mine market also lived on the Plots and Farms and with the youth were often prominent local party officials in their areas. They were also concerned to have U.N.I.P. support to protect their interests, for the Union had been attacking what it considered to be high prices for food and clothing. Furthermore, residents on mine property who were not mineworkers were subject to some insecurity of tenure. The Management periodically attempted to conduct surveys in their areas to gauge the number of non-mining residents and declared an interest in evicting those who were not in mine employment. Those in this category on the Plots and Farms felt particularly threatened. Many of the mineworkers felt antagonistic to them and considered that they had illegitimate access to mine facilities. It was here too that the non-mining population expected support from the Party.

Another section of the mine community which was interested in Party support was, of course, the Staff. This was especially so given the virulent opposition shown towards them by the Union. Indeed, many of the Staff were senior local officials in U.N.I.P. Senior party positions at the Branch and Constituency levels were at this stage in the history of the Party held by upper status members of the general African urban community[8].

Members of the mine population who either were not miners or were members of Staff became militant organizers for U.N.I.P. in the mine township. Because their interests diverged from and frequently opposed those of most of the miners there was an intensification both in the opposition between the Party and the Union and between the Union and the Staff. In order to improve attendance at political meetings U.N.I.P., through Staff on the Township Council, exerted influence on Management to close the mine beer halls at times scheduled for political gatherings. This provoked the expression of hostility by the miners, not so much towards U.N.I.P. but rather towards the Council.

In the first part of 1963 U.N.I.P. was relatively unsuccessful in its mine township activities. My explanation for this also applies to its unimportance, relative to the Municipal areas, in earlier years on the mine. U.N.I.P. emerged, after its breakaway from A.N.C. in 1958, as a major political force principally in the Municipal areas of the towns. It operated in a context where there were no single overriding authorities which affected most areas of urban African social and economic life. U.N.I.P. in its organizational aspects began to embrace and intrude into all areas of Municipal African life. Herein lay its strength. It achieved its greatest success in those urban areas where it was operating in virtually an uncontested environment. In what Epstein has called the 'atomistic' social organization of the municipal sectors of the mining towns it developed a 'unitary' framework drawing together the diverse interests of the residents. Local officials assisted in the making of funeral arrangements and the collection of money to buy the food and beer consumed by the mourners. Party officials settled domestic disputes and differences which occasionally arose between neighbours. They exerted pressure on local authorities in matters of housing and welfare. Officials became particularly active in the sphere of industrial relations. In the control of Municipal, commercial and light-industrial employment where the labour unions were weak (Epstein 1958 : 124; 1964 : 93-5; and Kapferer 1972), U.N.I.P. became an effective organization in the defence of worker interests.

But the mine context was different from that of the municipality. Here an organization, the Union, already existed which had emerged specifically in response to the needs of the mineworkers and their families. The Party was unable to exercise the same organizational role. The Union already possessed effective negotiating machinery by which it could bargain with the Management in most areas of the African workers' everyday social and industrial lives. Like U.N.I.P. in the Municipality, the Union helped in the organization of funerals, the settling of domestic disputes, housing, welfare and so on. The key area, of course, where the Union's influence and power rested was its ability to negotiate directly over industrial matters with Management. U.N.I.P. had no industrial agreement with the Company and thus, in the pre-Independence period, could not be an effective competitor with the Union. Not, therefore, having influence in these matters U.N.I.P. could not present, as it did in the Municipality, a convergence between the wider nationalist aims of the Party and the local interests of the mineworkers. Indeed, for the miners themselves there was no necessary contradiction between their support for the Party and their allegiance to the Union. I was repeatedly told by miners, even after the contradiction between the interests of the Party and the Union became more apparent, that their support of U.N.I.P. related to matters of national concern and the right of all Africans to self-determination. The affairs of the Union were separate and referred specifically to local Management/worker industrial relations.

Despite the attempt by U.N.I.P. to increase its influence in the mine it was not very successful. Those who actively aided its efforts were seen by most of the workers as opposed to their interests or peripheral or separate from them. If the Party was to ensure itself of more active support from the miners it had more directly to affect their immediate interests as mineworkers. Rather than act at the margins of mine township life it had to enter more fully the mine political arena, directly confront the Union and compete with it explicitly for control over the same resources. Ideally the Party required an organizational framework similar to the Union and a capability to enter into industrial negotiation with the Management. Such an opportunity was provided by the formation of the United Mineworkers Union in September 1963 on the Copperbelt and the establishment of local branches in Broken Hill and other mine centres[9]. Although U.N.I.P. leaders at the national level did not publicly express their support, U.M.U. organizers covertly understood that they had the backing of the Party. The policy statement of the new union, prepared in September, allied itself with what it viewed as U.N.I.P. industrial policy. At political meetings in the major urban centres U.N.I.P. national leaders repeatedly stressed the need for economic stability as the country progressed towards independence. One way this could be effected, it was stated, was to have 'One union, one industry'. The U.M.U. policy statement also declared an intention to bring the mineworkers back under the aegis of the U.N.I.P.-dominated United Trades Union Congress, which A.M.U. had recently left. Furthermore, the statement promised to meet the demands of all mineworkers, both Staff and non-Staff, regarding a new wage agreement and the implementation of an effective programme of African advancement in the industry – a concern which not only involved those at Broken Hill but throughout the Copperbelt as well[10].

Progress to the strike

U.N.I.P. leaders at Broken Hill threw their support behind the new union The U.M.U. executive, up to the eve of the February 1964 strike, included five U.N.I.P. officials[11], three of whom were also mine Staff. On October 29, 1963 during a U.N.I.P. political rally in the Mine Township it was announced that the local party officials supported U.M.U. and all mineworkers were urged to join. The multiple group affiliations of the U.M.U. leadership were clustered in that set of relationships which differentiated and opposed them to the bulk of the mine work force. Only two members of the executive were from non-Staff categories. The remainder were Staff, as might be expected given that U.M.U. had been initiated from within the Staff Association. More than this they were also either prominent local Association officials, or Township Councillors or both. The African Mineworkers Union easily portrayed the loyalties and interests of the new union as representative of sectional and opposed Staff interests. That this was accepted by the ordinary Union members was demonstrated by the failure in the early days of its formation of the new union to attract membership away from the African Mineworkers Union. However, there were areas of interest and loyalty, represented by the new union, which crossed over structural divisions internally dividing the mineworkers. Thus it appealed to the growing discontent felt in all sections of the mine African work force relating to a need for a new wage scheme and African advancement policy. It also appealed to the wider nationalist political loyalties which inter-linked the African mine population. These were to be exploited to some effect in the ensuing political events on the mine.

At the local level the new union emerged in response to a developing set of conflicts and oppositions on the mine. It provided a potential framework within which U.N.I.P. leaders in their attempt to win more overt support from the mineworkers, given the national political situation, could compete with the Union on its own ground. Dependent on U.M.U.'s ability to win recognition from the Management and to work out a new industrial agreement, it presented a discontented Staff with the opportunity of rectifying its grievances with the Company. The appearance of the new union on the local political scene was to alter radically existing relationships on the mine and lead to a further intensification of conflict and the outbreak of community violence.

The new union was immediately beset with problems. The Management refused to meet its leaders. For this reason it was forced to attempt to negotiate through already available channels provided by the Staff Association. This procedure was bound not to lead to the attraction of membership away from A.M.U. But membership had to be attracted if it was to demonstrate itself as a major representative of general mining opinion which could then be used to win Management recognition. However, the Staff Association as a channel for approaching Management ended when the latter eventually refused to meet with Association officials on the grounds that they were acting as a cloak for U.M.U. and by purporting to represent all mineworkers had broken the terms of their industrial agreement.

Staff, except through U.M.U., were now without any representation. Their opposition to Management deepened and it became a matter of urgency that the new union be firmly established. The problem of membership was crucial. Staff in their positions as industrial training officers and welfare workers began an active recruiting drive. This naturally brought forth accusations from the Union that they were illegitimately using their work positions. But it was the relationship of U.M.U. with the local U.N.I.P. organization that presented Union leaders with the greatest consternation and which was used most effectively for recruitment. Party political meetings of U.N.I.P. became a guise for statements on U.M.U. policy and occasions for public attacks on the Union and its leadership. A U.M.U. Planning Committee decided on the use of the Party organization to recruit new members. U.N.I.P. Youth Brigade members, most of whom were not mine employees, prowled the mine township demanding Party membership cards and urging miners, often violently, to join U.M.U. Partly because of the obvious link between U.M.U. and the Staff, attacks by Kabungo and other Union officials intensified, especially in the direction of the Township Council. But because of the common association of councillors with U.N.I.P. through U.M.U. these attacks were presented by the victims as not simply against Staff but upon U.N.I.P., its local representatives and its national aims. A conflict which had initially developed along the main lines of internal differentiation within the mine community now transformed into a conflict between the Union and the Party. There emerged a fully expressed contradiction for the miners between this loyalty to the Party and to the Union. No more could they successfully maintain that these pertained to separate sets of relations and interests. Kabungo especially, and some other members of the Union executive, were drawn increasingly into forced opposition to the Party. Kabungo openly attacked local U.N.I.P. officials at Union public meetings. At one time he entered the Mine Plant area and publicly burnt U.N.I.P. membership cards. He began to organize a Union Youth Brigade and a Women's Brigade to combat similar units of organization in the Party. Fights and brawls between rival sections of the mine population became an everyday occurrence. U.M.U. leaders and members of U.N.I.P. responded in kind to Kabungo's and the Union's attacks upon them. Kabungo's house was stoned and all the windows broken. He was personally vilified. Accusations were made to the effect that he had squandered Union money. Reference was made to how he used the Union car for personal use and in fact had crashed it while on non-Union business. He was accused of living in the pocket of Management and being party to Management's withholding of the results of the job re-evaluation study.

An important consequence of the open disputing between Union leadership and the leaders of U.M.U. and U.N.I.P. was that it gave substance to some aspects of the accusations against the Union. Kabungo, supported by the Union executive, demanded that Management remove the chairman of U.M.U. and other militant Staff from employment. He even threatened use of the Union strike weapon. The Union Head Office at Kitwe supported Kabungo's demands. Management proposed a deal with the Union Head Office that it would transfer the U.M.U. chairman out of Broken Hill if the Union in return recalled Kabungo to the Copperbelt, and so remove the two basic causes, as Management viewed it, of the local troubles. This did not come off but Management was becoming increasingly alarmed at the general disruption and strife breaking out in the township, particularly as this was also leading to disruption of work in the Mine Plant area. Management, however, withdrew the use of mine facilities, such as the Mine Welfare Hall, for U.N.I.P. meetings and in fact began to threaten various Staff, prominent in U.M.U., with dismissal if they did not desist from their activities[12]. The Management, on the Copperbelt also, distributed leaflets urging the mineworkers against joining U.M.U.

The presssures which Management began to exert on Staff, its withholding of mine facilities from local U.N.I.P. officials, inevitably made it appear as if the Union had formed an alliance with it against the Union's opponents in the township. Certainly A.M.U. in its conflict with the Party, Staff and U.M.U. was dependent on Management opposition to them. The conflict on the mine, therefore, reduced the extent of the opposition and conflict between the Union and Management, described earlier, and brought it into greater conflict with Staff and other organizations on the mine.

Secondly, the activities of the Union leadership began to divorce them increasingly from the ordinary Union members. The conflict had taken on the dimensions of a battle between members of the mine African elite concerning who should wield power and influence in the community. Further divorced from the rank and file members, the Union leaders began to lose effective influence and control over them.

Finally, the conflict had become extremely personalized. Accusations focussed on the personal characteristics and behaviour of the antagonists. These were not unrelated to various interests which aligned and opposed the population, but they were at least one step removed from central issues. Much of the content of the conflict became focussed on the subject of political loyalties and aspects of personal behaviour rather than upon wage increases and job advancement.

Strife on the mine came to a head in December 1963 when Management advertised for the position of Assistant Community Services Manager. Kabungo applied, was appointed and began his duties in January. The local Union executive, which had not been informed of his application until the post was filled, was acutely embarrassed. All that the Union had been accused of by its opponents suddenly appeared completely true to its members. It was at this point that many Union members went over to U.M.U., and the latter's membership grew to over three hundred. The African Staff were furious. Some among them, with experience well-suited to Kabungo's new position, had applied for the job. More than ever it seemed that a clear promotion and advancement scheme was needed.

Given the angry mood of the African mine population, a strike seemed inevitable. But the expected did not happen for over six weeks. Various factors might explain this. Most important, January was the month of the national elections and U.N.I.P. national leaders urged that nothing else take precedence over them. Indeed there was a temporary suspension of local hostilities over the election period. The leadership, by which strike action could have been initiated was, until February, confused. The local chairman of the Union was on a trade union course in England. (This was organized by the Company as part of its policy to defuse the situation in the strife-torn community. There was similar purpose behind Kabungo's promotion too.) With the absence of the chairman, members of the Union executive were competing among themselves for power within the local Union hierarchy and this was not resolved until February. In January the local U.M.U. leadership was undergoing some re-organization. The chairman of U.M.U. had left mine employment in December. During January, with the cross-over of a number of non-Staff employees to U.M.U., there were attempts to reduce the control of Staff over U.M.U. affairs.

On February 19th, a strike supported by all mine employees was called. It was organized through the local branch and came with little prior warning to Management and without, at first, the official backing of the Union Head Office. Indeed as far as the miners were concerned the Head Office never gave them the support which they expected. No financial aid came from the Copperbelt and in the view of local Union leaders, the ability of the workers successfully to stay out for over five weeks was due to their being paid their Metal Bonus during the strike period. Also mentioned was the fact that the maize gardens cultivated by the miners on the outskirts of the mine township were being harvested at the time[13].

The strike was successful in its declared aim of effecting the removal of Kabungo from his post. The workers did not return until the Management agreed to transfer him out of Broken Hill. Although the strike was organized and negotiated to conclusion by local Union officials, their influence and control over the strikers was limited. They were effective in the organization of picket lines, in the broadcasting of the progress of events to the strikers and in all other matters consistent with the dominant mood of hostility to Management and Kabungo on the mine. But they were not effective in controlling outbreaks of violence on the mine and more especially in getting a return to work before the demands for Kabungo's removal had been met.

U.N.I.P. had been successfully elected to power at the January elections and now embarked on its policy of effecting industrial restraint. Considerable pressure was brought to bear on the local Union officials by national government leaders to force a return to work of the Union's members. At one time Broken Hill Union officials were taken to Lusaka where they personally confronted government leaders. U.N.I.P. officials outside the mine township and mine employment exhorted the miners to return to work. The miners became the subjects of attack at Party public meetings in the Municipal areas. At Union meetings, in the later stages of the strike, members were asked to return to work by their officials but the members refused to concur.

Violence and other expressions of division within the mine community continued throughout the strike. Members of the elite in the mine, Union officials and prominent Staff leaders, were relatively united. The acting Union chairman (later to become chairman) was driven around the mine by a Staff member in his car, while he broadcasted the strike's progress through a loudspeaker. But the feeling of the non-Staff miners still ran high against the mine African Staff. Many Staff, particularly those in the Industrial Relations Department, continued to go to work. Even though they donated money to the strike effort they were seen as strike-breakers. Interviews with miners, which I conducted after the strike, were expressive of the feeling that Staff were against the strike and had weakened the strike effort. Clashes occurred between Party members, not employed in mine work and living on the Mine Plots and Farms, and groups of miners. Unemployed youths living on Mine Property offered to break strike and approached the Management for employment. Party officials of the U.N.I.P. Mine Market Branch actively opposed the miners, but this became more evident towards the end of the strike when the 'out-of-pocket' miners began to affect their trading seriously.

Undoubtedly, the lack of control which Union leaders had over many aspects of the strike was related to the disillusionment which the workers felt towards the Union. There was a marked symbolic character to the strike. The Union Head Office had begun preliminary negotiations with the mining companies for wage increases and on the subject of African advancement. The Broken Hill miners were aware of this. However, they were dissatisfied with an established pattern whereby the Union Head Office engaged in negotiations with the Companies on the Copperbelt in relation to the Copperbelt situation. Separate clauses in these agreements were made covering the special conditions of the Broken Hill mine without, it was felt, proper consideration for the interests of the Broken Hill miners. When strike action was called by the Union to support a negotiating position, it was the Copperbelt miners who were invariably called out and not those at Broken Hill. In the 1962 strike on the Copperbelt over wages and advancement, for example, the Union Head Office specifically requested the Broken Hill miners not to come out. The miners at Broken Hill generally felt, therefore, that their voice was not being given sufficient hearing. Thus the strike can be seen as a symbolic expression of the workers' ability to pursue their interests independent of the Copperbelt and as a protest against the marginal significance apparently accorded Broken Hill by the Union Head Office.

While there were many issues underlying the strike, including a general concern for a new wage and advancement scheme, those which were at the forefront concerned Kabungo's promotion, and were of a highly symbolic character. At the conciliation hearings (Record of Evidence 1964) no mention was made of the many crucial issues which had generated much of the developing conflict on the mine and which were vital to the miners' interests. No reference was made to wages or to advancement. The complaints raised all related to Kabungo's alleged misdemeanours in his new Management post, and were connected to his new identity as a renegade and traitor to the miners. Underlying the accusations was the deep social and emotional rift between Staff and non-Staff. All the miners who gave evidence against Kabungo were non-Staff members. One, although a non-Staff worker, was a Party and U.M.U. official. Many of the complainants were miners' wives. The complaints concerned Kabungo's usage of abusive English and Afrikaans words to the miners and their families, and his alleged insistence that they clear around their houses, a reversal of his approach when he had been the Union secretary. Evidence was given that he had not followed Management policy in the allocation of new housing, that he had unwarrantedly evicted miners or their families from their homes and that he had not helped workers in receiving medical attention provided by the Mine.

Cohesion, change and the definition of issues

Many of the aspects to which Gluckman and others have drawn attention in the analysis of conflict are evident in the above account. Conflict is emergent from and expressive of the many features which organize the mine African community. It defines separate groups and interests. In my description I have paid explicit attention to Gluckman's stress that conflicts within a community should be related to wider forces operating upon it. I have also made use of his emphasis on relating conflict and its development to the basic social cleavages which align and oppose not just individuals and groups within a specific social context but also in the wider social arena, an approach which he derived from Marx and perhaps more obviously from Evans-Pritchard's study of the Nuer. While Gluckman was acutely aware of the dynamic properties of conflict, its force as an agent of change, he concentrated, as Coser (1965) does in his presentation of Simmel's ideas, on the way it can paradoxically lead to order in the social system as a whole, on its socially cohesive properties. Indeed, Gluckman (1965 : 109; 1969; 1971) repeatedly makes a distinction between two kinds of conflict, 'conflict' and 'struggle'. 'Conflict' and 'struggle', for Gluckman, both relate to core organizing principles in a society (though not necessarily of a material productive kind but also to other socio-cultural factors, what he sometimes calls 'customary' principles). They differ in that 'conflict' is expressive and eventually system-maintaining while 'struggle' is transformative. 'Conflict' does not challenge the principles organizing the system at its very heart, whereas 'struggle' does. This bears obvious comparison with his well-known distinction between 'rebellion' and 'revolution' (1954). Gluckman's main concern is, therefore, with conflict in the terms of his definition. While I acknowledge the significance of Gluckman's distinction between 'conflict' and 'struggle' I am doubtful of its applicability to forms of conflict in specific situations. It seems to me that they are *post hoc*. They give insufficient attention to the fact that what might start out as 'struggle' in the sense he defines it may end up as 'conflict'. This could skew analysis away from a concern with social and political behaviour as process which he advocated. It could subvert the raising of such questions as why political action which begins as a struggle against basic contradictions in a system should give way to conflict and become merely expressive of them. I return to this later.

Of course it is not accurate to state that Gluckman was not concerned with the factors which militated against individuals and groups organizing to overthrow the system in which they were placed. This is the central concern of his *Social Situation in Modern Zululand* (1958) and later books and articles. Certain aspects of how he handles this problem are bound up with his interest in conflict as socially cohesive[14]. It is to this that I now turn. In his examination of conflict as a force in producing social cohesion he concerns himself with the role of ties cross-cutting horizontal and vertical social and political divisions. Briefly there is order and the system is maintained when such ties are in evidence. But disorder, and perhaps radical social change, occur when ties cross-cutting a dominant social and political cleavage are negated and groups on one side of a social cleavage become united. This unity is produced by ties interlinking groups previously opposed on one side of the dominant cleavage and by the identification of common loyalties. A further element in his argument, one which he develops in relation to material on the Nuer and Colson's work among the Tonga, is that ties cross-cutting groups opposed on the basis of one set of loyalties and interests bring into play loyalties and interests common to the parties concerned at a higher level of socio-cultural organization. This principle is used by Gluckman to explain how disputes, quarrels and strife are resolved. It might also be used to account for why, in his terms, 'conflicts' do not become 'struggles' and *vice versa*.

This argument can be applied to the mine situation I have described. The strike broke out at a time when all sections of the African mine work force had become opposed to the Management and 'united' as African workers *vis a vis* the European Management. A further basis for this unity was a common antagonism to Kabungo and his appointment. I drew attention to the dynamic and changing qualities of the developing conflict situation on the mine, for example, the way in which Staff complicity with Management in the formation of the Township Council more firmly opposed the Union to Management and brought out the deep seated hostilities of the Union members to Staff, increasing the Staff/non-Staff opposition. Gluckman might have argued that the 'imbalances' in one part of the system were balanced out by countervailing processes in other parts of the system, producing an overall equilibrium. But this was not so. Later developments led to an increasing disillusionment of the Union rank and file with their leadership and this in association with other factors produced a further dislocation in the life of the community leading it, inevitably I consider, to the events in the latter part of 1963 and early 1964.

Strife on the mine led to the awareness of cross-cutting loyalties and affiliations. With the formation of U.M.U. the multiple group affiliations of the Staff, particularly into the Party, became apparent. Union members and Staff belonged to the one nationalist political party and broadly were in agreement with its political objectives. But this loyalty at a higher level in the system did not override or subvert lower-level loyalties and interests of a more exclusive and less unifying nature. The conflicts produced internal divisions within the various opposed groups among the African mine population. They related to the emergence of competition for control of the Union among the Union executive and also a change in leadership within the ranks of U.M.U. But these conflicts continued to be founded on major divisions subdividing the African community. In U.M.U. Staff were progressively excluded from local leadership positions; this if anything increased the opposition between Staff and non-Staff and furthered divisions within the ranks of non-Staff employees.

The developing conflict did, as Gluckman and Simmel have both suggested, generate the proliferation of social ties and their manipulation. But these often extended to individuals and groups who had divergent interests in the industrial mine context. For example, ties were extended to those who were not mine employees on the Mine Farms and Plots. They became involved in the mine political arena and contributed extensively to the local disorder and violence. Later they came to oppose the strike but they were not important in effecting any resolution. Their opposition only served clearly to define their interests and those of the mineworkers in general as distinctly opposed.

At the time of the strike there was certainly a consensus among the mineworkers, their opposition to Kabungo's appointment and at a deeper level their concern for wage increases and advancement. The conflicts had produced no overall cohesion provided by a network of criss-crossing ties and affiliations. On the surface they were united in their stand against Management but the African community was as fundamentally divided as ever.

It was this lack of cross-cutting ties (as having cohesive properties) and the continued internal divisiveness of the mine African community which contributed to the long drawn-out nature of the strike (and, perhaps, the attainment of its limited objective, the removal of Kabungo), despite the considerable application of external political pressure. The Union and U.M.U. leaders were competing either to retain or build-up their membership in their fight to legitimate their right to represent the workers and to exercise power and influence over them. If the Union had backed down in the face, for example, of outside pressure then it risked a further disillusionment with its leadership and a greater loss in membership leading to a strengthening of U.M.U. I stress that the conflict situation was cohesive in the sense that it locked the various groups together in a field of opposing forces. It was this rather than cohesion through conflict-producing cross-cutting ties which generated the apparent 'unity' of the mine community. That the various individuals and groups were so 'locked' was undoubtedly contributed to by their common interest (*see* Gluckman 1971) in the industrial system. But even so this does not deny conflict as a process which can lead to a tranformation of the principles on which this system is based.

Earlier, I referred to Gluckman's distinction between 'conflict' and 'struggle'. The developments on the mine progressed in relation to basic issues which structured the mine population. The demands for wage increases and the implementation of a policy for African advancement were aimed at changing fundamentally the mining structure. The mines were based on a dual wage structure which gave Europeans, in the same kind of work as Africans, vastly higher wages. Certain jobs were reserved for Europeans and there was no way in which Africans could be promoted to them. African mineworkers were concerned to overthrow this system. These issues formed the basis of a growing opposition across the Management/Worker horizontal cleavage. However, certain aspects of this opposition were affected by vertical oppositions internally dividing the African mine population. As events proceeded, in fact, the conflict in terms of vertical oppositions began to dominate the nature of relationships and the conflict across the Management/Worker structural cleavage. This process, in addition to the fact that the issues which aligned and opposed members of the African mine community were different from those which generally opposed them to Management, led to a subversion of such fundamental issues as wages and advancement. It led to a deflection away from a conflict framed in terms of an opposition to principles at the core of the mine industrial system, to conflict less challenging to the system as a whole.

An explanation I advance for this process (why issues relevant to vertical cleavages subverted issues central to the dominant horizontal cleavage) is the personalization of the strife on the mine. Kabungo and his opponents vilified one another in terms of their total social identities. There are pressures to this in the structure of the mine community itself. The mine community, as Epstein has described for Luanshya, is one where the same individuals and groups come together in a great many separate, but interrelated, situations and contexts. An individual's social persona in one situation or context cannot be readily treated as distinct or separate from his persona in another. The presentation of one identity in one context cannot easily be treated as distinct from the presentation of a different identity in another. Inconsistencies in personal presentation, political or otherwise, become speedily apparent and contribute to the generation of dispute and quarrels. Once personal attacks are launched and the conflict moves away from a focus on restricted aspects of their identity (e.g., as Staff or non-Staff) and begins to embrace the totality of that identity, then the conflict becomes deeply imbedded in the persona of the antagonists and begins to lose sight of the major aspects of the situation which the individuals and groups represented. The more the conflict becomes grounded in the total persona the more this as a content of conflict will flow into and obscure other issues more central to other specific defined oppositions which emerge. This is precisely what happened in the events leading up to and including the strike. Kabungo progressively focussed his attack on the total social personae of those against whom he was drawn into conflict and in time was selected out for counterattack of a similar nature. The events on the mine developed from issues which opposed the mineworkers as categories to issues founded on the opposition of personalities. In that the latter became the focus of the conflict it clouded other more fundamental grounds on which the mine community was structured and allowed issues based on vertical divisions continually to dominate those grounded in the more basic horizontal opposition between **Management** and **Worker**.

While I stress the above I do not ignore other factors which can complicate a conflict situation and obscure other vital issues. Thus the process whereby the Party, and through it, individuals and groups not engaged in mine labour were introduced into the conflict also assisted a deflection of certain issues and probably heightened the centering of the strife on Kabungo and his antagonists.

The conflict on the mine was resolved with Kabungo's transfer by the Management out of Broken Hill. The situation in many ways returned to a state resembling that prior to the events I have described. Staff were edged out of their leadership of U.M.U. and reformed their separate Staff Association in the later part of 1964, the Kabwe Mine Local Staff Association (renamed in 1965 as the Mines Local Staff Association). Staff were also largely removed from the Township Council in 1964, their places being taken by staunch on-Staff U.N.I.P. supporters. As Gluckman would have predicted the conflict produced a change in personnel but it also cleared the way for the development of further conflict in terms of fundamental contradictory principles which organized protest on the mine shortly before and after I left the field. The appearance of U.M.U. (U.N.I.P. failed to gain Management recognition and dissolved in 1965) at Broken Hill and other mining centres was, as the Brown Commission (1966 : 24-5) on the mining industry noted, to influence radically the later negotiations between the Mine Companies and their employees.

Gluckman has provided an enduring and significant contribution to the study of social and political conflict. He concentrated, however, on the forces producing order, overall cohesion and stability. His analysis, although clearly related to the work of other scholars who examined conflict, like Simmel, nonetheless constituted an advance – particularly for anthropology which had by and large ignored its significance. He examined conflict through a concrete analysis of the structure of the systems, locating them within the particularities of their historical context. As such his work is not a simple duplication of the work of Simmel, Coser and other sociologists before him. Rather it is an extension and development, as is seen by his argument that conflicts develop around a dominant cleavage and his documentation of the specific forms this process takes. Gluckman does not neglect conflict as a dynamic force or as an agent in radical social transformation. To label him crudely as a structural functionalist interested solely in order, stable equilibria and system maintenance is to do him an injustice. But his emphasis is upon the expressive, socially reflective aspects, of conflict rather than its transformational properties.

Furthermore, when he does apply his approach to the study of change he confines his analysis to relatively long periods of historical time and adopts as Murphy notes a 'Big Bang' transformational perspective (Murphy 1972, 235). Gluckman advocates the analysis of social process through historical time in terms of successive 'temporary equilibria' (Gluckman 1958, 46-52; 1968). He does not stress that the dialectical forces which he isolates over a longterm time span are often constantly present leading to major transformative events. 'If dialectics operate in social life, they do not do so every century or so, when the peasants take to the hills and the students to the streets. The process is continually operative, and it is even more evident in the microhistorical span of our ethnographies than in history writ large' (Murphy 1972, 234-235). I have attempted, while in large measure adopting Gluckman's analytical framework, to demonstrate in the microhistorical context I have selected, the continual operation of dialectical forces in the mine community, how they led to changes in the structure of relationships and in turn culminated in the emergence of violent political clashes and strife. I have attempted to move away from the treatment of conflict as simply reflective and expressive of underlying contradictions and oppositions but rather, as it surfaced, as an active element in producing changes in the structure of social and political relationships on the mine. Also, in doing this, I have outlined for one context at a brief moment in its history, some of the factors which inhibit or limit some of his explanatory principles in the analysis of conflict. His work still stands and will for future generations of anthropologists as a monument to a significant scholar in the history of anthropology.

NOTES

1 Versions of this paper were read at the Manchester and Adelaide anthropology seminars. The late Professor Gluckman discussed aspects of the arguments with me. I acknowledge my deep intellectual debt to him as teacher, friend and colleague. Others who have assisted me in the writing of this paper are John Gray, Jacki Gray, Roy Fitzhenry, Adrian Peace, Tom Ernst and Morris Sheftel.
2 In 1928 the Cell Room in the Mine Zinc Plant was constructed. This involved a new process of which Management was duly proud. Workers in the Cell Room were given special privileges. Thus they worked a 4-hour shift for which they received an equivalent of an 8-hour shift pay. At the time of fieldwork the Management was considering cutting some of these privileges but had not yet found a way to do it (*see* Kapferer 1969 for a description of this work context).
3 My use of the terms 'field' and 'arena' is in accordance with their definition in Kapferer, 1972.
4 Wives of miners often employed men living on the Farms or Plots to hoe their gardens on the outskirts of the mine township. This was often expressed by miners as a reason for holding the non-mining elements of the Farm population in low esteem.
5 When the Township Council was first instituted, it was to be composed of members nominated from each of the mine labour associations. The Union initially agreed to this. But, shortly after the first Council meeting, the Union withdrew its support. Selection to the Council was changed to one in which councillors were to be selected from each of the mine housing sections. There was little response from the mine population (only 20% of it voted in the first election) and councillors became, until 1964, largely Management nominees.

6 All except one of the councillors on the 1962 and 1963 Township Council were Staff. All had an education of Std. VI or above, a high level of education when taken in relation to the mine African labour force at the time.
7 This was virtually essential especially in view of the fact that the Community Services Manager who presided at the meetings from 1963 on was not acquainted with any of the major African languages. Just before I left the field in March 1966, when events on the mine had resulted in the Council's being largely composed of non-Staff workers, the Council was suspended. A major reason for its suspension was that the Community Services Manager was faced with presiding over a meeting in which only one councillor was fluent and literate in English.
8 Burawoy (1972: 239) states that U.N.I.P. derived its support both before and after independence from the poorer sections of Zambian communities. This is true only up to a point for the observation ignores the fact that in the immediate pre- and post-independence periods, the Party leadership, especially at the Constituency and Branch levels, often consisted of individuals from the better-educated and better-off elements of the urban communities.
9 The United Mineworkers Union was formally constituted out of the Miners African Staff Association at the General Council Meeting of this association on September 21 and 22, 1963 in Kitwe. The general managers of the Copperbelt and Broken Hill mines were notified of the new union by letter on September 23, 1963. It was not until October, however, that officials representative of U.M.U. at Broken Hill began pressing Management to enter into negotiations with them.
10 I itemize some of the more relevant clauses of this policy statement as an illustration.

'The General Policy of this Union is:

1) To improve and maintain the standard of living of people as specified in the Union's Constitution.

2) Bring unity among the mineworkers by establishing one said organization in the mining industry.

3) Combat unemployment and under-employment in conjunction with employers and Government.

4) Africanize unskilled and semi-skilled jobs in order to enable capable mine workers to acquire skill and managerial ability by practice without disturbing the efficiency of the industry.

5) Provide progressive increases in real income of the work people and at the same time see that employers remain in business and are not penalized unfairly by the Union demands.

6) See that wages are maintained in accordance with the changes in the cost of living. That gains in productivity are shared with workers.

7) Reduce the gap between skilled and semi-skilled by giving higher differential increases in pensions and other fringe benefits to lower graded people.

8) Establish Workers Co-Operative Movement in conjuction with the United Trades Union Congress.

9) Fight against any attempts to drive capital out of the country or against any tricks designed to hinder economic growth.

10) To provide social benefits to subscribing members of the Union.

11) Agitate for the establishment of one contract in the Mining Industry.'

11 These were respectively the U.N.I.P. Constituency Chairman, Constituency Secretary, Branch Trustee, Branch Secretary and Branch Youth Organizer.
12 At one point Management even considered taking legal action against the Staff Association.
13 Powdermaker (1962: 124) refers to a similar aspect of strike activity on the Copperbelt in the 1950's as does Epstein (1958: 96).
14 Gluckman distinguishes between consensus and cohesion. For example see Gluckman 1969a, 385-386.

LITERATURE CITED

Anglo American Corporation of South Africa L'td. Minutes of Meeting in Kitwe, September 16, 1960.
BATES, R. H. 1971. *Union, Parties and Political Development, a Study of Mineworkers in Zambia*. New Haven: Yale University Press.
BERGER, E. L. 1974. *Labour, Race and Colonial Rule*, Oxford.
BURAWOY, M. 1972. Another look at the mineworker, *African Social Research* XIV.
COSER, LEWIS. 1965. *The Functions of Social Conflict*, London: Routledge & Kegan Paul.
EPSTEIN, A. L. 1958. *Politics in an Urban African Community*, Manchester: Manchester University Press.
–. 1959. Linguistic innovation and culture in the Copperbelt, Northern Rhodesia, *Southwestern Journal of Anthropology* 15: 235-530.
–. 1964. Urban communities in Africa in *Closed Systems and Open Minds*. Edited by M. Gluckman, pp. 83-102. Chicago: Aldine.
GLUCKMAN, M. 1948. *Malinowski's Sociological Theories*, Rhodes Livingstone Paper 16. Manchester: Manchester University Press.
–. 1955. *Custom and Conflict in Africa*. Oxford: Basil Blackwell.
–. 1958. *Analysis of a Social Situation in Modern Zululand*. Manchester: Manchester University Press.
–. 1961a . Anthropological problems arising from the Africa industrial revolution, in *Social Change in Africa*. Edited by A.W. Southall. London: Oxford University Press for the International African Institute.
–. 1961b. Ethnographic data in British social anthropology, *The Sociological Review* M.S. 9, No. 1: 5-17.
–. 1963. *Rituals of Rebellion in South-East Africa*. Manchester 1954; reprinted in *Order and Rebellion in Tribal Africa*, London: Cohen and West.
–. 1965. *Politics, Law and Ritual in Tribal Society*. Oxford: Basil Blackwell.
–. 1968. The Utility of the Equilibrium Model in the Study of Social Change, *American Anthropologist* 70(2): 219-237.
–. 1969a. The tribal area in South and Central Africa, in *Pluralism in Africa*. Edited by L. Kuper and M.G. Smith, pp. 373-409. Berkeley and Los Angeles: University of California Press.
–. 1969b. Interhierarchical roles: professional and party ethics in tribal areas in South and Central Africa, in *Local-level Politics*. Edited by M.T. Swartz, pp. 69-93. London: University of London Press.

—. 1971. Tribalism, ruralism and urbanism in South and Central Africa, in *Colonialism in Africa 1870-1960 No. 3. Profiles of Change.* Edited by V. Turner, pp. 127-166. Cambridge: Cambridge University Press.

HARRIS, M. 1969. *The Rise of Anthropological Theory*, London: Routledge & Kegan Paul.

KAPFERER, B. 1966. *The Population of a Zambian Municipal Township,* Lusaka: Communication No. 1, Institue for Social Research, University of Zambia.

—. 1969. Norms and the manipulation of relationships in a work context, in *Social Networks in Urban Situations.* Edited by J. C. Mitchell, pp. 181-244. Manchester: Manchester University Press.

—. 1972. *Strategy and Transaction in an African Factory.* Manchester: Manchester University Press.

MURPHY, R.F. 1972. *The dialectics of social life: alarms and excursions in anthropological theory.* London: Allen & Unwin.

POWDERMAKER, H. 1962. *Copper Town.* New York and Evanston: Harper and Row.

Record of evidence heard by the Conciliator at Broken Hill Mine (Doubleday Conciliator), 1964.

Records of the Township Council 1961 to 1966.

Report of the Commission of Inquiry into the Mining Industry (Chairman, Roland Brown), Lusaka, 1966.

SIMMEL, G. 1955. *Conflict;* tr. by Kurt H. Wolf, and *The web of group affiliation*; tr. by Reinhard Bendix. Glencoe Ill.: Free Press.

VAN VELSEN, J. 1967. The Extended-case Method and Situational Analysis in *The Craft of Social Anthropology.* Edited by A. L. Epstein, pp. 129-49. London: Tavistock.

Of Signs and Symbols: The Transformation of Designations in Israeli Electioneering

SHLOMO DESHEN
Tel Aviv University

Signs and Symbols

Philosophers and linguists have for many years grappled with the problems of defining and delimiting designations such as signal, sign, symbol, icon, index. They concentrated mostly on the semantics and logics of the designations, and their approaches were orientated accordingly[1]. For anthropologists symbolism and symbols held great fascination ever since the Victorian founding fathers. Anthropological work, however, especially that of British and American anthropologists, while luxuriantly and vividly descriptive, has often been marked by a lack of concern for specification of concepts, leading to weak analyses. Only since the mid-1950s, possibly under the influence of Susanne Langer's popular *Philosophy in a New Key,* have anthropologists increasingly taken note of the studies of scholars such as Peirce and de Saussure in the new field of semiotics. The traditional interest in ongoing ritual and in symbolic activities, stimulated now by a heightened awareness of the multiple semantic and logical properties of symbols, has greatly advanced study in the field. As a result, anthropological research has become more sensitive and precise.

As is so often the case in matters of terminology, anthropologists in the field of symbolism have not arrived at a common detailed terminology, while in agreement on the essential issues (see for instance, Firth 1973: 74-5, Turner 1967: 19-47, Beattie 1964: 69-71). In both semiotics and anthropology we now find a proliferation of concepts and classifications of designations. For the anthropologist, in common with social scientists generally, the specification of the various types of designation is primarily a problem of specifying different types of action within the broad sphere of designative action (see Salomon 1964). It is not only a question of abstract logic and semantics.

The general recognition by social scientists of symbols as the elemental components of culture has long stimulated the study of symbols and systems of symbols. Hence the many anthropological monographs elucidating systems of symbolic action that have cropped up over the years. However, anthropologists beyond interpreting designations substantively have not devoted much attention to the actual variety of types of designations because of the disregard of relevant work in the field of semiotics. Nor have anthropologists devoted much attention to dynamic processes whereby designations change their character and mutate (but see recently Harris 1973). Given the premise that symbols (and designations generally) are the elemental components of culture, the study of culture change demands precise study of the dynamic processes pertaining to symbols. Yet anthropological studies of changing cultures are not noted for precise examinations of the processes of symbolic change. Mostly, these studies content themselves with presenting blanket discussions of the constriction or abandonment of traditional symbols and the adoption of new ones. In this paper I seek to contribute to the study of the dynamics of change in the area of symbolism. I describe a particular phenomenon of mutating designations and explain it by considering the broader socio-cultural context. For heuristic purposes I operate with one of the several sets of classifications offered by semiotics.

The great variety of designations can be located on a continuum, pointing to an extensive range of activities. At one pole they indicate very specific, clearly delimited actions; at the opposing end very diffuse and unspecified actions. I suggest that *designation* be the inclusive generic term, with those clustering around one pole classified as *signals*, those near the opposing end *symbols*, while *sign* be applied to designations of an intermediate type. We shall remain close to conventional linguistic usage in terming a polysemous designation (one which generates a variety of meanings of whose existence the actor may not be aware) as a symbol. The complexity of the symbol renders it opaque to the actor, and even when the different meanings are explicated, the symbol is likely to remain vague. The opposite designation, on the other hand, with its simple direct meaning known to the actor, is a signal. The term sign, culturally more loaded than the barren signal but less so than the symbol, suits designations of the intermediate type. This conceptual frame is not in my view inherently superior to that of alternative classifications; it is merely useful for practical purposes of social science. I grind the axe of studying the mutation of designations, and I use these concepts only as convenient pegs for the presentation of data. I am not directly concerned with the semiotic problem of constructing concepts and classifications of designations.

In many countries holding democratic elections political parties are represented by various culture designations, such as pictures and letters of the alphabet. The phenomenon is common among electorates with low levels of literacy, such as in India and East Africa. But occasionally one encounters it also in literate societies; the Democratic donkey and Republican elephant are outstanding U.S. examples. The manipulation of cultural designations in electioneering poses many problems for the social anthropologist, in connection with the mechanisms of manipulation and the pertinent socio-cultural conditions. At the same time these phenomena of manipulation lend themselves readily to analysis. First, electioneering actions are dramatic and closely concentrated in time and space, rendering them amenable to full observation in the field. Second, designations that figure at electioneering are of a simple type in comparison with the maze of complex ritual symbols that usually confronts the anthropologist of symbols. Third, the phenomena often have considerable comparability. Anthropology however, has hardly devoted them any serious attention[2].

For the present, I propose to pursue the study of mutating designations in the field of electioneering manipulations, and within this field, in the Israeli electioneering scene.

The Activation of Signs

Coming to the Israeli scene, we find a variety of cultural designations being manipulated in the course of electioneering. Such typical Jewish religious rituals and symbols as *Torah* scroll presentations, traditional feasts, and the readings of holy texts serve as vehicles to project political messages. In other words, religious symbols are being charged with political content (see my descriptions in Deshen 1970, ch. 7, and in Deshen & Shokeid 1974, ch. 5). At the same time, the converse process also takes place, i.e., political signs are charged with religious symbolic content; stated differently, political signs are religiously activated. In the present paper I am concerned with the latter process. I shall describe this particular kind of symbolic transformation and seek to show what social forces are operative therein.

At the polls, the Israeli voter is faced with lists of candidates (rather than with individual candidates), which represent the various political parties. Since the names of most of the parties are long and rambling, each party, as a matter of convenience, campaigns under an alphabetic sign, decided upon by a central elections committee. The choice of the particular alphabetical letter (or letters) of each party is often arbitrary, a barren sign, devoid of any partisan content and close to the signal pole of the continuum of designations. For example, the *Rakah* party ('New Communist List') was assigned the leter 'v'[3]. The campaigners, however, prefer a letter that figures prominently in the name of the party, which in actual fact is usually the case. Thus the *Liberalim Atzmaiyim* party ('Independent Liberals') campaigned under the 'LA' sign. Sometimes the party is assigned a letter that expresses something of the political image the campaigners wish to convey. Thus, for many years, the *Mapai* party ('Labor') campaigned under the sign 'A'. While the letter was prominent in the party's name, its major political thrust was that 'A' generated the notion of primacy, that *Mapai* was a party standing vanguard. This sign is capital political propaganda value in a future-oriented society beset with external conflict and committed to building its nationhood. The sign was changed some years ago when *Mapai* merged with other parties which had their own election signs, and a new common sign had to be formulated. The new party, now called *Ma'arakh* ('The Alignment: the Israel Labor party, the United Workers' party, and Non-partisans') campaigns under the letters 'AMT'. Similarly, 'B' is the campaign letter of Mafdal ('Religious National Front'), assigned to it after 'A' had already been given to *Mapai*. 'B' does not figure at all in the name of the party, but neither does 'A'. However, 'B', as 'A', is a prominent letter since it is near the beginning of the alphabet and thus is acceptable as a good second choice. A most colorful choice of election sign occurred in the 1973 general elections when a protest group calling itself *Hapanterim Hashehorim* ('*the Black Panthers*'), composed of disgruntled young men mostly of Moroccan origin, many of them from poor and deprived homes, insisted on being assigned the letter 'Z' whose pronunciation is *zain*. In Hebrew slang *zain* means phallus and the election sign 'Z' was thus intended as a symbol of the group's contempt for society and its values. In the past 'Z' had not been used as a sign in national elections and it was assigned only relectantly after heated arguments by the elections committee[4].

From an analytical point of view these election labels are 'signs' in the technical sense outlined above, certainly the 'V' sign and even the 'LA' sign, the latter though slightly less (since it has an inherent relationship with its referrent). The 'A' and 'B' signs are also barren, but less so. 'A' and 'B' carry some inherent cultural content and therefore tend to be a little further removed from the signal pole of designations. The 'Z' sign is, of course, much closer to the symbol pole. As a whole, however, all these signs refer to a reasonably clear and delimited reality. Their meanings are simple, direct, and known to the actors. These signs are a far cry from fully developed symbols, such as a national flag, the cross, the Torah, whose referrents are extremely diffuse, complex, and ambiguous.

During electioneering, however, a process is at work which activates and transforms barren political signs into designations of a far more powerful symbolic nature. The Israeli electorate is highly heterogeneous and the discussion which follows focuses on that specific sector in which I was a participant observer – first-generation immigrants hailing from traditional communities in the lesser developed regions of Muslim countries. On the whole, these people have only a very limited education, and their civic experience is minimal. Prior to immigrating to Israel they had never participated in a free election campaign. My observations were carried out mostly in a town that I call Ayara, among immigrants from Southern Tunisia, and to a smaller extent among immigrants from Southern Morocco (see Deshen 1970, 1972). Most intensively I studied the election campaigns of the *Mafdal* party.

The alphabetical signs of the parties were often featured on poster-size placards, with the full name of the parties appearing in small print below. Also in oral campaigning the signs figured prominently in the slogans of the campaigners. People, especially those not conversant with the techniques of political campaigns and electioneering, were puzzled by the political signs. Sometimes, after hearing a lengthy political harangue, at which partisan ideology and policy had been aired and the name and sign of the party repeatedly mentioned, people would voice their confusion with such an emphatic question as 'But what does 'B' mean?' While the ranting politicans had elucidated the practical political meaning of 'B', it had failed to register in these people's minds.

Those politicians who came to address mass meetings and rallies in Ayara from large party centers, such as Tel Aviv and Jerusalem, and were of an ethnic and cultural background very different from that of the local electorate were often quite insensitive to the effect their speeches and comport had on their audience. Most of the smaller campaign gatherings however, were addressed by comparatively minor local politicians whose social background was identical, or similar, to that of the electorate, and they were more attuned to the mood of their listeners. These politicians quickly reacted to the confusion of their audiences, obviating questions and misunderstandings by offering symbolic meanings to the signs. The *Mafdal* campaigners whom I often observed commonly interpreted their sign homiletically (but not only they), drawing it within the range of comprehension and familiarity of the electorate. I quote from my observations of a small election meeting in an Ayara home:

> Towards the end of the meeting only one practical issue was raised. Since nearly all the women were illiterate, one lady asked how would they remember and recognize the 'B' ... of the party? [The politician] reacted to the question as to a challenge. He perceived it as being more than a mere demand for information, but also as implicit disagreement and rejection of the arguments he had presented. He countered by presenting emotional slogans, i.e., a string of homiletic associations of the

Hebrew character 'B'. The women would remember the symbol by bearing in mind that it figures in such hopeful phrases as 'in the beginning the L-rd created...' (*bereishit bara*...), the opening verse of the Bible. 'B' also stands from *beriut* (health), and for *berakha* (blessing). As against this, [the politician] warned in conclusion, let no one by mischance vote *Ma'arakh*, whose alphabetic sign was AT. The AT sign is ominously symbolic: it stands for *ayn Torah* – no Torah! Each woman was advised to tuck a scrap of paper marked with a 'B' in her bosom before entering the polling booth, and in the booth to choose the election slip according to the model. Upon this the meeting was closed and all went home.

(Deshen 1970: 168)

The reactions of this particular group of voters were not solely prompted by the very practical matter of their illiteracy. Evidently the politician considered these women literate enough to be able to compare the letters in the ballot booth with the sample letter they were advised to bring with them. And in any case his homiletical interpretations of the sign 'B' were in no way relevant to the practical question of identifying the letter. The politician had perceived the woman's question in much more profound terms: 'What is the inherent meaning of the party's sign?' and his answer was on that level. He transformed the strictly technical political sign into a veritable religious symbol by associating 'B' with some of the major themes in popular Judaism: the fundamental creation myth related in the *Torah* (by stressing the opening verse in particular), the universal quest for welfare, and diffuse blessing. Yearnings and feelings, traditionally articulated in theological or liturgical terms, were here expressed in a form that suits modern political action – namely through the sign 'B'. The politician sought to endow the 'B' sign with such profound religious feelings as the deep sentiments evoked at the ritual reading of the opening *Torah* verses, to which traditionally is attributed the joy of being part of the nation that studies the Holy Writ and practices its precepts, and the firm resolution (also traditionally called forth by the reading) to be steadfast in continuing to study and practice. By investing the election sign with these meanings, the politician offered his audience a clever mnemonic device. They would now be less likely to forget the sign of his party. But thereby they also transformed the 'B' sign into a religious symbol: it has acquired a variety of meanings, some of them referring to very deep layers of Jewish religious sentiment, which the actors are able to articulate only with great difficulty, if at all. The religious message attains form and shape in terms of concrete political action and is now somewhat akin to this: by selecting the 'B' slip in the voting booth the voter expresses joy and satisfaction at being one of those who trust in the Creator of the world, who treasure the Holy Writ and exemplify it personally, and he acts to assure that the Holy Writ will also be treasured by society at large. For this good deed the L-rd will grant health and blessings. The politician in fact creates a new religious symbol that is in consonance with the election procedure[5].

Not only are religious symbols created in the process of electioneering, but derogative religious meaning is attributed to the signs of rival parties. The 1965 'AT' sign of *Ma'arakh*, the rival of *Mafdal*, was interpreted by the religious politician as having the substantive content *ayn Torah* ('no *Torah*'). By driving home to the voter this particular interpretation, the politician cautioned him that if he votes the 'AT' slip, he in fact repudiates *Torah*, the holy teaching. In 1969, when the *Ma'arakh* sign was 'AMT', I encountered variations on this theme at gatherings of *Mafdal*. One was *ayn emuna* ('no faith'). This was a somewhat clumsy play on the letter 'M' in the party's sign, but the interpretive effect was similar to the one previously mentioned. Another 'anti-AMT' slogan is remarkable for its political rather than religious symbolic interpretation. Since Hebrew writing is usually not plene (vowels are rarely used), the letters AMT' can be read as *A Met*. During an election address, a campaigner of Mafdal interpreted the 'AMT' sign as meaning *Aleph Met* ('A is dead!'). The letter 'A' had for many years been the election sign of *Mapai*, the main component of *Ma'arakh* formed in the 1960s, which had in the past attracted many observant voters to the distress of the religious parties. *Ma'arakh*, however, included labor groups whose position on religious issues was much more adverse to religionists than that of the old *Mapai*. Hence one of the arguments of the religious parties in 1969, voiced orally and in written propaganda, was that the old *Mapai* no longer existed and that the new *Ma'arakh* was inimical toward religious policies. *Mafdal* thus attempted to wean some of the traditional support among religious voters away from *Ma'arakh*. The *Aleph Met* slogan of *Mafdal* transformed the 'AMT' sign into a political symbol through which the voter expressed a view of developments within the party in recent years.

Also the other political parties in Ayara engaged in symbolic innovation. The new *Ma'arakh* sign, 'AMT', lent itself very neatly to homiletic manipulations. It is in fact reasonable to assume that the party leaders exerted themselves at the central elections committee to be assigned this particular combination of letters. The letters *A*, *M*, and *T*, read as a single word, form the wordt *emet* (the diphtong *a* receiving the vowel *e*), meaning 'truth'. *Ma'a-*

rakh campaigners sometimes exploited this fact gleefully. One address that I heard closed emphatically with the following words:

> I have told you the truth ('emet'), the whole truth ('emet'), and now we shall all go and vote Emet!

Ma'arakh campaigners developed the pun very imaginatively and systematically. During the 1969 campaign, throughout the country, buses along their entire length were plastered with the slogans *Emet Ve'Emuna* ('True and Trustworthy') and *Emet Ve'Yatziv* ('True and Firm'). These expressions, prominent in Jewish liturgy, come immediately after the recital of the verses beginning with 'Hear, O Israel' (Deut. 6 : 4) that form the credo of Judaism and climax religious services. They convey the worshiper's approval and confirmation of the credo and in their liturgical context are vehicles through which a mood of unconditional trust and ecstasy is generated.

One of the most pervasive campaign arguments of *Ma'arakh* was that since the creation of the State it had been the mainstay in the formation of all governments. *Ma'arakh* campaigners argued that the party should be returned because it had proved itself in the past and its leaders were experienced in statecraft, whereas the opposition politicians had never wielded power and were inexperienced. The latter should, therefore, not be entrusted with forming a government and should not be supported at the polls. These politicians transformed the bare 'AMT' sign into the resonant word *emet* and associated it with powerful liturgical phrases which arouse sentiments of rock-firm trust, belief, and constancy: feelings that suited the party's political slate admirably. *Ma'arakh's* 'AMT' did not become as sweeping and imaginative a religious symbol as *Mafdal's* 'B', but it was infused with very potent and intense feelings rooted in Jewish liturgy.

A dramatic instance of symbolic creation occured during the 1965 Ayara election campaign with a small religious party (*Poalei Agudat Yisrael*, in short called *Pai*), whose election sign 'D' was devoid of any substantive significance. The letter is one of the many that compose that party's full Hebrew name. On one occasion a politician closed his address to a group of immigrants from Southern Morocco with the dramatic call,

> 'Hear O Israel, the L-rd is our G-d, the L-rd is one (*ehad*)! This is the D, the great D, the D of *Pai*, Vote D!

We have two designations here: a religious symbol, the text 'Hear O Israel...' and a political sign, the letter 'D'. In an earlier study (Deshen and Shokeid 1974, ch. 5) I have discussed the religious symbol and the way it changed in this instance; here I wish to analyze the political sign and indicate how it was activated and transformed into a religious symbol.

Throughout Jewish history intense religious feelings have been aroused by this ancient monotheistic call. These emotions erupted particularly during periods of persecution, and generations of Jewish martyrs have died with this verse on their lips. There is a traditional form in which the credo is written in *Torah* scrolls. The last letters of the first and last words of the verse are in characters larger than the rest, a form copied in all prayer books. This verse, richly charged with associations, the politician grafted unto the election sign of his party, which happened to be the Hebrew character made prominent in the credo. Thereby he imbued the colorless and bare election sign with a repertory of religious references. The politician is suggesting to the electorate that by selecting the 'D' slip they are in fact expressing the credo and all that is traditionally evoked by its liturgical expression. The associative content of the verse is of such theological and existential profundity that virtually a whole literature of rabbinical homiletics has developed around this single verse. All this is now linked to the 'D' of the party in the context of the selection of slips in the ballot booth.

I present finally the most radical instance of symbolic creation that I observed. It occurred at a 1969 election discussion among a group of Moroccan immigrants in Ayara. One man, a staunch supporter of *Mafdal*, was enthusiastically expounding his views to his more sober companions. He stated emphatically:

> When I go to vote, I take the 'B' slip in my hand. I kiss it! I say the *Lesheim yihud kudsha*! And I drop it into the ballot box!

This is routine behavior in the performance of acts of ritual devotion in Judaeo-Moroccan tradition. Had the man referred to orthodox actions of standard ritual, his description of the kissing and uttering of *Lesheim yihud kudsha* would have been quite common. Remarkable is the fact that he was referring to voting actions. The *Lesheim yihud kudsha* is prefaced to numerous standard ritual actions, such as the daily prayers, putting on phylacteries, the eating of unleavened bread of Passover. Frequently, when the ritual hinges on a concrete artifact one kisses the object prior to performance of the act. In this incident, however, the actor atrributed to the 'B' slip and the voting act the religious behavior of tradition. The *Lesheim yihud kudsha* prayer is a mystical text of the late *Kabbalah* that, according to certain variants of Jewish rite (including those of North Africa), is prefaced to a great variety of ritual actions. The text is in Aramaic, the content highly esoteric, and it is virtually untranslatable without engaging in a preliminary discourse on its complex theosophical terminology (see Jacobs 1972: 140-153). The ordinary worshiper does not usually have a full understanding of the text. What he does understand, and the meaning he gives the text, is the point relevant for present purposes. By reciting the *Lesheim yihud kudsha,* the worshiper expresses his hope that the ritual act he is about to perform be carried out in pure devotion without any extraneous, secular attributes or intensions. He prays that the act have certain profound mystical effects, one of which is to hasten the ultimate Redemption and the coming of the Messiah. The voting act just described has thus become not a medium to effect political aims, not even to effect religious policies, but a definite ritual action that has been endowed with the appropriate behavior customary in Judaeo-Moroccan tradition. Remarkably, this instance of symbolization was neither the work of a propagandist nor of an outsider, but of an unsophisticated local. Here it can be seen that the process of symbolization of political signs, far from stemming only from the machination of advertisers, is also rooted in the culture of the electorate.

The North African Immigrant Electorate

Having documented the activation of political signs and their transformation into designations of a more symbolic nature, we must now consider the social background of the actors that we may understand why these phenomena occurred. As mentioned above, the sector I observed was mostly composed of recent first-generation immigrants from Muslim countries. They stem mainly from closed traditional Jewish communities and to most of them traditional Jewish symbols are highly resonant. These immigrants constitute a large portion of the electorate and at election time their vote is naturally highly sought after. The politicians in trying to attract the popular vote exert themselves in a variety of strategies: one general line of electioneering is the manipulation of religious symbols.

The parties are divided over a great variety of issues: economic, foreign, social and religious. In the present context the religious issues are noteworthy. There are recurring controversies in Israel as to the extent to which Judaism, as currently interpreted by religious authorities, should be accorded legal status. This problem has many practical ramifications that reach down to the individual citizen. The most debated of these are such questions as: Should public transport run on the Sabbath? Should commercial amusement places be open on these days and on religious holidays? Should personal law be formulated according to canon or civil law? The problem of personal law has been particularly acute. Until the present time personal law is enacted and executed by rabbinical authorities. In practice this means that, among other things, all marriage and divorce contracts are religious acts and certain categories of marital unions are not legal because they are prohibited by religious law. The attitudes to this setup of the various sectors of the population and their political organs run the gamut of opinion – from radical secularism, through liberal forms of traditionalism, to fundamentalism and extreme orthodoxy. At the latter end of the continuum there are several religious parties whose major election plank consists of assuring legal standing to various requirements of canon law as currently interpreted by rabbinical authorities. The major political parties in the country generally support the orthodox position, while a group of small secular parties is consistently pitted against it. In general, however, the present setup enjoys a good deal of support rooted in Jewish folk sentiment.

First-generation immigrants coming from such places as rural North Africa do not differentiate very clearly between the variegated motivations and aims of the different parties. To them all parties and politicians are novel and foreign[6]. Though personally attuned to the policies and aims of the religious parties, their concrete organizational phenomenon is profoundly baffling to the immigrants. This paradox is rooted in socio-historical factors. In North Africa, particularly among Moroccan Jewry, religious authority was often invested in charismatic individuals, who were more or less self-appointed, or in the scions of aristocratic families that provided religious leaders generation after generation. In either case, religious authority did not stem from a very broad base of communal decision. Among European Jewry, on the other hand, religious authority was, to a much more considerable extent, a function of communal decision. Oligarchic community leaders had much more say in the 'making' and 'unmaking' of rabbis than they had in North Africa. In traditional European Jewry, even since late medieval times, the communities, moved by a powerful sensation of corporate identity, were autonomously governed by formal institutionalized bodies that acted in accordance with written statutes. The communities were administered by lay officers who, while themselves bound by statutes that delimited their powers, appointed the local clergy. The role of the latter was clearly defined by formal general statutes and personal contracts. The local rabbis usually commanded their flock's deep respect, but at the same time they were subject to the community as a corporate body.

Among Oriental Jewries clerical leadership was usually not so clearly differentiated from other types of communal leadership. The rabbis did not have formally defined positions in relation to those of other local wielders of power. Organizationally Oriental rabbis were often much more the masters of the local community than their European counterparts. This is typified by the Moroccan situation where synagogues were very often the private property of rabbinical families and were operated by individual rabbis. They were not owned and run by the community as such (Bénech 1940: 116-18). North African Jewish community power was often highly concentrated. Not only was there a general lack of formal community statutes that act to inhibit the power of the individual, but often religious and lay leadership roles were united in the same person. Particular families often producing rabbis *cum* general community leaders for several generations (Goldberg 1972: 22-34, Goulven 1927: 101, Zafrani 1972: 124)[7].

Finally one has to bear in mind the particular marabout tradition of all North Africa (see for instance Geertz 1968), which has also colored North African Judaism and which accords great power to religious personalities generally. The consequence of all this is that the role of the traditional Oriental rabbi is a much more potent one than that of the traditional European rabbi.

This background is relevant to Israeli politics. Both the traditional European rabbinical role and the lay leadership role have been carried over into the modern context of Israeli democracy. But the latter role is strange to Oriental and particularly to Moroccan immigrants. They are perplexed by the phenomenon of laymen propagating religious policies (as they are altogether struck by the novelty that persons who wield authority have to seek popular support). From their experience in Jewish communities abroad, these immigrants expect religious policies to be promoted exclusively by aristocratic, venerable, and saintly rabbis. They expect the propagators to exhibit the qualities of patrimonial behavior associated with the aristocratic rabbinical leadership of old, such as generosity, charity, and dignity (see Flamand 1956: 218-9 for a sketch of a Moroccan rabbi). Instead, the immigrants are confronted by small politicians seeking bits of power. The fact that the politicians of religious parties promise, by and large most sincerely, to use their powers for religious purposes does not make them less novel and strange a phenomenon than their counterparts in other parties. All politicians competing for power in a democratic system are for these immigrants a novelty, but religious politicians even more so; and the latter are not only baffling to them but also deeply disappointing. A father of nine, from Morocco and deeply religious, characteristically remarked to me during the 1969 election campaign:

> I dislike *Mafdal*. They ought to go around asking people what is bothering them. There are large families in need who are ashamed to ask

for assistance. True, none of the parties do this, but the religious party ought to help because that is its *raison d'être* (*ha'ikar bishvilam*). It would then not need to spend much money on campaigning because people would vote for it anyway. Now only people of deep piety (*sheyesh lahem yire'a va'fahad*), who understand the need for religious schools and the other things that *Mafdal* aims for, vote for them.

The man expressed his bitterness at religious politicians who do not live up to the noble patrimonial role that he envisages for religious leaders. In his opinion, the religious party is now popular only among persons who dissociate the attractive aims of the party from its unattractive organizational and personal features, but not among ordinary folk.

I now suggest that the infusion of religious content into the otherwise quite colorless signs of political mechanics should be seen in conjunction with the whole electoral atmosphere outlined above, i.e., campaigning among an electorate to many of whom the workings of elections and democratic politics generally are novel and strange, to whom the phenomenon of religious policies propagated by laymen is foreign. The phenomenon of religious policies promoted by laymen and expressed at the crucial stage of ballot selection through religiously neutral, technical, and unaffective signs is utterly frustrating to these people. The frustration is rooted in the situation of an electorate undergoing change and moving from a comparatively simple structured, relatively undifferentiated society to a far more complex and differentiated society.

Democratic electoral procedures, such as those in Israel, imply considerable social and symbolic differentiation, which the electorate neither experienced nor even conceived of in its North African past[8]. It is the reactions of the electorate to the practices they encountered in Israel that underlie and prompted the transformation of political signs into religious symbols. Thus, in the case of the women who asked for the meaning of the 'B' sign, we have the quest for elucidation of the political sign at a deeper symbolic level. Going beyond the simple technical message, they wanted an interpretation in religious terms.

The people involved, both religious politicians and the electorate, resolved the problems of making democratic elections intelligible by causing the mechanics of elections to fall into the grooves of activities more familiar to the electorate, namely activities pertinent to religious symbols. This, in fact, was the only feasible thing to do. On the level of social differentiation, the politicians could be conformable only to a very limited extent. After all, they were not saintly rabbis, and the role of an Israeli politican and that of a rabbi, as conceived by traditionalists from North Africa, are not easily bridged. Theoretically, the politicians might try to assume the role of rabbinical figures and the electorate, for its part, might elect only traditional rabbis. In fact, such developments are present, but only very marginally. Powerful political and social processes operating in Israeli society obviate such developments. In the matter of symbolic differentiation – political aims articulated by political signs and not by religious symbols – the politicians were able to be much more pliable and compliant (see also Cohen 1970: 612-13). As a consequence, the electoral procedure as a whole became more understandable and the parties projected their messages more effectively.

My analysis concentrated on the transformative activities of politicians and supporters of religious parties among North African immigrants. However, parties, such as *Ma'arakh*, that are indifferent to religion and do not seek support exclusively among observant voters also engaged in such activities. Some of them I have documented above. These parties, when approaching the electorate, do not face the complex problem of their religious rivals. Then why do they sometimes engage in similar transformative practices? The answer I suggest may lie in the fact that the Labor party and other secular parties cannot idly stand by while the religious parties develop such powerful campaign techniques as the creation of religious symbols. All the more so since Labor traditionally draws many of its votes from first-generation immigrants from Muslim countries. Secular politicians therefore engage, often quite consciously, in the manipulation of religious symbols[9].

I have demonstrated the activation and transformation of political signs into symbols. Where does this lead us to in the study of symbolism? Many more and systematic studies of the phenomenon are, of course, needed before we attain a firm empirical base for any kind of generalization. Many data on mutating designations, embedded in anthropological and historical monographs, need to emerge and to be explicated in the light of our interests in the present context. Our theoretical aim should be toward uncovering the general pattern whereby designations mutate. This entails discovering the kinds of designations that are more (or less) prone to mutation, the direction and extent of mutation, and the socio-cultural conditions under which the phenomena occur.

NOTES

The paper is based on fieldwork that was supported by the Bernstein Fund for Research on Israel, which was organized and directed by Max Gluckman. Early versions were presented at the 9th I.C.A.E. Chicago 1973, and to seminars at the universities of Tel Aviv, S.U.N.Y.-Albany, Utah, U.C.-Berkeley, Sussex and U.C.-London. I am grateful to the colleagues who helped with comments; particulary M. Aronoff, Erik Cohen, H. Goldberg, R. Kahane, G. Kressel, M. Nash, M. Schwartz, M. Shokeid, S. Weil, W. Zenner. Also to Mrs. A. Sommer (Goldberg) for editorial help and Mr. R. Attal for bibliographic advice. Lamentably, Max Gluckman is not among those who commented. Shortly before his death I sent him the paper for comment, but he did not live to do so. A superb critic, loving friend, unforgettable teacher, Max had always been generous. Only very few of my papers in many years did not benefit from him directly. Regretably, this is one of them. As such, incomplete in a poignant way, it is a humble expression of my sorrow.

1 For a summary of some of this work see, for instance, Schutz 1964.
2 For minor treatments see Rigby (1965), Kressel (1972: 144) and Firth (1973: 23-25); also Shridharani (1954) for an interesting journalistic discussion.
3 The Hebrew letter V(*vav*) is not at all associated with 'victory' as in European languages, so that 'V' as an Israeli political sign is absolutely barren of inherent content.
4 *Hapanterim Hashehorim* campaigned under the ambiguous slogan *Sim Zain*, literally meaning 'place a 'Z' slip,' but also meaning 'screw them'; they failed dismally at the elections. For details see Cohen 1972.
5 At this juncture I should like to dispose of a possible *caveat*. One might argue that in the context of political propaganda campaigners unscrupulously manipulated cultural symbols, and that an interpretation in cultural terms, such as I am attempting here, is inappropriate. To this I would counter that the presumed unscrupulousness of propagandists and advertisers generally, rests largely on popular belief whereas sociologically this remains an open question. Furthermore, granting popular belief, one still faces the problem as to why advertisers choose to manipulate particular symbols in particular ways. The work of the advertisers is evidently based, partly at least, on the judgement of his clientele, and is anything but random. Thus the manipulations of advertisers in order that they may be understood sociologically must be discussed in terms of broad social reality.
6 This characterization of this particular sector of the Israeli electorate is based on first-hand experience of the Israeli immigrant scene in recent years. It has been graphically pictured and caricatured in a movie such as Kishon's 'Sallah Shabbati'.
7 These generalizations on Jewish leadership in North Africa and in Europe necessitate a grounding in socio-historical research. For European Jewry the facts have been well established in such works as Katz (1961), ch. 17; Ben-Sasson (1959) chs. 11, 12 and appendix 2 particularly; and in studies by other scholars. There is no comparable research in the social history of traditional Jewish communities in Muslim countries on the eve of their breakdown. My argument relative to North Africa falls back on oral data on the recent past which fieldworkers in Israel have collected in recent years among immigrants from North Africa (see Goldberg 1972: 22-34, Shokeid 1971: 15-33 and n.d., Willner 1969: 253-302). But also the documentary evidence points in the direction that I have indicated. Flamand (1956, particularly pp. 218-35) and Bénech (1949, particularly pp. 116-36) in accounts of Jewish communities in southern Morocco in the first decades of French rule, describe in general a relatively undifferentiated community leadership with many functions united in a small number of people. We find in the sources details of specific institutional arrangements typical of relatively undifferentiated political and religious institutions. For instance, whereas in Europe, ever since the late middle ages, rabbis were exempt

from paying communal taxes, in Morocco this was a debated point (see Zafrani 1969: 37 and 1972: 138-40). And again in contrast to European practice, rabbis in Morocco did not always draw a salary from the community (Zafrani 1972: 122). Some rabbis had an income from commerce (Bénech 1940: 133) and, when acting as judges, held court in their private homes, not in community offices (p. 135). All this leads one to a picture of a situation where the dividing line between the lay community leadership and the religious leadership was not very clear. (In parantheses it is notable, that whatever evidence there is of rabbinical exemption from taxation comes from the towns of North Morocco; in the small communities of the Atlas mountains rabbis were probably not exempt, and differentiation there was even less clearcut than in the north). See also Benayahu 1953: 100-3, for some further relevant documentary evidence.

8 In my usage of the concept 'differentiation', and its derivatives 'social differentiation' and 'symbolic differentiation', I follow such works as Eisenstadt 1973, ch. 7, and more generally Eisenstadt 1963.

9 A point relevant to the sociological study of migration and directed change: All too often one comes across studies which discuss the change experienced by people subjected to directed change, or migrant groups such as the Israeli electorate of North African origin, only in terms that are strictly delimited to the people who are presumably changing. Thus there are many studies on the changing economy, political organization, or culture of this or that migrant or remote tribe, which focus strictly on the group undergoing change. These studies obviate, because of their limited focus, the very plausible fact that the dominant society and its institutions might concommitantly be undergoing changes. Therefore while they may illuminate their delimited fields, such studies create a distorted perspective, because their silence on the wider field of the absorbing or colonial society implies that no concommitant changes take place elsewhere in that society. In a rather neglected paper on the economic practices of new farmers in Israel, Weingrod (1962) forcefully pointed out that studies of directed change or migration should not be rigidly focused on the delimited population that is presumed to be changing and demonstrated that changes flowed in at least two directions. The administrators of the new farming projects indeed caused profound occupational and economic changes among the immigrants, but the latter also provoked very considerable modifications of the economic institutions to which they were supposed to adapt. Weingrod applied the term 'reciprocal change' to this process. Discussing social change in terms of a variety of levels of change, or at least in terms of 'reciprocal change,' affords a more sophisticated view of reality than that which one gains from the more traditional approaches in studies of social change. The process of 'reciprocal change,' I argue, operates also in Israeli election procedures as analyzed here, and in many other social institutions (see again Cohen 1970: 612). The new voters adapt to democratic practices, as Weingrod's farmers adapted to new economic pratices. However, just as the latter cause the economic institutional arrangements to change, so do the new voters cause certain aspects of electioneering practices to be modified.

REFERENCES

BEATTIE, J. 1964. *Other Cultures: Aims, Methods and Achievements in Social Anthropology*. London: Routledge & Kegan Paul.

BENAYAHU, M. 1953. *Marbitz Tora* (Hebrew), Jerusalem: Harav Kook Institute.
BÉNECH, J. 1949. *Essai d'Explication d'un Mellah*, Baden-Baden.
BEN-SASSON, H. H. 1959. *Hagut Ve'hanhaga* (Hebrew) Jerusalem: Bialik Institute.
COHEN, E. 1970. Development Towns: The Social Dynamics of 'Planted' Communities in Israel, in *Integration and Development in Israel*. Edited by S. N. Eisenstadt, R. Bar-Yosef and C. Adler, pp. 587-617. Jerusalem: Israel Universities Press.
—. 1972 The Black Panthers and Israeli Society, *Jewish Journal of Sociology*, XVI: 93-109.
DESHEN, S. 1970. *Immigrant Voters in Israel: Parties and Congregations in a Local Election Campaign,* Manchester: Manchester University Press.
—. 1972. 'The Business of Ethnicity is Finished!'?: The Ethnic Factor in a Local Election Campaign, in *The Elections in Israel, 1969*. Edited by A. Arian, pp. 278-304. Jerusalem: Academic Press.
DESHEN, S. & SHOKEID, M. (co-authors) 1974. *The Predicament of Homecoming: Cultural and Social Life of North African Immigrants in Israel*, Ithaca, N.Y.: Cornell University Press.
EISENSTADT, S. N. 1963. *The Political Systems of Empires*, Glencoe, Ill.: Free Press, 1963.
EISENSTADT, S. N. 1973. *Tradition, Change and Modernity,* New York: Wiley, 1973.
FIRTH, R. 1973. *Symbols: Public and Private*, London: George Allen & Unwin.
FLAMAND, P. 1956. *Les communautés israélites du Sud-Marocain: essai de description et d'analyze de la vie juive en milieu berbère*, Casablanca.
GEERTZ, C. 1968. *Islam Observed: Religious Developments in Morocco and Indonesia*, New Haven: Yale University Press.
GOLDBERG, H. E. 1972. *Cave Dwellers and Citrus Crowers: A Jewish Community in Libya and Israel*, Cambridge: Cambridge University Press.
GOULVEN, J. 1927. *Les Mellahs de Rabat-Salé*, Paris: Geuthner.
JACOBS, L. 1972. *Hassidic Prayer*. London: Routledge & Kegan Paul.
HARRIS, G. 1973. Inward-Looking and Outward-Looking Symbols. Paper read at the 9th International Congress of Anthropological and Ethnological Sciences, Chicago, September 1973.
KATZ, J. 1961. *Tradition and Crisis: Jewish Society at the End of the Middle Ages,* Glencoe, Ill.: Free Press.
KRESSEL, G. M. 1972. *The Dynamics of an Israeli-Arab Community in a Process of Urbanization*. Unpublished Ph.D. dissertation, Tel Aviv University (in Hebrew).
LANGER, S. 1942. *Philosophy in a New Key,* Cambridge, Mass.: Harvard University Press.
RIGBY, P. 1967. 'Ugogo: Local Government Changes and the National Elections', in *One-Party Democracy: The 1965 Tanzania General Elections*. Edited by L. Cliffe, pp. 77-104. Nairobi: East African Pub. House, 1967.
SALOMON, A. 1964. Symbols and Images in the Constitution of Society, in *Symbols and Society*. Edited by L. Bryson, pp. 103-129. New York: Cooper Square.
SCHUTZ, A. 1964. Symbol, Reality and Society, in *Symbols and Society*. Edited by L. Bryson, pp. 135-202. New York: Cooper Square.
SHRIDHARANI, K. 1954. Symbols and Signs in the Indian Election, in *Symbols and Values: An Initial Study*. Edited by L. Bryson et. al., pp. 405-412. New York: Harper and Row.

SHOKEID, M. 1971. *The Dual Heritage: Immigrants from the Atlas Mountains in an Israeli Village*, Manchester: Manchester University Press.
–. n.d. From Personal Endowment to Bureaucratic Appointment: The Transition in Israel of the Communal Religious Leadership of Atlas Mountains Jews. Unpublished ms.
TURNER, V. W. 1967. *The Forest of Symbols,* Ithaca: Cornell University Press.
WEINGROD, A. 1962. Reciprocal Change: A Case Study of a Moroccan Village in Israel, *American Anthropologist* LXIV, 115-31.
WILLNER, D. 1969. *Nation-Building and Community in Israel*, Princeton, N.J.: Princeton University Press.
ZAFRANI, H. 1969. *Pedagogie Juive en Terre d'Islam*, Paris: Maisonneuve.
–. 1972. *Les Juifs du Maroc: vie sociale economique et religieuse,* Paris: Geuthner.

Conviviality Versus Strife

Peacemaking at Parties among Atlas Mountains Immigrants in Israel[1]

MOSHE SHOKEID
Tel Aviv University

Abstract

Many anthropological studies have described and analyzed some of the methods and dynamics by which peace is maintained or by which a settlement is achieved when strife flares up. These studies have often emphasized the influence of standardized forms of solving strife, e.g., crosscutting loyalties, patterns of personal avoidance, joking relationships, rituals related to seasonal changes and the life cycle, and peacemaking ceremonies. They seem to have stressed the one-dimensional 'man in strife' individual, guided by ritual and formal buffers, but have neglected the counterbalance facet, 'the convivial man' who is guided by an etiquette of sociability and polite behavior. The observations reported here were made in an Israeli community of immigrants from the Atlas Mountains. The community was composed of bitterly opposed patronymic groups. Nevertheless, persons who usually were in strife, met in a jocular and friendly manner at festivities given either by members of a lesser status in the community, or by those less involved in politics, and at impromptu leisure activities. These social gatherings were occasioned neither by the life nor the seasonal cycle, nor by any other normative obligation. Introducing these types of informal encounters into the analysis of the dynamics of social relationships in rural and other 'face-to-face' societies, the research reveals social mechanisms which may help to explain how it is that 'face-to-face' societies, despite the prevalence of endemic oppositions, do not disintegrate.

> 'How, in spite of it [the never-ending bitter competition and strife], do peasant villages continue without flying apart from centrifugal forces?' (Foster 1960 : 176)

Introduction

Many anthropologists have been fascinated, and sometimes misled, by the paradox of relationships in 'face-to-face' societies. The two contrasting faces of the Tepotzlan society reported by Redfield (1930) and Lewis (1951) still present an enigma to modern anthropology. Redfield defended his ' rousseauean' image of society saying: 'The hidden questions behind my book is 'what do these people enjoy?' The hidden question behind Dr. Lewis' book is 'what do these people suffer from?' (1955:136). Lewis, on his part, replied: 'It seems to me that concern with what people suffer from is more important than the study of enjoyment because it is more productive of insights about the human condition, about the dynamics of conflict and the forces for change' (1960:179). Redfield's approach is not substantially supported by later studies; those of Foster (1960), Bialor (1968), and Bailey (1971), among others, stress the evidence for the apparent universality of competition, tension, and bitter struggles in 'face-to-face' societies. Foster, who limits his discussion to peasant societies and brings forward economic factors related to a static technology as explanation for that phenomenon, states that ... "underlying these overt expressions of competition is the harsh economic fact that 'the pie is constant in size' ... if someone is seen to get ahead, logically it can be only at the expense of others in the village" (1960: 177). Bailey, who also deals mainly with rural societies, nevertheless pursues the phenomenon beyond the borders of a static peasant economy and society. He emphasizes the apparent universality of the struggle between people who are related to one another by various types of links and who compete to remain equal (1971: 19).

It seems that both Redfield and Lewis, and probably other researchers, have failed to consider the 'other face' of the society they studied. I contend that joy and suffering are components of the one phenomenon: And that is the subject of this essay.

Following a lengthy study of immigrants from the Atlas Mountains in an Israeli village (Shokeid 1971, 1974), I became interested in the dynamics of 'enjoyments' amid 'suffering' (in Redfield's terms) in a society. The tension and strife in Romema (the name I gave to the village) stood out sharply. The inhabitants of Romema (whom I shall henceforth call Romemites) were continually involved in a struggle to maintain equality. That struggle appeared, to the outsider at least, to be wasteful and comical (as generally stated by Bailey 1971). This state of strife impressed me as it had Lewis and other researchers in comparable situations. At first, it seems as if much more is at stake during conflict than during times of enjoyment. The Romemites, however, were frequently also spending much time, energy, and material resources on social gatherings and celebrations which rarely were a success, (as I shall describe later). These parties included those which could be defined, *inter alia,* as standardized forms of peacemaking. But, more important to our discussion were the parties that appeared to provide informal patterns of peacemaking. In the latter category I include parties dictated neither by the life cycle nor the annual cycle, nor by any other normative obligation. Although the occurrence of some of these parties and attendance at them could be anticipated and be explained as a response to a certain accepted etiquette of polite behavior, this etiquette implies a relatively voluntary code of behavior rather than an obligatory set of norms. Thus, for example, there were people who gave parties at certain events while others did not under similar or identical circumstances.

Foster (1960) asks, how is it that peasant societies do not disintegrate in spite of never-ending oppositions? A search into, and analysis of, the informal patterns of peacemaking in Romema, as well as in other 'face-to-face' societies, groups, and associations of 'equals', may reveal some integrating mechanisms of social behavior which may partly answer Foster's question.

An outline of the studied community

The data which follow were collected during 18 months of field work (October 1965 - March 1967) in Romema, an Israeli community of immigrant farmers. The settlers of Romema had come from Amran, a village in the Atlas Mountains of Morocco which had been inhabited entirely by Jews. Before describing the present social and economic structure of Romema, I shall reconstruct the general patterns of social life in Amran.

Amran, with a population of about 60 families, was situated near the larger center of Demnate. Its inhabitants had made their living mainly through the performance of a few limited functions for the Berbers. They had been craftsmen, such as shoemakers, carpenters, smiths, and tailors; and pedlars of a few processed goods - sugar, candles, and oil. Some of the inhabitants of Amran helped to finance the Berbers' farms and herds, whose products they later shared and traded in nearby market towns. It was natural for a son to take up his father's occupation, especially since he had little other choice. Those in the community who had neither craft skills nor property usually served the more prosperous members, either by working in their businesses or their homes. They lived almost entirely within the fold of the Jewish religion which they had inherited, and which had been kept alive mainly through an oral tradition handed down from generation to generation. Due to the isolation of Amran, this tradition had hardly been influenced by the mainstream of Jewish culture developed in the large centers of Jewish learning.

In 1956, the entire population of Amran migrated to Israel and, in 1957, 33 families settled in Romema, an agricultural village in the semiarid zone of the nothern Negev, in southern Israel. Romema was planned by the settlement authorities[2] according to the *moshav* pattern, a type of settlement introduced into Israel in the 1920s by young Jewish pioneers from Europe who were looking for a new social way of life. The *moshav* is an agricultural settlement organized on the basis of moderate economic and social cooperation (in comparison with the extreme form of the *kibbutz*). Each family cultivates its own farm and privately owns its household and farm equipment. The land belongs to the nation and each farmer is allocated the same amount of land and facilities by national administrative institutions. While the *moshav* ideology intends its members to remain economically equal, in practice differentiation may occur as economic success depends also on individual efforts, talents, and family size. Economic cooperation takes place in many important activities, such as the marketing of agricultural products, the supplying of farm and household needs, and the sharing of such services as those of dairy and granaries. The most important administrative organs are: an executive committee, the general assembly, and many other committees whose functions are specific and circumscribed. The incumbents of all offices and members of committees are elected democratically every year.[3]

On their arrival in Romema, the settlers defined themselves, and were identified by others, as members of three groups of relatives known by their family names: Sebag, Biton, Mahluf. Each of these core groups consisted, in the main, of kinsfolk plus a few members from other patronymic groups who had committed themselves to one or another of the core groups. The groups were soon involved in competition and strife, called '*hamulot* feuding' by the administrators (representatives of the settlement authorities who initially helped in the running of the *moshav*), a term also adopted by the Romemites. In the Middle East, *hamula* (singular) is a common term applied to a corporate group formed by a mimimal agnatic lineage. In the context of an Israeli immigrant society, this term is also applied to groups that do not necessarily conform to this definition. The struggles between the so-called *hamula* groups in many of the villages were expressed particularly through the fierce competition for positions in the village administration and for economic resources.[4]

I have analyzed elsewhere (Shokeid 1971) the relation between present rivalries of Romemites and the social differentiation which existed in Amran. In Amran, the Sebags, who had been wealthy merchants, had enjoyed a better economic and social position than the Bitons, who in the main had been the poorer, traveling craftsmen and the unskilled residents of Amran. The

Mahlufs had held an intermediate position: some of them had practised crafts of higher skills and they were counted among the better-educated Amranites. In Romema, however, the Mahlufs gradually declined in number. The Sebags, according to my observations, tried to preserve their earlier superior position; while the Bitons tried to reverse their lowly station of Amran. The Romemites competed in various spheres of life: (1) in the economic sphere; (2) over leadership positions in the *moshav*; (3) in the sphere of ritual.

In 1962 Romema was merged with Torem, a small planned village across the road from Romema, which was also founded in 1957, but only settled in 1962. At its foundation the village had been called Torem, but at settlement the administrators treated the village in connection with official and municipal matters as part of Romema, and the name Torem ceased to be officially used. For the convenience of the present research, I shall continue to apply the name Torem to this part of the village. The newcomers in Torem, who were unrelated immigrants among themselves and mainly from different towns in Morocco, were reluctant to remain in Romema. They neither took up independent farming nor did they interfere in the veterans' administration of the *moshav* organization. They worked at various jobs in the vincinity of Romema with many of them laborers on the farms of neighboring villages; some were regularly employed by veteran Romemites. I shall refer to this population as the Torem settlers in order to differentiate between them and the first settlers, the Romemites. The Romemites themselves used to call the Torem settlers 'newcomers' (*olim*), while the latter called the Romemites 'veterans' (*vatikim*).

Parties in Romema

Public life in Romema seemed to be swayed by strife and quarreling. The general assemblies, often held on Saturday nights, usually disintegrated into chaos. Occupation of the different offices of the *moshav* organization was a permanent source of friction between the Romemites; the holders of these offices, if they were locals, were held in contempt and were often humiliated. Such posts as those of secretary, rabbi, and shopkeeper were held by outsiders. Every discussion of an occasional problem or a current issue – the shortage of water supply, the prices of vegetables, the planning of crops, etc. – quickly turned into a dispute. Both groups of relatives and individuals were in a constant state of competition which expressed itself whenever a subject, or problem, arose that was connected with the administration of the village, or with the routine life of the farmers. The competition was also manifest during ritual when the synagogue often became the scene of bitter quarrels between Romemites, or between the Romemites and the officiating rabbi, who was an outsider. These quarrels were due either to the Romemites' daily competition, or to their annoyance at the performance of ritual, or to their disagreement with the ways in which contributions for the synagogue, or for charities, or for the poor, etc., were collected (see Shokeid 1974:64-94).

But the Romemites also indulged in relaxation, friendly meetings, and joyful entertainment. Sometimes a scene ripe with animosity and strife would change, and the Romemites would relax and joke. Thus a meeting of farmers, at which tensions ran high and tempers flared, might turn into a gay party.

Below I classify three types of celebrations given by Romemites, including mainly parties at which a large number of Romemites – friends and foes alike – could meet convivially, thus setting aside temporarily their constant strifes and competition. Not included are Sabbath and festivals repasts at which only close relatives and friends were invited. Nor have I listed occasions at which Romemites might meet amicably, but which had not been purposely initiated by the Romemites (among these may be cited pilgrimages to holy sites or celebrations by relatives residing elsewhere in Israel).

1 *Religious Festive Celebrations*

Life and family cycle ceremonies, such as weddings, circumcisions, as well as gatherings on the memorial days of deceased parents fall into this category.[5] Also included are celebrations in commemoration of famous ancient scholars and at the acquisition of religious books, and similar occasions.

2 *Celebrations not related to Religious Events*

Among these are children's birthday parties, as well as shindigs thrown when an expensive commodity for the home or a tool for the farm was bought.

3 *Parties which Appeared to be Impromptu*

These parties evolved out of a spontaneous action, such as betting in the course of an argument, an instant personal decision, or the change of mood at an official meeting of farmers.

The sharing of food with guests (whether relatives or not), a custom highly esteemed in Morocco, and perpetuated by Moroccans in Israel, was important and compelling in Romema, whether this was at parties or merely on a casual visit. My observations in Romema led me to the conclusion that refusal to accept the food offered a guest was tantamount to refusing to establish close social relationships.[6] The consumption of some meat (chicken but preferably mutton) and liquor formed a main part of any party. The first course was either fish or a type of cake made mainly of eggs, while a variety of pickled vegetables and olives garnished every meal.

Often given on the Sabbath or festivals, these parties were nevertheless held for such reasons as classified above. On these days people were free, relaxed, and easily available for gatherings. The celebrations, intended for large crowds, were bound to include people beyond the host's circle of friends and close relatives and consequently had, *inter alia,* to cut across the family groups. Rarely would a party be deemed successful if the host had to rely solely on the attendance of his family group. The success of a party was marked by the size of the Romemite crowd that gathered, the conviviality of the guests – gauged by the large intake of liquor, the singing, and the storytelling – and whether it lasted long. The early dispersal of the guests (soon after the meal was over) was a sure sign of failure, while a successful party went on for hours.

Although the Romemites tended to give parties at almost every available opportunity, to gather enough people for a successful celebration was quite difficult. A Romemite would never attend a party only publicly announced by the host, whether in the synagogue or elsewhere. For the Romemites, the announcement was merely a first communication, which had to be followed by personal invitations. The publicity a party enjoyed bestowed presitige on the host, since the throwing of a party was a sign of generosity and sociability. But unless the host extended his invitation personally, at least more than once, the invitee would not attend. The Romemites considered formal invitations a sort of politeness which did not reflect the host's true attitudes. A personal invitation and its acceptance were expressive of a further affirmation of the existing relationship and commitment between a host and his guest, or of a new development in the relationship. The host in coming to a person's home in order to invite him to his party appeared to be asking for a favor. The success of his party and the social esteem he gained through that success depended, to a large extent, on the number of guests, their social status, and the presence of members of various groups in the village. The host thus was indebted to his guest for accepting his invitation. On the other hand, in attending the party, partaking of the meal, the guest became indebted to his host (see also Pitt-Rivers 1968). We should also consider in this 'exchange' the guest's opportunity to be sociable with people with whom he otherwise might have refrained from interacting, even had he wished to do so.

In view of the relationships of debt and the implication underlying attendance of a party, a host would carefully consider every invitation and how he extended it. He would either call on his guests personally or send his father, mother, wife, child. On the other hand, he might desist altogether from extending any kind of a personal invitation to a guest, depending on his calculation of the latter's attitude and status. On the eve of a party, the host would be seen calling on his guests, going either by tractor, cart, or walking. Some of his close relatives and friends would help him gather his guests. This type of behavior between hosts and guests was particularly noticeable when compared with the behavior of the settlers of Torem, who had immigrated to Israel from various towns and villages in Morocco. They used to come to parties given by the Romemites without expecting to be repeatedly invited to the one affair. Unless they were on bad terms with the hosts, or had other commitments, many of the Torem settlers would attend a party only announced in the synagogue. Not involved in the complex and intense relationships that existed between the Romemites, the Torem settlers could afford, with only the first public invitation, to come to parties. In fact, at many parties given by the Romemites, Torem settlers greatly outnumbered the Romemite guests. While the Romemites rarely went to parties in Torem, quite often celebrations in Romema could not have properly been held had it not been for the attendance of the Torem settlers. At most parties thrown by Romemites, seldom more than 10 Romemites attended, and these were mainly, or only, members of the host's group of relatives. However, to those parties that were attended by many Romemites, especially members of various groups of relatives, few Torem settlers came.[7] It is these parties which are of particular interest to my discussion. When I asked Romemites why few of them came to parties in Romema and why they had need to 'court' guests, the usual reply was that it was because of the 'envy' which prevailed in Romema.

The nine parties described below are typical, as to what prompted them, of the very many celebrations I observed in Romema and among the Romemites. Some were given by influential members in the community, others by settlers of lesser status. The celebrations were similar both in the pattern of hospitality and in the actual proceeding of the gathering. Some of the parties outlined were thrown for similar occasions, a few of the others for different events. My observations show that the occasion for celebration cannot alone

Conviviality Versus Strife 109

explain the success of a party. The following short description illuminates *inter alia* the common phenomenon that parties by the more influential settlers of Romema, who were often involved in village politics and strife, were poorly attended by other Romemites. Those present were mainly from the host's family group. In contrast, celebrations by persons not involved in local politics and even parties thrown by persons of low status in the community were often largely attended, and by members of various groups at strife in Romema. Bitter opponents in political and daily life met at the latter parties in a friendly manner.

1 *Birth of Nahum Sebag's Daughter*

Nahum Sebag was quite a successful young farmer and though he did not indulge in the instigation of intrigues, he was overt and strongly outspoken in his attitudes and feelings toward other people and the policies followed by the *moshav* leaders and officers. Only 10 Romemites attended his party. There were, however, 15 persons from Torem. Present also were close relatives of Nahum's wife, who had come from another village. The Romemites counted 7 Sebages and 3 Bitons, including the husband and the affinal nephew of Nahum's sister. The latter, although they were distant relatives of the Bitons, were usually considered followers of the Sebags. The guests dispersed shortly after the meal, which had not been followed by much drinking, singing, or storytelling.

2 *Birth of Asher Biton's Daughter*

Attendance at a party by Asher Biton in celebration of the birth of a daughter, was quite different. A man of somewhat peculiar physical appearance (because of the disproportion of facial and other physical features), who often used to be the butt of laughter due to his odd remarks and arguments, Asher Biton was a poor farmer of low status in the community. Nevertheless, 12 Romemites came to his party, among them 6 Bitons, 4 Sebags, and the 2 Bitons mentioned above, distant relatives of the Bitons who were affinally related to the Sebags. Among those attending were some of the leading members of the Biton and the Sebag groups, including such bitter opponents as Levy Biton and Aziz and Shlomo Sebag (all 3 of them members of the village committee – at whose meetings they were usually at loggerheads). There were also 4 guests from other villages, relatives of Asher. Only 2 settlers from Torem came. The celebration was very gay and there was much drinking. Aziz Sebag entertained the audience with songs, and David Biton, the leader of the Biton's congregation (which had seceded from, the communal congregation, see Shokeid 1974: 71-74) honored the gathering with a homily. Aziz also joyfully organized the collection of monetary gifts, following the custom that had prevailed in Morocco. The party continued late into the night.

3 Birthday of Meir Biton's Daughter

Meir Biton held the influential offices of water controller and egg marketer in Romema, and he also aspired to other offices in the administration of the village. He was related to the Bitons (through his father and wife) and to the Sebags (through his mother). Few Romemites attended a party celebrating the first birthday of his only child, a girl. The participants included only close relatives: his father, 4 Bitons (his wife's father and brothers), 2 Sebags (his maternal grandfather and maternal uncle), and a guest from another village. Since he had not announced the party in the synagogue, none came from Torem.

4 In Commemoration of a Scholar and the Passing of a Driving Test

A few months later, Meir Biton gave another party, both to commemorate Rabbi Meir Ba'al Ha'Ness (a popular figure in Oriental Jewish tradition),[8] and to celebrate his passing the driving test for a tractor and his receiving the license. Only 6 Romemites attended the party: Meir's father, 3 Sebags, one Biton, and one Amzlag (member of a small family cluster usually considered followers of the Bitons), and 8 settlers from Torem. Neither of the parties given by Meir Biton lasted very long, nor were they gay or convivial.,

5 In commemoration of a Scholar

The day following Meir Biton's party also Aziz Sebag, the eldest son of the last leader of the community of the Romemites in Morocco (Amran), festively commemorated Rabbi Meir Ba'al Ha'Ness. Aziz, quite a successful farmer, was also a member of the village committee. Most Romemites assumed that he aspired to a leading position in Romema. The pattern of attendance at his party was not much different from that at Meir Biton's. Only 9 Romemites were present: 6 Sebags, the related Meir Biton and his father, and an Amzlag. The attendance of 10 Torem settlers provided the gathering with the atmosphere of a party. Soon after the meal was over, the guests left.

Conviviality Versus Strife 111

6 Celebrating the End of a Zohar Reading

At the end of a cycle of reading of the *Zohar* (a text of Jewish gnosticism), Shlomo Sebag insisted on giving a party. One of the most successful farmers in Romema, he was also a member of the village committee and he distinguished himself as a shrewd politician. The pattern of guests at his party did not vary from that of the parties of Meir Biton and Aziz Sebag. The 6 Romemites who came: 2 Sebags, 2 Mahlufs, one Biton, and one Amzlag were those who regularly attended the *Zohar* meetings (Shlomo himself rarely sat in); also present were 9 Torem settlers. The general atmosphere was not particularly gay, and the guests dispersed soon after the meal.

It should be noted that although among the Romemites attending parties 4, 5, and 6 there were members of various family groups, these were the more congenial, the old, or unimportant among their kin.

7 Celebrating the Purchase of Zohar Books

The largest gathering of Romemites was at the party given by Yehuda Mahluf to celebrate the purchase of the books of the *Zohar*. A successful farmer, who had no political pretensions, Yehuda was a member of the weakest group of relatives in Romema. Nineteen Romemites (5 Mahlufs, 7 Sebags, 5 Bitons, and 2 Amzlags) and 8 Torem settlers came to the celebration, which turned out to be very gay. The participants happily read from the *Zohar* and discussed stories and legends related to the Bible. They sang and amicably engaged in a contest of alcoholic drinks. When the food and drinks had nearly been consumed, Aziz Sebag delivered a speech concluding with the thought that since the Romemites lived together they had to 'keep up one language (*safa ahat*) and one heart (*lev ehad*).' He thus applied to the situation in Romema a traditional phrase which called for the avoidance of dispute and ill feelings. His message for peace was pronounced in the presence of most of the influential members of Romema, among whom there were those who were bitter opponents in daily life.[9]

8 Circumcision Ceremony

Levy Biton, one of the most influential and powerful settlers in Romema, was a very successful farmer, a member of the committee, and a shrewd and dangerous enemy to his opponents (particularly the Sebags). While many Romemites, young and old, attended the circumcision ceremony of his son, most of them left as soon as the ritual of circumcision was concluded. People had come for the ritual of circumcision, which is a *mitzvah* (religious precept), regardless of personal relationships. Only 13 Romemites (6 Bitons, 3 Sebags, 3 Mahlufs, and one Amzlag), 4 Torem settlers, and 2 guests from outside the village remained for the meal given at Levy Biton's home. The 3 Sebags did not include their more influential members. Nobody expected many Torem settlers to attend because they had had little contact with Levy and his close relatives since the establishment of the Bitons' synagogue. Most of Torem's settlers had remained in the communal congregation. Altogether it was considered a small party for that type of occasion, nor was it gay, but a rather solemn and dull gathering which did not last long. Some of the younger and more active participants went to Yehuda Mahluf to partake of a jolly repast. The gay atmosphere there and some of the remarks made by his guests clearly indicated that attending Levy Biton's party was a duty rather than a pleasure.

9 *Celebrating the Purchase of a Horse*

Yoram Sebag, Shlomo's (party 6) youngest brother, took the occasion of the purchase of a horse to throw a shindig. Though a prosperous farmer, he seemed not to be involved in village politics, and consequently was not thought to aspire to any office in the Romema organizational framework. Fifteen Romemites came to his party: 6 Sebags, 3 Bitons, a Mahluf, an Amzlag, the related Meir Biton and his father, and 2 Mamans (who were usually considered Sebag followers), but only 2 Torem settlers. The various sections of Romema society were well represented at Yoram's party. The guests drank much, and the singing went on late into the night.
Table 1 shows some of the main points about the reported parties.

We can conclude that the attendance of a fairly large number of Romemites, effectively representing various groups of relatives, and the existence of a gay and convivial atmosphere were due neither to the occasion of the celebration nor to lack of leisure time. A large attendance seems rather to be inversely related to the degree of the host's involvement in village politics. The most successful parties were those given by: Yehudah Mahluf to celebrate the purchase of *Zohar* books, Asher Biton on the birth of a daughter, and Yoram Sebag upon purchasing a horse. None of the 3 hosts held, at that time at least, an important social position in Romema. The success of Asher Biton's party is particularly illuminating (in spite of the relatively smaller attendance), since of the 9 hosts he was least seriously considered by the Romemites in any aspect of daily life in Romema. At the parties given by Ro-

Conviviality Versus Strife

Table I

The following table indicates: (1) the occasion of the celebration; (2) involvement of the host in village politics; (3) the attendance of Romemites and Torem settlers; (4) the degree of conviviality and of representation of members of various groups and people at enmity:

Parties	Occasion for celebrating	Political involvement of host*	Romemite attendance	Torem attendance	conviviality and representation
(1)	Birth of daughter	involved	10	15	NO
(2)	Birth of daughter	not involved	12	2	YES
(3)	Birthday of child	involved	7	–	NO
(4)	Commemoration of scholar	involved	6	8	NO
(5)	Commemoration of scholar	involved	9	10	NO
(6)	End of *Zohar* readings	involved	6	9	NO
(7)	Purchase of *Zohar* books	not involved	19	8	YES
(8)	Circumcision celebration	involved	13	4	NO
(9)	Purchase of horse	not involved	15	2	YES

* Involved are those who held offices, were members of the committee, and took an active part in arguments and quarrels.

memites of lower status, or by those not directly involved in political conflict (as holders of offices, members of the committee, etc.), bitter opponents met in an atmosphere of leisure and conviviality and for a while forgot their enmity and strife. On these occasions they even entertained the idea of love and peace reigning in Romema in the future.

I have analyzed earlier the careful consideration of invitations to parties both by the host and the invitees, guided as these were, *inter alia,* by some norms of reciprocity. In attending a party given by a lesser personality, the guests were neither as much committed nor as much indebted to the host. The favor a guest bestowed on his host in attending the party outweighed the guest's expected commitment to exchange hospitality. The prestige the host gained through that attendance and the guests' general goodwill was his main gratification. His hospitality did not imply that he might make important demands on his guests in the future. It was, therefore, easier for a host of a minor social position, or one who was not fiercely involved in village politics, to recruit a larger and more varied attendance of Romemites. At these parties, influential members could show their amiability and readiness to be convivial by meeting their opponents in a friendly manner without offering any real concessions, even if the party was given by a member of an opposed group of relatives.

Till now we have discussed parties planned in celebration of religious and life cycle occasions, as well as to mark special events and achievements. However, there were also parties which seemed to spring up impromptu, and these are of much significance. Thus, for example, one evening, at the meeting-place of the sentries, Shlomo Sebag, Levy Biton, Noah Biton, Reuben Mahluf (who were members of the committee), Daniel Sebag (who until a few months earlier had been produce marketer), Nahum Sebag, and Nathan Maman were arguing about the large number of empty vegatable boxes that were missing and for which the village would be obliged to pay. During the discussion, Shlomo remarked on the careless attitude of the farmers and mentioned that Reuben Mahluf himself had 20 boxes scattered around his house and yard. Reuben denied the charge, but Shlomo insisted that it was true and backed his allegation by betting a bottle of brandy.

Reuben, Shlomo, and a neutral attendant, an Amzlag, went to prove Shlomo's claim. They found, in fact, 22 boxes. Reuben was now obliged to invite all those who had been present at the wager to his home in order to meet his end of the bet. None expected Shlomo to keep the bottle to himself, nor could Reuben invite the others only for a drink. He was, in fact, expected to serve a meal. A Romemite rarely allowed a visitor to leave his house without offering him some food. But Reuben was unable to feed his unexpected guests properly that same evening. At this point Nathan Maman intervened and, in a bold manner, declared that he was going to demonstrate manly behavior by inviting all present for a meal and drinks at his home. Those who eventually came to Nathan's were Levy Biton, Shlomo, Daniel, and Nahum Sebag, Reuben Mahluf, and the Amzlag mentioned earlier.

At the end of that joyful gathering it was decided that they would all meet at Reuben Mahluf's house the next evening. All came, except Nahum Sebag who had been on bad terms with Reuben since the year before when their partnership in the ownership of a tractor had been dissolved with much bitterness. Since Nahum could not be persuaded to come to Reuben's, it was decided to inflict on him a party to be given the following evening.

At first, Levy Biton did not touch the food offered to him at Reuben's. The others told him that he could not suspect Reuben's food of not being fit on religious grounds. I do not think that Levy had any suspicion of that sort, for Reuben shared his household with his old father who was one of the most venerated personalities in Romema. It would have been most imprudent of Levy to suspect Reuben's food. I think, however, that Levy was embarrassed by a situation in which he was entertained in the company of some of his opponents, and those whom he had publicly humiliated. Here he was a guest of Reuben Mahluf, who offered him food and whom he, Levy, under other circumstances, usually despised and addressed in a rude manner. He thus tried to escape the social commitment implied in the partaking of food.

The following evening all, except Reuben Mahluf, were present at the home of Nahum. Levy Biton and Daniel Sebag went together to Reuben to persuade him to come. They talked to him for about half an hour, but he firmly refused. Though their effort was futile, it carried import, both in respect of Levy Biton's relationship to Daniel Sebag and in his relationship to Reuben Mahluf. Only a few months earlier Levy had instigated the removal of Daniel from the office of produce marketer. Daniel was finally dismissed, as a consequence of which his economic and social positions were badly affected. Levy also constantly attacked Daniel who was continually aspiring to offices in the *moshav* organization. But on this occasion they went together to Reuben Mahluf, on a 'peace mission', chatting and joking in a friendly manner. Reuben, whom Levy usually held in contempt and humiliated, was now flattered by Levy's attention and effort to take him to Nahum's home. The party turned out to be very gay, lasting till about one o'clock in the morning. Satiated with food and drinks, yet excited and a bit high, the participants decided to oblige Noah Biton, the chairman of the committee, to give the next party. Although Noah had been present at the wager between Shlomo and Reuben, he did not attend the parties which followed[10]. Nahum and his guests went in search of Noah, who was on watch. Noah refused to give a party the following evening, but agreed to the coming Sunday. However, as far as my records show, the party given by Nahum was the last in that series.

The Romemites were soon involved in other problems, quarrels, and parties. But for three consecutive evenings, members of all groups of relatives, including some of their leading figures, who were usually at odds with one another, met in a close circle and in a very friendly atmosphere. Apart from other differences, the closeness of the circle of participants greatly differentiates this type of impromptu party from other parties, including the most successful ones described above.

It is interesting to quote in this context Yehuda Mahluf, who, during the little party we had at his home after we left the circumcision ceremony at Levy's, told me: 'We, Romemites, have a dirty mouth (*peh melukhlakh*) but a clean heart (*lev nakee*). We quarrel, spit it all out, but afterward nothing bad remains in our hearts, and then we can be friends again.' This confession was often made to me by other Romemites as well. The rabbi, however, could not come to terms with this kind of reasoning and its implied pattern of behavior. Thus, when we attended the party at Shlomo Sebag's to celebrate the end of the reading cycle of the *Zohar,* the rabbi told me bitterly: 'These people [implying Shlomo and other Romemites] make trouble at the synagogue and afterward they want people to come and eat at their table. It is all right if a person once commits a sin and regrets, but a man who repeatedly sins, his apologies are not accepted. That sort of eating together is meaningless.' But the rabbi's condemnation and moral judgment did not disprove the Romemites' anxiety to make peace and to prove before God and men their better character and manners, which were often betrayed by the impulse of daily life.

An important feature characteristic of the impromptu parties was that they were initiated on neutral territory. Thus, the series of impromptu parties described above began at a wager made at the meeting-place of the sentries. This feature, *inter alia,* greatly reduced the personal commitment implied in an outright invitation to the host's home, for otherwise people involved in politics would have been prevented from attending each other's parties.

A second type of impromptu parties was the one that sometimes evolved at the height of heated discussions at meetings which dealt with matters of village administration or farming. Suddenly one of the debaters might disappear and return with a case of soft drinks and bags of peanuts which he had bought at the local cooperative grocery. Now, while people were munching away and busily opening bottles, the arguments were kept in a mild and low key. The two occasions I witnessed took place shortly after a new committee had been elected (none of the old members who had held office for three consecutive years sat on it). Both times the food offered came from the two younger of the new members of the committee. The new committee, as a whole, was still in a precarious position and its members tried to pacify the crowd which, incited by some of the former committee members, who were still influential, called for the committee to resign or to be dismissed. Here we see that the young members, who were not entrenched in their political positions, could still afford to court their opponents by offering hospitality. The food, willingly accepted, became in fact a peace offering and the young members' humulity was rewarded by a milder and more friendly ambiance.[11]

On one of these rare occasions, before we left the assembly hall, the young committee member who had treated the meeting to refreshments declared that the Romemites should all live together like brothers. The secretary of the *moshav*, an outsider, who also attended the meeting, laughed, remarking ironically to me that the very one who now preached brotherhood had but moments before actively sown discord. Thus the secretary, as the rabbi, judged the Romemites by norms of consistent behavior. Shlomo Sebag (mentioned earlier), one of the chief debaters (a prominent member of the former committee), said to me afterward in despair, 'We should live here together in peace!' On a later occasion, the last time I dined with him before leaving Romema, he continued his plaint, 'Only envy rules here. What is the good of our staying here together?' The Romemites were however destined to stay together and give momentum to the pendulum swinging between persistent strife and sporadic spells of peace and friendlines.

Conclusions

Both sociologists and anthropologists have tried to analyze the existence of continual strife within persisting sets of social relationships and to relate these paradoxical processes to each other, in society in general and in rural communities in particular (see, e.g., Gluckmann 1955; Coser 1956; Foster 1960; Beals and Siegel 1966; Shokeid 1968; Bailey 1971; and many others). Some of these studies have also described and analyzed the custom arrangements which are connected with the mechanisms and processes that in various societies maintain peace, in spite of the many persisting tensions, as well as those set in motion to settle strife when it flares up. We could probably classify the various forms of prevention of strife, and of peacemaking when strife breaks out, reported and analyzed in the field of research, into three main categories:

1 relationships through which the occurrence of conflict is reduced and its severity is mitigated (such as affinal links which cut across corporate groups);
2 judicial methods (such as courts and institutions of arbitration);
3 the great variety of standardized customs, ceremonies, and modes of behavior, which in turn could be divided into two main types:

    a those customs, ceremonies, and modes of behavior through which strife is avoided, tensions are reduced, and solidarity among the groups is enhanced (such as the patterns of avoidance and joking relationships, and the festivals and ceremonies which are related to the annual and life cycles);
    b those customs and the ceremonies held, which pacify belligerent parties (such as the norms and ceremonies which guide and follow blood compensation).

I find, however, that the studies discussing the forms of avoiding and settling conflict are wanting because they overemphasized the standardized and formal patterns of peacemaking. These studies have often presented conflict and the efforts made to prevent it as virtually distinct phenomena. They also neglected an important facet of social behavior, which is guided by a code of politeness and of pride in the situational concealment of enmity.

In this paper I have tried to report and analyze those occasions when people, who were usually at odds and often at strife with one another, met cordially at ceremonies and at entertainments. These opportunities for friendly meetings of enemies were neither standardized forms of peacemaking nor were they necessarily part of the cycle of ceremonial life. They evolved out of, and occurred within, the routine of daily life (in which ceremonial events occasionally take place). Notably, I reported the sociable and friendly encounter of enemies, who behaved according to a code of polite etiquette, at parties given by members of a lesser status in the community, or by members who were not intensely involved in the political life of the village and the continued animosity at work there. But probably more important is my report of the impromptu parties, initiated on the spur of the moment, on neutral territory, by bitter opponents. At these parties enemies, prompted by a code of polite behavior and the presentation of a magnanimous self, met in a close circle for recreation. In this category I also include the sudden arranging by one person of a refreshing interlude in a situation of dispute which gradually dissolved in the purposefully created relaxed atmosphere.

Although the belligerent parties who met at leisure (either at parties given by 'nonpolitical' members or at the impromptu parties) did not, in fact, change for long their attitudes and actual relationships of mutual animosity, these occasions nevertheless formed an important break in the series of hostility and dispute. Moreover, the sudden changes of heart prompted the belief and fostered the illusion that the prevailing conflict might one day vanish forever. I assume, however, that these irregular and apparently informal patterns of temporary peacemaking and relaxation in the course of continued animosity are not peculiar to Romema. My hypothesis is that in most 'face-to-face' (or rather 'back-to-back' as M. N. Srinivas put it) societies where suspicions, rivalries, hostility, and disputes are endemic, we are always likely to find spells of relaxation without which life would have become unbearable. This has to be set against the persistent strife arising from various forms of conflict. Such spells of relaxation are likely to occur whenever people, who may be at loggerheads, live or work within a single set of social relationships.

I perceive these patterns of occasional relaxation in social relationships – which are not part of a scheduled cycle or ceremonial life and which are not conceived as standardized forms of peacemaking – as an indispensable complementary mode of social behavior to the other more standardized modes and social mechanisms which contribute to the avoidance of conflict and the reduction of tension in society. It is in this direction of observations and analysis, which perceive and present the two dimensions of social behavior – man in strife versus the convivial man – that we may find at least a partial answer to Foseter's question which this paper has broadened: 'how, in spite of it do peasant villages [*and other 'face-to-face' societies*] continue without flying apart from centrifugal forces'?

NOTES

1 Revision of a paper presented at the 9th International Congress of Anthropological and Ethnological Sciences, Chicago, August-September 1973. The research on which this paper is based was carried out during the period of October 1965 to April 1967 while I held a research fellowship in social anthropology at Manchester University, financed by the Bernstein Israeli Research Trust. My first draft was written during the summer of 1971 when I held a second tenure of the same post at the invitation of the same research project. I am grateful to Prof. S. A. Deshen

of Tel Aviv University and to Dr. D. Handelman of the Hebrew University for reading and commenting on the manuscript. More than to anyone else, however, I am indebted to the late Professor Max Gluckman who supervised the research under the Bernstein Trust and whose generosity, encouragement, and advice greatly influenced my professional career. But a few months before his death he read this paper with much care and made invaluable comments. Its dedication to his memory is a small token in a debt too immense ever to be repaid.

2 These were the government, the Jewish Agency, and the central institutions of the settlement movements whose members lived in veteran villages of different orientations.

3 For more details about the *mosha*v see Weingrod (1966), Weintraub *et al.* (1969), Willner (1969), Shokeid (1971), and Baldwin (1972).

4 For more details see Shokeid (1968).

5 Although the atmosphere at memorial gatherings was not particularly gay, these occasions were characterized by elements of a celebration such as the serving of food and drinks.

6 See Shokeid (1974: 231-234).

7 While in some cases it is clear why not many Torem settlers attended these parties, such as in a case where their relationship with the host was slight or when the party was not announced publicly, in other cases it is not.

8 For more details about Rabbi Meir Ba'al Ha'Ness see Shokeid (1974: 74).

9 In this context, as on later occasions, it is profitable to consider Szwed's analysis (1966) of the functions of drinking behavior.

10 Since I have not recorded the reasons why Noah Biton did not participate, I must refrain from considering this rather interesting absentee. He had not, however, been at odds with any of the people who gave the parties.

11 Aronoff (1974) provides a detailed case of changing of mood at a community meeting where strife prevailed (55-71).

LITERATURE CITED

ARONOFF, M. J. 1974. *Frontiertown: The Politics of Community Building in Israel.* Manchester and Jerusalem: Manchester University Press and Jerusalem Academic Press.

BAILEY, F. (ed.) 1971. *Gifts and Poison.* Oxford: Basil Blackwell.

BALDWIN, E. 1972. *Differentiation and Cooperation in an Israeli Veteran Moshav.* Manchester: Manchester University Press.

BEALS, A. R. and B. J. SIEGEL, 1966. *Divisiveness and Social Conflict.* Stanford: Stanford University Press.

BIALOR, P. 1968. Tensions leading to conflict and the resolution and avoidance of conflict in a Greek farming community, in *Contributions to Mediterranean Sociology.* Edited by J. G. Peristiany, pp. 107-126. The Hague and Paris: Mouton & Co.

COSER, L. 1956. *The Functions of Social Conflict.* Glencoe: The Free Press.

FOSTER, G. M. 1960-1961. Interpersonal relations in peasant society, *Human Organization* 19: 174-178.

GLUCKMAN, M. 1955. *Custom and Conflict in Africa.* Oxford: Blackwell.

LEWIS, O. 1951. *Life in a Mexican Village: Tepoztlan Re-studied.* Urbana, Ill.: University of Illinois Press.
–. 1960-1961. Some of my best friends are peasants, *Human Organization* 19: 179-180.
PITT-RIVERS, J. 1968. The stranger, the guest and the hostile host: introduction to the study of the laws of hospitality, in *Contributions to Mediterranean Sociology*. Edited by J. G. Peristiany, pp. 13-30. The Hague and Paris: Mouton & Co.
REDFIELD, R. 1930. *Tepoztlan: a Mexican Village.* Chicago, Ill.: University of Chicago Press.
–. 1955. *The Little Community.* Chicago, Ill.: University of Chicago Press.
SHOKEID, M. 1968. Immigration and factionalism: an analysis of factions in rural Isaeli communities of immigrants, *British Journal of Sociology* 19: 385-406.
–. 1971. *The Dual Heritage: Immigrants from the Atlas Mountains in an Israeli Village.* Manchester: Manchester University Press.
–. 1974. Deshen, S. and M. Shokeid (co-authors). *The Predicament of Homecoming: Cultural and Social Life of North African Immigrants in Israel.* Ithaca and London: Cornell University Press.
SZWED, J. F. 1966. Gossip, drinking and social control: concensus and communication in a Newfoundland parish, *Ethnology* 5: 434-441.
WEINGROD, A. 1966. *Reluctant Pioneers: Village Development in Israel.* Ithaca: Cornell University Press.
WEINTRAUB, D., M. LISSAK and Y. AZMON. 1970. *Moshava, Kibbutz and Moshav: Patterns of Jewish Settlement and Development in Palestine.* Ithaca and London: Cornell University Press.
WILLNER, D. 1969. *Nation-building and Community in Israel.* Princeton, N.J.: Princeton University Press.

The Periphery of a Political System

The Cottica Djuka of Surinam

A. J. F. KÖBBEN
University of Amsterdam

Introduction. Max Gluckman once said, with the thought provoking exaggeration that was so much part of his personality, that formerly anthropologists studied institutions, nowadays they study the way people manipulate their institutions. This short paper is, in fact, a specimen of the latter kind of anthropology: it depicts how the Cottica Djuka of Surinam interpret their tribal political institutions so as to promote their own aims and interests.
The Djuka are Bush Negroes or Maroons[1] (descendants of runaway slaves) living in the vast interior of Surinam along the Tapanahony, Marowijne and Cottica rivers (see map). Population figures are not precisely known but they probably number about 15,000-18,000. They live in villages averaging some hundreds of inhabitants, the core of which is formed by one or more matrilineages. The largest village is Dritabiki, the seat of the Paramount Chief (*Granman*) with a population of about 500. Basically their political system is quite simple: apart from the *Granman* at the tribal apex every village has one or two village heads and from two to four *basia* (heralds, policemen). Their relationship to the Surinam national state is quite peculiar. Although *legally* the Djuka are not in a special or separate position at all, *de facto* the authorities recognize the tribal hierarchy, upholding the dignity and power of the Granman and other tribal functionaries and even paying them a small salary.
In Dritabiki, the Granman's residence, and in the villages nearby, he is very much the centre of attention and activities. His permission is even sought for quite trivial acts: the laying of a concrete floor in a hut; the buying of an outboard motor; the invitation of a stranger (a non-Djuka) to stay as a guest in a village; a journey to Paramaribo (the country's capital). When Granman himself is absent, e.g. for a stay in the capital which may last for months, all official activities should come to a halt ('except funerals') and what is more, for the most part people stick to this rule (Thoden van Velzen, 1966: 74-75).
Granman disposes of very few physical sanctions – the main one is ordering

The Periphery of a Political System

Distribution of Djuka in Surinam

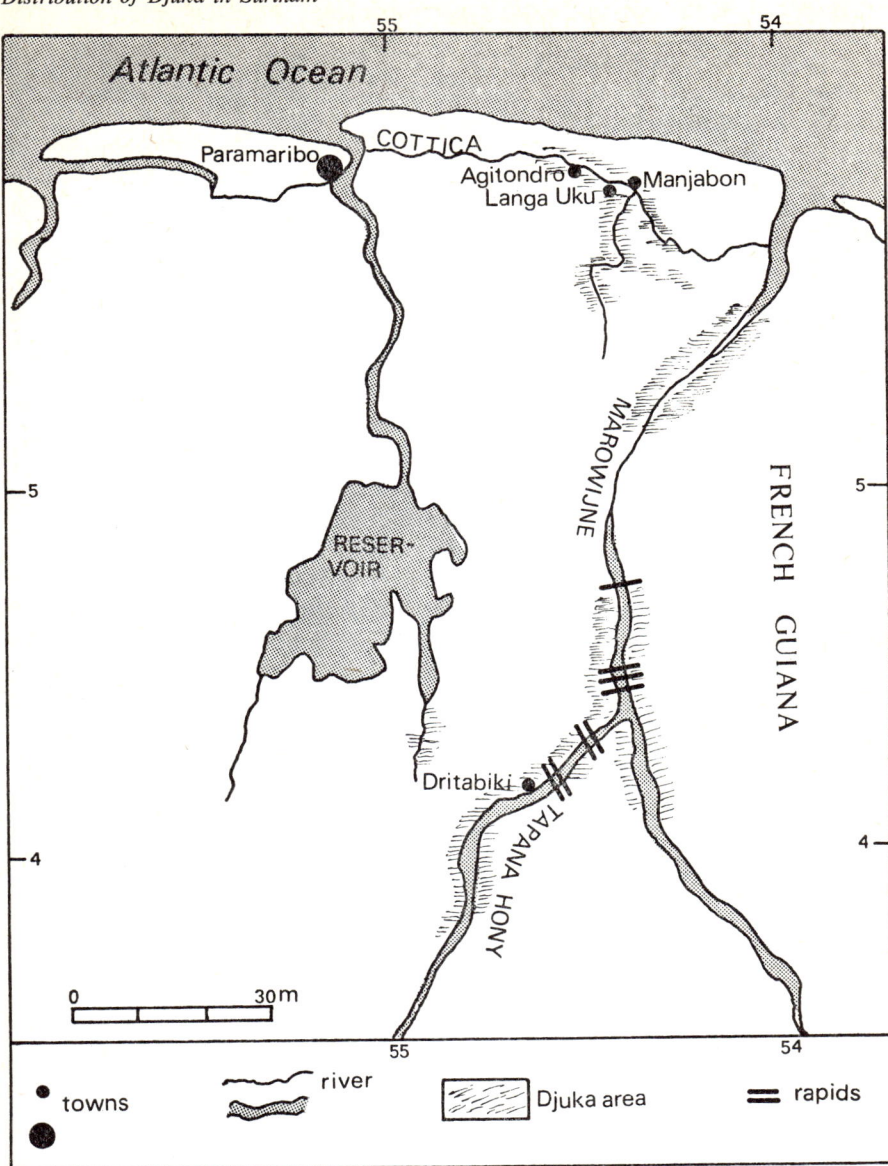

a culprit to sit in the burning sun for an hour or so. Still, his prestige and the religious sanctions at hand are such than most people are obedient to him, although this calls for quite some political manoeuvring from his side (Thoden van Velzen and van Wetering: 1975).

I did my fieldwork[2] in the Cottica area where there are many relatively populous and prosperous Djuka villages but which is far removed from the tribal political centre. Although the distance between Dritabiki and the Cottica villages is no more than about 125 miles as the crow flies, it means a hazardgus journey by outboard motor boat of three days over falls and rapids; the return journey upstreams takes even 4 to 5 days (see map). Still, many selfstyled experts on the Bush Negroes in Paramaribo agree that somehow, mysteriously, mystically, Granman is kept informed of everything that happens in his entire tribal territory and that the awe for him is such that he manages to have things under control everywhere (see also Van Lier, 1940: 155-156). Therefore before I started my fieldwork proper I went to Dritabiki to ask Granman's permission to work in the Cottica area which was graciously accorded. One of the topics on my research program was precisely to look into his position in this peripheral area.

The case of the mourning widow. Some two months after my arrival in the Cottica village of Langa Uku a young man suddenly died. He had lived his whole life in Langa Uku, although this was not his matrilineal village; he was the son of a male member of Langa Uku's matrilineage (nr. 7 in diagram 1) and married to a daughter of another male member of the same matrilineage (nr. 6). Such classificatory parallel cousin marriages are preferential in Djuka society (see Köbben, 1967: 36). Given this double link with the

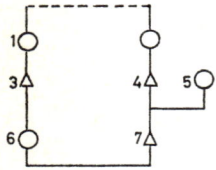 means: classificatory sisters

diagram 1: ties of deceased with Langa Uku

village, his position there was not at all unfavorable, but he 'really' belonged, of course, to the village of his mother, the nearby village of Manjabon, although he had never lived there.

After the funeral, the moot question which rapidly triggered off into a serious conflict, was in which of the two villages mentioned the widow should pass her obligatory year of ritual mourning. Both had excellent claims on her, as is apparent from the above.

As considerations of prestige were involved and also matters of a more material nature, neither of the parties was inclined to give in. Intricate diplomatic steps followed. Within a few weeks, the poor girl was brought from one village to the other at least four times, each time appropriately accompanied by about 50 mourners with beating drums and flags at half-mast.

In earlier times a fight between the villages (*botofeti*) might have cut the matter, but nowadays the proximity of the police station prevents this; so a stalemate situation ensued.

Then, in discussions about the situation, the opinion was voiced time and again that there was only one Person who could really decide the issue: Granman. And thus it was decided that the question should be put before him.

I was duly impressed: so it *was* true, after all, that Granman was the decisive factor even in these peripheral villages!

However, when I asked people what the proper procedure was to be, they were disconcertingly vague: well, either a notable who would go to Dritabiki for one reason or another, would talk about it to Granman, or perhaps a notable from there who would come and see his friends here would be a proper intermediary, or else they might wait until Granman himself would come and visit the area. Of course nothing of the kind happened. In the following months less and less was talked about the matter, new occurrences excited people's emotions and finally the affair simply petered out.

Only gradually I became aware what the real situation was: Granman's name is invoked whenever there is no feasible solution to a conflict and when at the same time there are so many crosscutting ties between the parties involved that there can be no question of cutting relations altogether. Then parties come to an uneasy factual compromise without any of them having to give in: 'it is up to Granman to decide who is right'. As it is exceptional indeed that affairs of this kind are really laid before him, both parties can maintain the illusion of being absolutely in the right.

Granman: authority at a distance. When I began my fieldwork it was four years since Granman had been in any of the Cottica villages. Quite a few people from the Cottica go and see him over the years (cf. below). Still, he is so far away, and communications are so few and far between (and so imprecise) that almost everyone can strengthen his case by referring to his authority: 'it is Granman who ordered this'; 'Granman does agree with this proposal'; 'Granman is of the same opinion'. Whoever can falsify such statements?

Some examples. (1) In the Cottica region the principle obtains that the village headmanship should rotate over the matri-segments of the village; so a man should not be succeeded by his real brother but by a *distant* (matrilineal) kinsman. 'The ancestors (*ganjorka*) want it so and they sicken the disobedient ... (follow examples of people that have died because they disregarded the rule) ... and besides, it is the will of Granman'.

Again, when I did my fieldwork, the Cottica villages had only one headman per village although the Surinam government was ready to pay for two. 'But Granman says that there should not be two in one village as they would quarrel', or so people explained.

In fact, however, the rotating rule does not even exist in the Tapanahony area where Granman lives. Also, in that part of the tribal area, most villages, even very tiny ones, have two headmen (Thoden van Velzen, 1966: 69). So there can be no question of Granman holding the opinions ascribed to him. Some years after I did my fieldwork, at least some Cottica villages finally got their second headman ... 'because Granman said it would be better', as the argument then ran. (This last argument, by the way, happens to be correct: I myself have heard Granman remark that the Cottica villages, like the Tapanahony ones, should make use of the opportunity to have two headmen, hence two salaries).

Example 2. In former times Djuka lineages were exogamous. Nowadays, however, in the Cottica area intra-lineage marriages are permitted, on condition that the partners don't belong to the same matri-segment. At present there are seven such marriages in Langa Uku, including those of the village head and his two *basia*. Still, such marriages are not yet a matter of course but are lively discussed. Among the Djuka of the Tapanahony river, intralineage marriages are much more exceptional (Thoden van Velzen, 1966: 33-34). Nevertheless, those strongly in favour of them in the Cottica area quote the authority of the Granman to sanction them. As an elder asserted: 'It was a former Granman who instituted those marriages. He said there was no wrong in them, not even in the case of children of full sisters marrying.' Needless to say this is an apocryphal statement.

It will not cause wonder when I say that the same innocent subterfuge is used vis à vis inconvenient requests of the ethnographer. Instead of saying: 'We won't allow you to attend the burial of a witch', they say: 'Granman won't allow you'.

The headmanship of Agitiondro. In the course of my stay in the Cottica area

The Periphery of a Political System

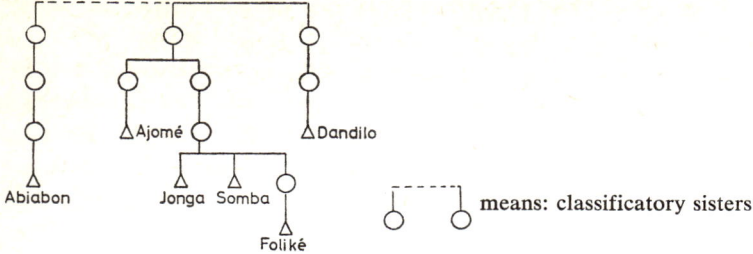

Diagram 2: participants in the struggle for the headmanship

a struggle took place over the succession to the headmanship of the village of Agitiondro. The intrigues and passions this struggle gave rise to remind one of the making of the presidency of the U.S., although the village in question hardly numbers 500 inhabitants.
Three factions fought to get the nomination, the faction of Da ('Father') Abiabon, Da Ajomè and Da Jonga[3] respectively (see diagram 2). I tell the story here as seen from the viewpoint of one of the protagonists, Da Jonga. I cannot well do it otherwise as Da Jonga was one of my best friends and informants; being a friend of one of their foes, I was held quite expertly at a distance by the other factions.
Da Dandilo, the deceased headman, as everybody knew, had a preference for Da Jonga as his successor. However, after his death, when they consulted his spirit in the usual way[4], to everyone's amazement Da Abiabon was designated (*naki*). Again, the designation was confirmed by the Great God (*Grangado*), the most dreaded and awe inspiring of all Djuka gods. But this outcome was the result of fraud and treachery of perfidious human beings who had even had the temerity of fooling the supernatural powers, – at least according to the interpretation of Da Jonga and his followers. In the meantime, Da Ajomè, the third aspirant, had succeeded in being nominated as acting headman for the interim period between the designation and the installation of the new headman, – which period may last for many months or even years. He profited by this advantageous position to further his own candidacy for the position of permanent headman.
All this caused great indignation in Da Jonga's faction. Then, in their midst rumors began to circulate that Granman was going to interfere. 'He has sent a message that the installation should be postponed, that he'll come himself and put things right'. Later on it was said that Granman had written a letter to the same effect: 'If they would install Da Abiabon' or so the letter was said to run, 'he would die soon. I, Granman, know very well whom Da Dan-

dilo wanted as his successor and I'll see to it that his wishes will be respected'. Great rejoycing among Da Jonga's following!
I must confess that at the time I believed in the reality of this letter, although by then I should perhaps have known better. I was led astray by the fact that so many different people talked in such details about the letter, as also by the fact that Agitiondro is by far the most important village of the Cottica area. After Dritabiki it is the main centre of the *Grangado*-worship, the god who is also called *Granman-gado* because of the intimate ties between him and Granman[5]. For this reason the headman of Agitiondro enjoys extra prestige in the whole of the Cottica region, so I did not deem it too farfetched to think that Granman would personally interfere in this special case.
A few weeks afterwards I went to Dritabiki together with my regular informant Ba Folikè, the sister's son of Da Jonga and as such very much involved in the struggle. We went to pay our respect to Granman and, after chatting about this and that *Granman asked us who had been designated as the new headman of Agitiondro*. He simply did not know that it had been Da Abiabon! Interestingly, young but wary Ba Folikè replied that he did not know, explaining afterwards to me that he thought this to be the most diplomatic answer. This poses the question whether Granman's question was as ingenuous as it sounded. Circumstantial evidence, however, makes me think that it was not just a political move.

A Machiavellian society? In my introductory paragraph I talk about the Cottica Djuka as using their political institutions in order to 'promote their own aims and interests.' This expression as also some of my examples may suggest that this paper is wholly in line of what one might call the Machivellian approach to political anthropology. In this approach society is seen as being under the sway of the political entrepreneur who cunningly, consciously, rationally seeks to maximize his power as a goal in itself. In the words of one of its pioneers: 'The politicians of whatever culture who appear in [my] book are all caught in the act of outmanoevring one another, of knifing one another in the back, of tripping one another up and they all appear to be engrossed in winning a victory over someone' (Bailey, 1969: xi). Basic in Bailey's approach is the distinction between normative and pragmatic rules: a political leader will *say*: 'I do this for the common good', whereas *in fact* he does it so as to promote his self-interest (Bailey 1969: 5-6). In the words of Machiavelli (1532, cited from Crick, 1970: 47): 'Whenever a Prince wants to take advantage of someone, he should not do so without a convenient justification or apparent moral cause.'

This model of society has several attractive elements, the main one being the emphasis on the role of the individual and of individual choice (although outstanding older anthropologists from Malinowski to Max Gluckman have never neglected the individual). All the same, however, it is a highly one-sided model, for one thing because most people are not that rational and self-conscious (cf. Thoden van Velzen, 1973, for this and other points of critique). Take the Cottica Djuka. Although they are masters of diplomatic subterfugue, it is not so that they consciously create myths about Granman as a 'convenient justification', nor do they as a rule belie people about his stance in political issues. I am sure, for instance, that most, perhaps all of Da Jonga's faction sincerely believed that there *was* a letter by Granman. Again, when a notable asserts that Granman wants only one headman in each of the Cottica villages, he really thinks this to be his point of view. The stronger one's conviction, the surer one is about Granman's support. The same attitude prevails vis à vis the gods, and for the same reason. As one elder put it: 'When we feel something is right, the gods cannot help to feel likewise (fortunately, we in our society are very far from such primitive notions). Again, there is real awe and veneration for Granman. 'Apart from the great gods, whoever can be more powerful than he?' people use to say. Those who are akin to him, however much at a distance genealogically, and those who have lived near to him have extra prestige. Even the suggestion that Granman is dishonored in public – or is not honored sufficiently – arouses genuine dismay. (Only in private people utter critical remarks about him; one elder even said: 'It is four years that Granman has not been here in the Cottica, we should have our own Granman!', but then he is widely known for his *enfant terrible*-like qualities). People genuinely think that one who resists Granman's wishes will fall ill and, in case of his not giving in, will die.

Ba Folikè, who accompanied me when I went to see Granman, had never met him before. Hours in advance he was nervous, asking himself what would be the proper costume for him to wear and racking his brains for the appropriate phrases to say.

Finally, it should be stressed that there *are* contacts between Granman and at least a number of notables in the Cottica region. The headman of Langa Uku has been in Dritabiki twice, altogether about six months. The first time he went in order to be installed by Granman and to learn the profession: 'Granman made me attend palavers (*kutu*) on his side, in which I had to keep silent and look how things were done'. (People will even say that 'all headmen are installed by Granman', although this is not true; it would, however, be a dishonour to him to say otherwise). Again, a few years ago, when a number of people died suddenly, and wild rumors of witchcraft circulated, most notables went to the Granman's residence as a group to be ritually cleansed by him (cf. Thoden van Velzen, 1966: 148-56). Finally, all individual villagers who for whatever business will go to the Tapanahony river will avail themselves of the opportunity to go and see Granman.

Finale. One day, a messenger came to Langa Uku to announce that before long Granman would pass by boat on his way to the capital and that he would give an audience in Agitiondro. People were thrilled. Many who had planned to leave for far away Tibiti to work as foresters, postponed their departure. When the great day had come, all villagers gathered at the riverbank clad in their colorful best, flags in hand. When the boat neared, drums were beaten, people danced and shouted for joy and pointed to a figure dimly to be seen on board. The audience in Agitiondro did not take place. A few days later, however, in Paramaribo, Da Jonga and some of his followers went to see Granman. I asked him whether he was going to plead his case. But he said: 'No, the gods have spoken. My foes have forced the decision on them against their will, still, if I were to contest it now, it would cause my illness and death. Even Granman cannot change that anymore'. True enough, when they met Granman they chatted urbanely about various subjects and did not even mention their political strife. (Two years later Da Jonga's brother Da Somba (see diagram 2) was made second headman of Agitiondro).

In 1964 Granman suddenly died. As Ba Folikè wrote to me: 'When we heard about it, in all Cottica villages people wailed. The headmen were called to Agitiondro. There for three days the big drums (*apinti*) were beaten. Da Abiabon who is the highest in rank, gathered the necessary money; we did all the rituals in the proper way'.[6]

NOTES

1 For an excellent survey of Maroon societies in the Caribbean and an overview of the extensive literature, see Price (1973).
2 I did fieldwork among the Djuka in 1961-62; some of the data in this article, however, are from later years and are derived from correspondence. Extensive data about the Djuka political centre are to be found in Thoden van Velzen (1966), Van Wetering (1973a and 1973b) and Thoden van Velzen and Van Wetering (1975). My thanks are due to the Netherlands Organization for Scientific Research in Surinam and the Netherlands Antilles (WOSUNA, now WOTRO) for financial support.
3 For obvious reasons I make use of pseudonyms.

4 See Köbben (1967: 24-26) for further details.
5 Thoden van Velzen (1966, ch. 7, 8, 9, 13) analyzes in great detail the church of Grangado as the power basis of Djuka politics. In recent years, as the consequence of a prophetic movement, the influence of the Grangado church has declined dramatically (cf. Thoden van Velzen and Van Wetering, 1975).
6 My thanks are due to M. Aronoff, H. U. E. Thoden van Velzen and W. van Wetering for suggestions and help.

LITERATURE CITED

BAILEY, F. G. 1969. *Strategems and spoils; a social anthropology of politics.* Oxford: Basil Blackwell.

CRICK, B. 1970. *Machiavelli; the discourses.* Penguin Books.

KÖBBEN, A. J. F. 1967. Unity and disunity: Cottica Djuka society as a kinship system, *Bijdragen tot de Taal-, Land- en Volkenkunde* 123: 10-52.

PRICE, R. 1973. Editor, *Maroon Societies; Rebel Slave Communities in the Americas.* Garden City: Anchor Books.

THODEN VAN VELZEN, H. U. E. 1966. *Politieke beheersing in de Djukamaatschappij* (Political control in Djuka society) 2 vol. Ph.D.-thesis, University of Amsterdam.

THODEN VAN VELZEN, H. U. E. and W. VAN WETERING 1975. On the political impact of a prophetic movement in Surinam. In: *Explorations in religious anthropology.* Verhandelingen Koninklijk Instituut voor Taal-, Land- en Volkenkunde no. 74. Edited by W. E. A. van Beek and J. H. Scherer. The Hague: Martinus Nijhoff.

THODEN VAN VELZEN, H. U. E. 1973. Robinson Crusoe and Friday; strength and weakness of the big man paradigm. *Man* 8 no. 4: 592-612.

VAN LIER, W. F. 1940. Aanteekeningen over het geestelijk leven en de samenleving der Djoeka's in Suriname (Notes on the spiritual life and the society of the Djuka in Surinam), *Bijdragen Taal-, Land- en Volkenkunde* 99: 131-294.

VAN WETERING, W. 1973a. *Hekserij bij de Djuka; een sociologische benadering.* (Witchcraft among the Djuka; a sociological approach). Ph.D.-thesis, University of Amsterdam.

VAN WETERING, W. 1973b. Witchcraft among the Tapanahony Djuka. In: *Maroon Societies; Rebel Slave Communities in the Americas.* Edited by R. Price, pp. 370-88. Garden City: Anchor Books.

Ritual Rebellion and Assertion in the Israel Labor Party

MYRON J. ARONOFF
Tel Aviv University
Netherlands Institute for Advanced Study in the Humanities and Social Sciences
(1974-1975)

Introduction

In this testimonial essay to the memory of the late Max Gluckman I attempt to show the wider application and theoretical implications of one of his important contributions to political anthropology, his essay on rituals of rebellion (Gluckman, 1954 and 1963). In applying and adapting Gluckman's concept to the contemporary Israel Labor Party, I stress both necessary revisions which must be made to Gluckman's original ideas and an additional level of analysis which owes a debt to the orginal contributions of one of Gluckman's most prominent former students, Victor Turner (cf. Turner, 1969 and Handelman in this volume). In so doing I analyze *one* aspect of the proceedings of the Standing Committee of the Israel Labor Party as a ritual of rebellion aimed at the reconciliation of groups which competed for leadership and power and as a ritual of assertion the consequences of which were the conciliation of an ideological world view which conflicted with the actors perceptions of social reality. I briefly introduce these two themes before presenting and analyzing the background and case material.

Gluckman has shown that rituals are frequently organized and licensed to protest against the established order; and his argument stressed that the ritual expression and even exaggeration of standardized conflict in the social order can only be socially beneficial when the participants accept their basic order and unity as a good they value. Gluckman has given cogent and convincing arguments why high ritualization of social relationships are primarily characteristic of traditional societies. He stated, '... that the licensed ritual of protest and rebellion is effective so long as there is no querying of the order within which the ritual of protest is set, and the group it self will endure' (Gluckman, 1955:130). Conversely, '... where the relationships involved are weak, there cannot be licence in ritual' (*Ibid*.: 132). Such rituals generally occur when there is an intricate mesh of relationships in which the same people are dependent upon one another. Gluckman stressed, 'The conflict can be stated openly wherever the social order is unquestioned and indubitable — where there are rebels, and not revolutionaries. In such a system, the licensed statement of conflict can bless the order' (*Ibid.*: 134).

The key to Gluckman's argument why we do not find rituals in societies such as our own is, 'Once there is questioning of the social order, the ritual of protest is inappropriate, since the purpose of the ritual is to unite people who *do not* or *cannot* query their social roles' (*Ibid.*, emphasis added). I attempt to illustrate that certain kinds of 'secular' rituals of rebellion can and do occur in so-called modern society in specific social and cultural contexts. I argue that the ideal type dichotomous division of societies into traditional and modern which we have inherited from our intellectual forefathers, e.g. Maine, Morgan, Tonnès, Durkheim, Marx, and Weber, has led to a tendency to reify these concepts into mutually exclusive categories on the part of many contemporary social scientists. We have tended to view the societies we study as being either traditional or modern according to the bundle of characteristics defining the theoretical ideal type, rather than viewing them along a continuum in which they more or less closely approximate the attributes of one and/or the other ideal type (cf. Wolf, 1974:260-1 for a similar point of view). One of the important contributions which political anthropology can make is to illustrate that subcultures and groups within so-called modern society can exhibit characteristics closely resembling those generally considered to exist only in so-called traditional society. For example, in this essay I attempt to show that secular political ideologies can take the place of religious and mystical cosmologies in ritual performances.

I maintain that in modern complex society one can find many examples of what Berger (1969:65) calls 'signals of transcendence'. I illustrate through examples in the Israel Labor Party modern men in a thoroughly contemporary institution who have sacraments, who place a high value on symbols which have a deep meaning for them, where taboos are observed, rituals take place, a modern version of a court jestor performs his role, and where even mysterious inspiration for the recreation of the modern state and its continued existence against formidable odds is believed by significant numbers, if not widely articulated by all who thus believe. I contend that in addition to being influenced by specific historical and cultural aspects of Judaism and modern Isareli society, these are particular forms of more general phenomena. As Berger succintly states: 'In the observable human propensity to order reality there is an intrinsic impulse to give cosmic scope to this order, an impulse that implies not only that human order in some way corresponds to an order that transcends it, but that this transcendent order is of such a character that man can trust himself and his destiny to it' (*Ibid.:* 70).

I suggest that terms such as 'court jestor', 'taboo', and 'ritual' have greater value for analysis of contemporary society than merely as metaphors. They can and should be developed and adapted to distinguish between the similarities and differences of the phenomena which occur in ostensibly 'traditional' and in ostensibly 'modern' social contexts. There is a clear danger that if concepts used in the analysis of traditional societies are applied uncritically stressing only the similarities between the phenomena which occur in different social contexts without adapting them to accomodate important sociological differences, the concepts may become merely metaphors or analogies having lost much of their explanatory value. (For an explanation of the differences between metaphor and analogy and their use in political analysis see Zashin and Chapman, 1974). For example there is a tendency in the work of Edelman (1964 and 1971) and even more so in that of Bobcock (1974) to apply the term ritual to such a wide range of socio-political phenomena in modern society, that by so doing the concept is not sufficiently refined to differentiate between specific types of modern ritual which much more closely approximate those which occur in traditional societies, and other types of activity which are analogies, but differ substantially (cf. Goody, forthcoming).

The problems generated by the developing structure of the Israel Labor Party in the context of a rapidly expanding and changing society provoked significant organizational changes and the need for the redefinition of central values and ideological concepts. The secondary echelon of party leaders, who were the participants in the ritual lacked the theoretical perspective to view the erosion of their positions and of central party values as a reasoned response to changes in the social system. They therefore attempted, in a controlled and bracketed ritual setting, to comment upon their roles and social order and to redefine their situation by reformulating and asserting their ideological perception of the social order, in which their own roles were given new meaning. When cumulative change has taken a society away from what ideology says it is, there is either a groping for a new transforming pattern, or the giving of a new interpretation to traditional patterns of symbolic action, or a reassertion of the traditional legitimating universe – in the face of a reality which is no longer meaningfully explained by it. The ritual performers in the Standing Committee created a bridge between affective situational reality (i.e. the erosion of the meaning of their roles and central values of party ideology), by asserting a desired normative structure (e.g. transforming their roles by giving them new meaning and reasserting central values such as the equality of all Jews, the importance of equal representation, democratic procedures, and so forth).

The following is a list of ten of the most important characteristics of con-

temporary rituals which I shall elaborate and illustrate throughout this essay:
1. takes place in controlled and bracketed social settings;
2. because of the controlled nature of the ritual performance, the actions of the actors are to a certain extent prescribed or constrained, but within these limits considerable freedom and innovation can take place (this appears to be particularly characteristic of certain types of modern ritual);
3. the actors are at some level conscious of performing ritual acts;
4. the ritual actions have serious implications for those who perform them;
5. the outcomes of the ritual are determined in advance at least to the minimal extent that it is known that the social unit will emerge united;
6. the ritual performers converse in symbols which, although multi-vocal, are understood by, and have deep meaning, for the ritual performers;
7. the ritual is an important means for dealing with ambivalent social roles, conflicting interests, and ideological world views which threaten the unity of the social unit in which they take place;
8. the ritual is an important means for dealing with cognitive dissonance between ideology and social reality, particularly when the latter has changed to the point that it is no longer meaningfully explained by the former;
9. the ritual presents reality symbolically in a selective and sometimes disguised manner thereby allowing discourse on it to take place which can produce the conciliation, affirmation, or transformation of symbolic universes;
10. The ritual takes place in modern society, not on a society-wide base, but in subgroups within society in which the necessary conditions of control and bracketing can be assured.

The analysis of ritual proceedings is prefaced by a brief account of relevant structural and cultural attributes of the Labor Party, and more specific aspects of the Standing Committee which are vital to an understanding of the social context within which the ritual performances took place. A description of ritual behavior without relating it to these contexts would be truly meaningless since the explanation of the meaning of ritual must be related to the specific social contexts in which they occur. An analysis of the characteristics of the actors in the performance and the audiences of reference groups to which the performance was directed, brings out significant differences in the roles of the three main levels of party leadership. The discussion of ritual form and process reveals the process through which the ritual performance was bracketed and controlled, thereby forming the formal constraints within which the freer innovative and creative aspect of the ritual process took place. The main focus of the analysis is on the theme of consensus and its meaning in different levels of social and symbolic contexts. Finally the outcomes of the ritual are related back to the various categories of actors and audiences in the concluding analysis.

Background: The Labor Party and The Standing Committee

I stress in this analysis the relationship between the political system and power structure and the ritual proceedings which took place within these political institutions. In particular I emphasize the significance of the fact that the Labor Party is the dominant party in Israel's multi-party system.
It has always been the dominant partner in every Government Coalition, having controlled the major economic and political resources and offices from before the State's independence to the present. It has provided the nation's most outstanding statesmen and leaders who were identified by most people as the pioneering vanguard who led the nation to independence, and played a dominant role in the shaping of the society. The Labor Party is a classic example of what Duverger calls a 'dominant party' which he defines as follows: 'A party is dominant when it is identified with an epoch; when its doctrines, ideas, methods, its style, so to speak, coincide with those of an epoch ... Domination is a question of influence rather than strength: it is also linked with belief. A dominant party is that which the public opinion believes to be dominant ... Even the enemies of the dominant party, even citizens who refuse to give it their vote, acknowledge its superior status and influence; they deplore it but admit it' (Duverger, 1963:308-9). Observers of the Israeli political scene concur that the Labor Party has enjoyed this unique position, at least up to the last election in 1973 (cf. Arian, 1972: 187-200 and 1975). It is particularly relevant to the present analysis that whereas Labor's dominance of political power was still intact during the proceedings of the Standing Committee, its members seemed to recognize that it's position of ideological or moral dominance had been gradually eroded as a consequence of rapid social, economic, and political change which Israeli society had undergone since independence. I shall return to this point in my later analysis after completing the outline of the structural and cultural setting in which the ritual took place.
The history of the Labor Party and its constituent factions has been charac-

terized by bitter power struggles for control of the party and intense ideological disputes which have led to several historic splits and mergers of the various factions which culminated in the unification of the former Mapai, Achdut Ha'avoda, and Rafi to form the newly united Israel Labor Party in January, 1968. This historic union, which took place in the aftermath of the war of June 1967, precipitated yet another struggle for succession to the control and leadership of the new party (cf. Aronoff, 1974).

The constitutional structure of authority in the Israel Labor Party resembles a four-tiered pyramid. The membership (approximately 300,000) elects delegates to the national party Conference (3,000 at the last conference) through internal party elections in the 84 branches, the kibbutz and moshav movements, and a proportion is selected by a central nominating committee. Constitutionally this body is supreme, but since it meets irregularly (once every few years), it delegates its authority to a Central Committee which it theoretically elects. The increasing demands for representation on the Central Committee have expanded its size to unwieldy proportions (presently over 600 members) necessitating the delegation of authority to a Secretariat elected by the Central Committee. The Secretariat in turn delegates authority to the Leadership Bureau which it elects. This body is the smallest official party institution which meets regularly, but in fact many important decisions are taken by even smaller informal constellations of top party leaders.

Medding (Medding, 1972:104) has noted the common saying in the former Mapai (the dominant faction in the Labor Party) that, 'the more supreme a particular party body, the less authoritative it was'. This inverse relationships between constitutional supremacy and real power is most blatant in the party Conference, the proceedings and decisions of which are dominated and controlled by an institution known as the Standing Committee which is in fact the 'real' Conference.

I stress two specific aspects of the party culture which have a direct bearing on the forthcoming analysis of ritual proceedings. The first aspect is the general prevalence of expressed feelings of political inefficacy. The feeling of a lack of influence, particularly with regard to decisions on important matters of national party policy, was so commonly expressed to me and in public that I do not hesitate to label it as universal among branch activists (cf. Aronoff, forthcoming).

The second important aspect of party culture was that outspoken criticism of the top national leadership, strong disagreement with the policies of the leadership, and an open expression of a wide range of conflicting views, loyalties and interests were generally forbidden to most of the members of the two largest national institutions. Strong normative and pragmatic political sanctions assured enforcement of the taboo except for specific members whose social roles gave them ritual license to break them.

For example, one individual had the social role of 'enfant terrible' and she was allowed and was even expected to act as an internal party critic. However, there were limits to the extent to which even a ritually sanctioned critic could go in their criticism. She evidently exceeded these limits and was punished by not being put on a 'realistic' position on the list for the next election to the Knesset. The 'removal' of this party 'rebel' from the Knesset served as a strong warning of the sanctions which could be applied to those who violated the taboo restricting criticism. The application of such sanctions emphasizes the vulnerability of the vast majority of members of the party's institutions and even the party's representatives in the Knesset. They are professional party functionaries and elected officials whose livelihood and careers are dependent upon the good will and support of the top party leadership. The process of nomination to all important political offices by small committees controlled by the top leadership ensures that the members of these institutions must be primarily answerable to those who appoint them from above (cf. Aronoff, 1975).

One of the most significant consequences of the Israel Labor Party's aggregative nature is that it is highly pluralistic. It contains within it a great diversity of interest groups and social categories, including young and old, people of European and of Oriental background, rich and poor, city dwellers and members of kibbutzim, religious and anti-religious. This diversity obviously expressed itself in different stands on vital issues. With such great demographic, ethnic and ideological diversity among its constituent interest-groups and membership, successful decision-making in its institutions obviously necessitates hard bargaining and compromise. However the type of issues and the kind of debate varies among the different party institutions. While there is a general sanction which enforces moderation on all fronts so as not to allieante any important segment of the party, there is a special occasion where free debate on all issues is allowed, and that is in the Standing Committee.

I am dealing with a case in which a ritual form was created within a context of a political institution which comes into being every four or five years (prior to the convening of the national party Conference), which functions for a period of two or three months, and the ostensable and explicit function of which is to accomplish clearly defined political goals. The Standing Committee prepares and runs the national party Conference (it is known as the Preparation Committee prior to the Conference and the Standing or Steering Committee during the Conference; the membership remaining constant with the charge in names). In the specific case at hand it, through a subcommittee drafted, and approved a new party constitution, debated and decided the proportion of members of the new Central Committee which were to be elected from the local branches of the party and the proportion which were to be 'appointed' by a nominating committee of the Standing Committee (Aronoff, 1975). It debated and formulated party policy on a wide range of ideological, social, and political issues which were passed on to the delegates of the party Conference for a 'ceremonial' debate and vote (Aronoff, 1973).

The Ritual Dimension Restated

In addition to these explicit goals and manifest functions of the Standing Committee, I examine a wide range of implicit goals, or what could be viewed at one level as latent functions of the Committee vis-à-vis the national party Conference. However, I shall attempt to go beyond the examination of latent functions at this level, including the allowing – in fact sanctioning of the open expression of discontent on the part of the participants, by analysing the creative aspects of the proceedings as a ritual of assertion through which the participants created a bridge between the affective situational reality of their roles which had lost their former meaning, and the desired normative structure of a true democracy. I stress that this level of activity was going on at different stages interspersed between, and sometimes simultaneously with the 'real' pragmatic political 'work' of the Committee, but the ritual behavior pointed out that something other than the political business was going on as well.

One of the commonly observed characteristics of a ritual is that it is a performance in which actions are prescribed, and in which the actors are conscious of performing, at least at some level of their psyches. I shall deal with the former problem first, and return to the aspect of self-consciousness late in the analysis. There are varying degrees of choice and determinancy for actors in different kinds of rituals. The ritual proceedings of the Standing Committee allowed the actors considerable freedom for expression and creativity. Ritual is particularly important in relationships where the actions have significant implications for the lives (moral and socio-political) of the participants. It appears that certain kinds of activities which bear strong resemblances to ritual, e.g. games and sport, can afford to be indeterminate when they do not directly affect the lives of the participants and audience, whereas rituals directly affect social relationships. In the former situations the audience is structurally free of commitment which is not the case for the participants in a ritual. It can be stated that ritual for those involved, is a serious business.

My application of the term ritual is more circumscribed and restricted than is that of Bocock (1974:65) whose broad classification of 'civic ritual' (in contrast to 'religious ritual'), '... carry few implications for other areas of life' and where 'neither the principal participants nor the onlookers need cultivate deep understanding of the inner meaning of the ritual actions and symbols involved.' I shall clarify in this analysis the serious implication of the ritual for the lives of the participants, the extent to which they were involved, and the degree to which they understood the meanings of the ritual actions and symbols involved. (cf. Langer, 1967 and Douglas, 1970 for excellent analyses of the concept 'symbols').

The conditions of the ritual forum of the Standing Committee appear to meet a criterion of a social ritual stressed by Gluckman, i.e. that the end is known in advance – the social unit must end united. There was no question that the final outcome of party unity was known in advance, and in fact one of the major purposes of the ritual proceedings was to attain this goal which was constantly emphasized. The two major conditional constraints which bracketed the freedom of debate within the Committee were:

1) that after the wide range of conflicting views, interests, and loyalties were expressed, all resolutions would reach compromised consensual formulations, and under no circumstances would minority proposals be submitted to the Conference; and 2) that all issues which would be likely to cause major conflicts or unpredictable outcomes in the Conference were suppressed by removing them from the agenda of the Conference. Within the confines of these rigorously applied constraints which determined the outcomes, the participants had practically unlimited freedom to innovate and express themselves in the ritual debates and proceedings. One additional element of constraint was imposed through the setting of the agenda by the chairman, in consultation with the top leadership of the party, but even in this area the participants could and did extend debates on some issues and cut short debate on others.

Most importantly, in spite of the good-humoured joking which characterized much of the proceedings, the participants were involved in serious business which affected their authority, power, statuses, mobility in careers, livelihoods, and individual and collective self-images as a category of leadership within the party. I shall explicate the different degrees of dependence and involvement of the various categories of actors and audiences, and then I shall assess the outcome of the ritual in terms of different levels of meaning and efficacy for these different categories.

Actors and Audiences

Although as I shall show, the actual participants in the ritual were a limited and fairly homogenious group, it is impossible fully to understand the meaning of their actions without placing them within the wider context of various levels of audiences of reference groups which had a significant influence on the form and style of the ritual performance. It is useful to think of the various categories of audiences and actors as constituting a pyramid, at the apex of which stand the elite, a small group of top national party leaders who hold the greatest power in the party (and indeed in the nation) and who have major influence in the making of key decisions. This group was most conspicuous by its physical absence (which was almost total) from the proceedings of the Standing Committee. I argue that the primary role of the top leadership of the party was one of control and manipulation behind the scenes. Their participation in the Conference itself was minimal, and when they appeared it was primarily in 'ceremonial' capacities. I argue, as has Gluckman in a different context, that, 'Prescribed absence from a ritual is thus a form of participation in it: though it is not a protest, it states that there is a conflict present in the social process' (Gluckman, 1955:139). I maintain that the prescribed absence of the elite from the debates of the Standing Committee was essential for the successful removal of taboos against criticism of this leadership, and that it allowed the free and open expression of extreme and conflicting views in the meeting. I suggest that had the top leadership been present this would have considerably inhibited the secondary leaders, who are so dependent upon them, from expressing freely criticism and views; and this restriction would have defeated one of the most important functions of the performance: here I consider I can justifiably call it a 'ritual'.

The next tier of the pyramid is composed of the major actors in the performance I consider to be ritual. They are the 134 members of the Standing Committee, who constitute the trusted and loyal, second echelon of party leadership. Practically 90% of them are elected party officials, Members of the Knesset, Mayors, Secretaries of Local Workers' Councils of the Histadrut or local party branches, or functionaries of the party and Histadrut bureaucracies, and representatives of the major interest groups. They are in fact very dependent upon the top leadership. While they have much higher status and more influence in national affairs than do the third tier of local-level leaders, they lack the support of solid grass-roots constituencies which the latter generally have. This is due primarily to their 'appointment' to office through 'nominations committees' rather than election to office in an open process. They were aware of their limited influence in the making of major decisions, and that they were primarily involved in executing the policies of the top leadership. Nevertheless they felt that, because of their high positions, their views and their opinions should be listened to attentively by the top leadership of the party. The Standing Committee was a ritually approved forum in which normal restrictions against open criticism of party policy and leaders and open expression of contradictory views were temporarily lifted. Because of their ambivalent position, involving high status yet with limited power, high dependence on the top leadership, and inability to express in public their opposition to, or disagreement with, the top leadership, the removal of these restraints in the proceedings of the Committee was vitally important to them.

The third tier, primarily the local leadership which made up the majority of delegates to the national Conference, acted as a very important reference-group for the former two categories whose actions were governed to a large extent by their estimation of the reactions of this audience. The local leaders, as I argued earlier, have a strong feeling of political weakness, because of their inability to influence national policy, but nevertheless have the security, generally, of strong local bases of support. I have shown elsewhere (Aronoff, 1972) that as new categories of local leadership, particularly local ethnic leaders in development towns, have consolidated positions based on local, rather than exclusively national, backing, they have successfully achieved greater local autonomy in internal party affairs. The uniqueness of this category, which differentiated it from the majority of the members of the Standing Committee, was due to the following factors: the differences in the nature of their relationships with the top leaders of the party, particularly the difference in the nature of their dependence; their relative newness to positions of party leadership at the local level; the fact that they frequently represented ethnic categories ('Oriental') different from the upper two tiers of party leadership (primarily 'European'); and the different processes of political socialization they had undergone, i.e. not having internalized party norms to the same extent as had the secondary leaders. From the point of view of the top leadership they were less reliable than were the secondary leaders; but they were more so than were the amorphous general party membership and public.

The increasingly wider circles of 'audiences' whom the performers in the ritual took into account were the 300,000 members of the party, the nation as a whole – particularly the voters, the Jews abroad, Israel's allies, and lastly Israel's numerous foes. Although the ritual performance was much more immediately influenced by the specific contextual relationships with the elite and perceptions of the interests and behavior of the elite and the local leaders, the wider context of Israeli society and its position in the Middle East and the world had an indirect, but significant, influence on the ritual.

Ritual Form and Process

In this section I briefly describe some of the major techniques through which the performance was bracketed and controlled, thereby forming the formal constraints within which the freer innovative and creative aspect of the ritual process took place. The membership of the Standing Committee was carefully selected through a series of nominations committees to ensure that the actors would abide by the rules of the game. In addition to the general dependence, already mentioned, of the secondary leadership on the top leadership, every member had either direct links to patrons in the top leadership or indirect links through their membership in common political networks. Throughout various stages of the meetings of the Standing Committee, after lengthy debates, final formulations and so-called technical decisions were relegated to sub-committees, thereby facilitating conciliation between opposed views and interests. The calling of special meetings on short notice, and the delaying of decisions until the last minute, were used effectively to overcome opposition, and to gain consent, to unpopular measures.

Control of the issues by the elite from behind the scenes was one of the most important constraints: on the one hand it assured the outcomes determining the ritual nature of the debates, but on the other hand it allowed freedom of expression and innovation in the performance. This control was expressed in the setting of the agenda, i.e. which issues would be discussed and when. It also meant control of which issues, once debated by the members of the Standing Committee, would be passed on to the delegates of the national party conference for their approval, in effect 'ceremonious', and which issues would be suppressed (cf. Aronoff, forthcoming).

Other issues were not actually suppressed, but because they were sensitive, were handled delicately. The stage of the proceedings in which the sensitive issues were discussed was marked by observable changes both in the atmosphere of the performance and in the behavior of the performers. One day's session had begun with the final stages of the suppression of the economic proposals concerning labor relations and the Histadrut; and this session was characterized by boisterous debate, sarcastic and joking exchanges, and a lot of hearty laughter.

The tone of the meeting began to change when a proposal was made to honor the families who had lost sons in Isarel's wars. The question was raised as to how this could be done in 'good taste'. The Chairman of the Organization Department of the party (who was to lose his own son in the forthcoming war of October, 1973) objected to debating such a 'sensitive' issue in the Conference, saying that it could not be discussed 'on the record'. After talking to a number of the members privately, he submitted a proposal for a 'blessing of Zahal' (the Israel Defense Forces); and this was accepted. This is one of many cases in which multivocal symbols were used to make indirect reference to issues that were so sensitive that direct reference to them was considered to be in 'bad taste'. Zahal not only represents the strength of the nation through its armed forces, but in different contexts represents, for example, the rebirth of the Jewish nation which after 2,000 years is capable of resisting persecution etc., and in this case symbolizes the sons of the nation who fell in the defense of the Jewish State and people.

A somewhat similar 'solution' was found to handle the highly sensitive issue of 'ethnic relations' in the party and in the nation. The issue was in a sense forced into the agenda by the spontaneous formation of a caucus of delegates to the Conference from 'Oriental' countries of North Africa. A speaker stressed this was an issue about which many members felt strongly, and if they wanted to show that it was not a problem, they must do something about it. When the chairman of the Committee suggested that the issue not be debated 'at the 12th hour' but be postponed for a future meeting of the Central Committee or the leadership Bureau, this attempt at outright suppression was rejected by the speaker who insisted, 'I still want this Committee to show that they are concerned'. When the Secretary-General of the party attempted to support the supression of the issue by assuring the speaker that the leadership and the nominations committee would 'consider this [ethnicity] at the top of their list of priorities', the speaker replied angrily: 'I am sorry, but this is too much'!' He insisted on a formal vote on his proposal.

I stress that there were few formal votes taken in the Committee. When one of the delegates objected to sending the proposal to the Conference saying, 'The problem will end in time', the speaker laughed nervously and angrily and said with bitter sarcasm, 'There is no problem at all'! There was an immediate vote in which his proposal was accepted unanimously.

I now look at this type of interaction and the use of symbols which typified much of the proceedings at two different levels. I focus first on the level of what might be viewed as the latent functions of the proceedings as a controlling mechanism. The potential for open strife in the Conference led the top leadership of the party to go to great lengths to control the issues brought to the arena of the Conference: the debates in the Standing Committee were a vital means to achieve this control. Through the careful selection of members who, because of their high degree of dependence on the elites and their strong internalization of party norms, could be trusted, the top leaders could allow a 'free' debate of the issues and could be confident that 'consensual' agreement would be reached in the final formulations. The Standing Committee could be relied upon to screen out issues which potentially might have disrupted the Conference or might have had unpredictable results. Even where the leadership did not succeed in removing the ethnic issue from the agenda, because of high salience and the unrelenting insistence of a trusted member of the secondary leadership, it was dealt with in a manner which was likely to be the least disruptive to party unity.

The critical importance of such control was manifested on several occasions during the Conference. I cite two brief examples related to the ethnic issue. A dramatic direct appeal was made by a young 'Oriental' on crutches who rose from his seat in the balcony of the Conference and shouted plaintively, 'Help me!', before he stumbled and fell. The young man (who was not an official delegate to the Conference) was given first aid, and was then escorted into a room where the talked privately with the Secretary-General of the party who promised him aid. He was then whisked off in a car. The man was promised aid because of genuine concern for his plight, but he was quickly removed from the Conference to prevent his case from becoming a 'cause célèbre' which might have precipitated a debate on this issue more laden with emotion and more divisive. As it was, the debate stirred many of the delegates to emotions which were difficult for the leadership to control. For example, when the speech of one of the 'Oriental' delegates in the Conference was interrupted by the chairwoman who told him his time had run out, there was a loud protest from the audience. They clapped their hands and insisted that he be allowed to continue, but the chairwoman insisted that he stop. When the next speaker (an 'Ashkenazi' or 'European') had run out of time according to the watches of some of the 'Oriental' delegates who were timing him, they shouted and clapped their hands demanding that he stop. The chairwoman said sternly, 'I am handling this meeting and he has another minute!'. But the speaker stepped down, when there was further protest from the audience against his continuing. These are just a few examples which highlight the importance of the latent 'controlling' function of the proceedings of the Standing Committee.,

But I am convinced that to leave the analysis at this level would be insufficient to explain the meaning of this behavior. For its deeper meaning, we must go to a further level, one which encompasses a wider social and symbolic context. When the speaker in the Standing Committee refused to allow the issue to be side-tracked or suppressed, and, by demanding a vote, insisted that his comrades demonstrate 'that they are concerned', he, through the symbols he invoked, was 'asserting' a major tenet of Zionist ideology – the ingathering of the exiles which proclaimed the equality of all Jews and the dream that in their new home the various communities would become rapidly merged into a newly reborn and re-united people in Israel. This is a value of such importance that it goes to the very heart of the 'raison d'être' which gives meaning to and legitimizes the re-gathering of the Jewish people in their national homeland. Any form of racial or ethnic prejudice or discrimination is reprehensible in Zionist ideology and in Israeli culture (cf. Deshen, 1970). But the historic circumstances of the immigration of the different ethnic groups have resulted in a correlation of socio-economic categories and political power with ethnic categories in which a very large proportion of the 'Oriental' immigrants are at the bottom of both the socio-economic ladder and the ladder of political power. The refusal of the speaker to allow the issue to be suppressed was at the same time a criticism of the breach of a central, even sacrosanct, norm of the ethnically pluralistic party and nation, and an assertion of the continuing vital importance of the norm in spite of reality. This is why I believe he insisted upon and received the unanimous vote which symbolized 'concern' and recognition of the legitimacy of his assertion that this norm was a central value in party ideology and an integral part of the ethos of Zionism and Israeli culture.

Consensus: Meaning in Social and Symbolic Contexts

The theme of consensus was at one and the same time a prerequisite for the success of the meeting of the Standing Committee, unquestionably the dominant theme of the meeting, and probably its most important outcome. I shall attempt to unravel the many facets of consensus through an analysis of its meaning at different levels of social and symbolic contexts.

The importance of consensus as a prerequisite for the success, of what I consider a ritual performance, has already been discussed. The members of the Standing Committee were selected because they represented a category of leaders who could be trusted and relied upon to play by the rules of the game. In addition to the nature of their dependence on the top leaders of the party, which I have already explained, I stress an additional factor which determined their actions. Gluckman has argued that ritual protest is inappropriate once there is a questioning of the social order, since the purpose of ritual is to unite people who do not or cannot query their social roles (Gluckman, 1955:134). While obviously the members of the Standing

Committee were capable of questioning their roles the constraints imposed by the political system are such that the costs of opting for other political roles are so great as to be perceived by almost all of them as prohibitive. The Labor Party has so dominated the political system that even attempts by the charismatic founder of the party and of the modern state, David Ben Gurion, to split off from the party led him into the political wilderness of the opposition. This precedent is a dramatic warning to ambitious leaders who have reached the second echelon of power in the party, that to opt for a different political role is not the most efficient means to achieve mobility. I stress also as important, that we are dealing with career politicians who have spent most of their adult lives in public service on behalf of the party and who have deeply internalized party norms. I shall return to this point later in the analysis.

Through an elaboration of concensus as the dominant theme of the ritual performance, the meaning of consensus in the other contexts will become clearer. The chairman of the Standing Committee introduced the first session with the following admonition: 'Whatever we do, we must decide in this committee. If the debate goes to the conference it will kill it. We must finish everything here!' Although he rarely used foreign words, throughout the proceedings of the Committee he constantly used the English term 'consensus': e.g. 'We must reach a 'consensus'. . . . ', or, 'I feel we have now reached a 'consensus' '. At times extreme positions were expressed and compromise appeared difficult. Issues were then submitted to a sub-committee called a 'formulation' committee, where, the chairman was certain a 'consensual' formulation (*nusach consensuali*) would be found. And it always was found.

In practice there are party members, e.g. a Minister-Without-Portfolio, who are known as experts in this special field and are called upon frequently in critical occasions. Although there is a Hebrew expression for 'general agreement' (*haskama klalit*) the use of the English term, 'consensus' particularly with the incongruous Yemenite accent of the chairman of the Committee, tended to highlight the central importance of the theme of consensus and at the same time lends itself more readily to wider and different meanings as a symbol than does the more narrow Hebrew term of 'general agreement' (cf. Bailey, 1972, for a framework for the analysis of conceptual systems).

The admonition that everything must be done in the Committee was constantly interwoven with openly expressed fear of the indeterminateness of outcomes in the Conference, and therefore a potential for chaos and uncontrolled strife. These 'threats' were carefully juxtaposed with pleas for the need for unity in the party. The potential threat of renewed factional strife based on the three former parties which merged to form the party, was invoked as a reminder of the need for unity. The size of the Conference (3,000 delegates) was emphasized in justifying the need to decide everything in the Committee and preventing anything but 'ceremonial' debates and votes in the Conference. The chairman constantly emphasized his fear of chaos if there would be too many debates and votes in the Conference: 'Not that I am afraid of democracy, but it could be chaos (*baligan*). Ceremonial votes are all right, but . . . '; and again he stressed the need to prevent chaos by maintaining order and controlling debates and votes, through the Standing Committee. The need for consensus in the Standing Committee in order to control the possibility of uncontroled and open strife in the Conference, the outcome of which was unforeseeable and threatening, was constantly expressed through the invocation of the overriding common value and goal of party 'unity'. This was done with constant attempts to legitimize what appeared to necessitate the violation of an equally strongly held value of democratic procedures. In order to resolve the paradoxes, they resorted to performance which I consider can be regarded as 'ritual'.

Whereas the members of the Standing Committee constituted a fairly homogeneous group in terms of party status, i.e. what I have termed the secondary echelon of leadership, they also represented a great diversity of group interests, ideological points of view and loyalties. I have dealt at length elsewhere (Aronoff, 1974 and forthcoming) with the factional divisions based on the three former parties merged to form the Labor Party. In addition, there are many more complicated subdivisions within the two broad cultural categories of 'Orientals' and 'Europeans', since these contain groups with quite different cultural traditions. These divisions are also related to various historical waves of immigration to Israel which also have significant socio-political ramifications. The three major categories by age, Seniors, i.e. founding fathers and veterans, Continuing Generation, and Young Guard were very important in the party where, at the time I am reporting on, the last of the founding generation still ruled, and the 'young' leaders of the Continuing Generation in their mid-fifties were growing increasingly impatient for their turn to take over the reins of power. The Young Guard, which officially includes members up to 35 years old (some of its leaders have long passed this fairly liberal definition of youth), complained bitterly about what they perceived to be their under-representation on party institutions and in the higher ranks of party leadership. Gluckman (1963:38) has noted that, 'the growing of younger men into adulthood in which they found their path to power blocked by their elders' was likely to have influenced the recurrent civil wars in some societies which he characterized as 'rebellions' as against revolutions. It is likely that the periodic and regular splits in Israeli political parties are related to the maturation of young cadres of leadership who have found their paths to power blocked by the entrenched veteran leadership. This was certainly one of several factors leading to the split of Rafi from Mapai in 1965. The potential threat of such rebellions necessitated the pacification and integration of the Young Guard through proceedings like the ritual in the Standing Committee. The knowledge that actual splits have not generally been the most successful means of gaining power was probably an additional incentive for rebelliously inclined Young Guardists to play by the rules of the game, and to remain within the fold of the party.

But the threat offered by such groups as the Young Guard was not restricted to their threat of potential rebellion or leading a faction into independence. They represented a new generation which posed problems of compliance with the operative rules of the game established by the founding generation, e.g. in leading in the charges against the violation of democratic principles and procedures. As Berger and Luckmann have stated (1966: 59), '... it is more likely that one will deviate from programs set up for one by others than from programs one has established oneself'. An analogous situation existed with the local leaders of newer immigrant and ethnic groups of the smaller branches of the development towns whose indoctrination into the institutional order was significantly different from that of the generation of predominantly European members of the secondary echelon of leadership.

Important interests were represented by the organization of branches of the party. The dominant party machine based in Tel Aviv, competed with the party machine of Haifa, and to a lesser extent that of Jerusalem. Each of them competed, and formed coalitions, with branches in the rest of the country. Many complaints were voiced during the proceedings about the domination of party institutions by the major city machines and by the kibbutzim which have disproportionately large overrepresentation at the expense of the smaller branches. In particular, severe criticism was voiced against the 'undemocratic' methods through which powerful groups gained more than their share of representation on bodies of the party. Representatives of the smaller branches voiced views such as the following: 'Members in the outlying areas need to be given rights!' Again, demands for fair and equal representation were juxtaposed with criticism that powerful groups perpetuated their dominance of others by undemocratic methods.

Other divisions, such as the division between the urban and agricultural sectors, represented not only conflicting economic interests, but also distinctly different ideological orientations. For example, the two kibbutz movements were autonomous institutions of the former Mapai and Achdut Haavoda parties with different ideologies and traditions; and in turn the moshav movement represented another set of economic and ideological interests with which they competed.

In addition the different institutions dominated by the party, represented a fairly wide range of different, and frequently competing interests, e.g. the marked confrontation of the conflicting views of the Ministry of Finance and the Histadrut (General Federation of Labor) over wage policies entailed considerably different interpretations of socialism. In fact a wide range of ideological conflicts were expressed in debates on almost all issues. For example, in the debate over policy on defense and security the protagonists ranged from extreme 'hawks' who were unwilling to consider giving back an inch of 'the Greater Land of Israel' to extreme 'doves' who favored the return of 'occupied territories' and the creation of a 'Palestinian entity'. These are only examples of the great diversity of conflicting interests and ideologies contained within what some Israelis call the 'supermarket' of the mass, pluralist, Israel Labor Party.

Obviously in a party which is characterized by such a diversity of conflicting interests and even conflicting values, there is a great need for procedures through which these interests and their norms can be reconciled in order to keep their protagonists together. This is particularly enforced because the dominant party is a microcosm of the wider society in which great centrifugal and centripetal forces tend, respectively, to pull the society apart as well as to enforce some unity. The social and political strains of a socially and culturally diverse society of immigrants, a society which is undergoing rapid social change within a context of a constant challenge to its physical survival, create tensions which are given symbolic representation through the ritual performance in the Standing Committee. As Da Matta (forthcoming) points out, the ritual life of a given society can express different ways of seeing, interpreting, and realizing the social structure. In complex societies these different domains compete for power; but only one of these views is legitimated at a given time, and that view's hegemony dominates the society.

The competition among the protagonists of these domains produces grave problems of legitimation, particularly when there is an overriding need for integration. This dominant ideology is constantly threatened by the presence of realities that are meaningless in its terms. 'The legitimation of the institutional order is also faced with the ongoing necessity of keeping chaos at bay. *All* social reality is precarious. *All* societies are constructions in the face of chaos. The constant possibility of anomic terror is actualized whenever the legitimations that obscure the precariousness are threatened or collapse'

(Berger and Luckmann, 1966: 96). The importance of specific procedures for maintaining order is critical when the symbolic universe is questioned. Although the human construction of society exposes inevitably its symbolic universes to question, some are more vulnerable than others, as in an institution where rival definitions of reality compete for power. Berger and Luckmann (1966: 114) state: 'The distinctiveness of ideology is rather that the *same* overall universe is interpreted in different ways, depending upon concrete vested interests within the society in question'. They point out that the pluralistic aspect of many modern societies means,' ... that they have a shared core universe, taken for granted as such, and different partial universes coexisting in a state of mutual accomodation' (Ibid.,: 115), or – I add – mutual antagonism. Pluralism is seen as an accelerating factor in social change '... precisely because it helps to undermine the change-resistant efficacy of the traditional definitions of reality. Pluralism encourages both skepticism and innovation and is thus inherently subversive of the taken-forgranted reality of the traditional *status quo*' (Ibid.,: 115).

Under such conditions the core symbolic universe may be very vulnerable. In societies of this type, where conciliation is an important cultural value, and when the character of the political regime makes it possible, I argue that arenas can be created for the exposition of these different views, but within limited and controlled borders, highly 'ritualized', because otherwise the taken-for-granted nature of reality would be challenged and even threatened. The dominant political party is a hierarchical system which cuts across and represents this wide range of divisions. Israeli society contains groups which view it differently, and which nevertheless have to, in order to survive, remain together without splitting apart. There is the attempt to conciliate the diverse interests and views through proceedings which necessarily are ritualistic.

Rituals stress basic principles in society, yet at the same time they mask these principles. They appear when there is a threat within the social structure, for they deal with the representation of conflicts, ambiguities, and disorder within society. Through ritual performances, social relationships are represented and affected. Reality itself is presented symbolicly, but in a controlled and disguised manner. Much like the 'encounters' analysed by Goffman, ' ... a disguise may function not so much as a way of concealing something as a way of revealing as much of it as can be tolerated in an encounter. We fence our encounters with gates; the means by which we hold off a part of reality can be the means by which we can bear introducing it' (Goffman, 1961:77-78). In this way rituals create an aura of authenticity by activating and selectively condensing reality in a convincing manner.

I have attempted to show for a segment of Israeli society how a controlled bracketing of a 'ritual' encounter provided a period in which the participants could reflect and discourse on their lives and on the social order. They orchestrated a meta-commentary on, and a critique of the social order, and through their performance tried to create a new authenticity which transformed their roles and gave them new meaning in a 'ritual of assertion'. Through their commentary on the mundane world they criticized the erosion of their influence and the meaning of their specific roles, and the erosion of such general norms of the party and the society, as democracy, participation, pioneering and equality.

In a sense the ritual was a temporary recapturing of the comradeship of an earlier period when mutual ideological commitment and a sense of mission bound the party activists tightly together in a common pioneering endeavor. Dramatic changes in Israeli socity led to the bureaucratization of the party and to marked decline in the role of ideology. The pioneering vanguard became a ruling elite and their dedicated comrades-in-arms became party functionaries (*askanim*, the Hebrew term, has a decidedly negative conotation in present-day Israel). As Turner has stated, 'Any developing structure generates problems of organization and values that provoke redefinition of central concepts. This often seems like temporizing and hypocrisy, or loss of faith, but it is really no more than a reasoned response to an alteration in the scale and complexity of social relations, and with these, a change in the location of the group in the social field it occupies, with concomitant changes in its major goals and means of attaining them' (Turner, 1969:147).

Terence Turner (forthcoming) has shown how rituals function to bridge a gap and transcend structural incommensurability which cannot be articulated at the lower level. He poses this as a predicament in which people must come to terms with, and regulate, what they cannot articulate – so, he argues, they resort to paradox and ritual. Cohen formulates a related point somewhat differently saying, 'When society changes, men tend for some time to continue, indeed to struggle hard to preserve their identity, their selfhood, in the old traditional ways. Social change is in a way always a threat to our selfhood, particularly if it involves changes in roles. We tenaciously try to maintain our selfhood by giving new interpretations to our patterns of symbolic action' (Cohen, 1974:58). Rapid social change in Israeli society has produced a reality significantly different from that which the symbolic universe of the party ideology proclaimed. The previous meanings of the roles of the secondary leaders and of central values in the party ideology had been eroded, and social reality was more than meaningless in its terms for it contradicted what ideology said it was. This indeed appeared to those involved in the proceedings as temporizing, loss of faith, and hypocrisy. It was beyond the cognitive perception of these actors to understand this as a reflection and consequence of social change. It presented them with conflicting cognitions of a real world which sharply contrasted with what it was supposed to be, according to the legitimating universe. They were pioneers; but people saw them as party hacks – all Jews are equal, but some are more equal than others; the party was democratic, but they were involved in and the victims of oligarchic manipulations, and so forth. Cohen has said of the disturbance in equilibrium between selfhood and disparate roles caused by these subversive processes of change: 'As a result, there is an active search for a new equilibrium, for a modified symbolic order to accomodate the self within the new alignments of power' (*Ibid*.,: 58).

From the alternatives open to them, i.e. creating a new ideology, giving new interpretations to old patterns of symbolic action, etc., the ritual performers in the Standing Committee sought to resolve the dissonance between their ideology and reality by affirming and reasserting the legitimacy of their traditional symbolic universe. They attempted to transcend this logical impasse by the assertion of meaning – both for their roles and their ideology, which short-circuited the real world which they thereby attempted to make fit their normative reality. I shall attempt to explain this particular choice in my concluding remarks.

Outcomes and Conclusions

In considering the outcomes of the ritual of the Standing Committee, I shall first relate them to the explicit purposes or manifest goals of the Committee. I shall then consider some of the latent functions of the outcomes, and conclude with a summary discussion of the more creative aspects of the proceedings in terms of the specific and more general social contexts in which they took place. The explicit pragmatic political work of the Standing Committee included approval of a new party constitution, nomination of a significant proportion of the members of the new Central Committee, and the presentation of the party's ideology through the formulation of the platform of issues presented to the Conference.

The primary implicit purpose of the Standing Committee was to control the Conference and thereby to guarantee support for the policies of the top leadership. This was accomplished through the careful selection of the performers, thereby maximizing the chances for the successful bracketing of the procedings within the constraints imposed, i.e. consensual formulations of policies, and the suppression of highly controversial issues. The fear of chaos in the Conference in the form of disordered conflict and indeterminate outcomes, was constantly impressed upon the performers in the Standing Committee as if to highlight the importance of the success of their performance, and the dangers to party unity were they to fail. There was a juxtapositioning of the need for minimal order, i.e. abiding by the rules, in the Committee in the face of disorder and possible chaos in the Conference. On the other hand, within the major constraints, the performers were permitted a wide range of freedom to improvise and express themselves. In contrast the full Conference was much more formal and restrictive, and allowed a minimum of initiative to the delegates, precisely because the threat of real disorder was greater.

I first discuss the immediate effects of the performance for the two major audiences or reference groups, i.e. the top leaders and the Conference delegates (grass-roots leaders), and then for the performers of the Standing Committee themselves. For the top leaders the most important outcome was that they succeeded in maintaining their control of the party, they kept the party intact, and their policies were approved without amendment by the overwhelming majority of the delegates to the Conference. In addition, despite the criticism in the Standing Committee (if not through it), the legitimacy of their dominant roles was reaffirmed and strengthened. However, I shall show that these effects were limited in scope and duration.

The Conference was an important occasion for the local leaders to come together and mingle with one another, to rub shoulders with and talk to the top leaders of the party, who on such an occasion were socially very accessible to them. For example, the Finance Minister (the most dominant figure in the party among the top leadership) held 'court' in which he received and talked with hundreds of delegates. In addition to more tangible political benefits they may have received from these consultations, and the semblance of participation in the Conference debates, this gave the delegates tremendous prestige and strengthened their own standing in their respecive local constituencies. For example, the ultimate status symbol among Israeli politicians, the 'James Bond' briefcase –, was temporarily edged out by the red plastic document case of the delegate to the party Conference. Local leaders could be seen demonstratively flashing them around for months after the Conference. I stress that the surface appearance of democratic participation felt by many Conference delegates was made possible through the tight structure provided by the successful proceedings of the Standing Committee.

The ritual had several results for the participants. In one sense, it was a performance of self-definition which emphasized the solidarity and uniqueness, as a socio-political category, of the secondary echelon of leadership. The exclusion of the other two categories was therefore not only practical in that it facilitated the successful ritual proceedings, but it gave symbolic representation of the uniqueness and importance of the secondary leaders. The rebellious aspects of the criticism raised against the top leadership, resemble in some ways analogous conduct of the Lozi priests in Barotseland, (Gluckman) and the chiefs designated by the kings of the Baganda as his messengers (Mair, 1934) as opposed to the Swazi where the entire people participate in the ritual rebellion (Gluckman, 1962 and 1963). Gluckman (1965, chap. 4-6) argues that rituals of rebellion of the Swazi type cease to occur in states where protoclasses have emerged. I contend that you can get the more limited type of ritual of rebellion, where the 'king' is conspicuously absent, e.g., among a segment of a dominant political party, under certain conditions. These conditions are that the dangers and high costs of opting for alternative social roles severely limit mobility and therefore freedom of choice; coupled with a high degree of internalization of norms, this allows for a successful rigid bracketing of a performance which I consider meets all the criteria of a ritual. Another factor is the multiplicity of social relationships. I differentiate the term 'multiple' from 'multiplex' (coined by Gluckman) in recognition that while socio-political roles of Labor Party politicians overlap with a whole range of other relationships, e.g. economic roles, friedship networks, and kinship relationships, they differ significantly from the multiplex relationships in traditional societies.

But the performance was ritual in more than mere self-definition or even rebellion; it was transformative in that it created new meaning for the roles of the performers through their assertion of an idealized normative structure. The strong criticism of the lack of internal party democracy raised in the Standing Committee reaffirmed belief in a valued ideal which had been blatantly breached. In a similar way, symbolic references to the inequality of ethnic groups involved criticism of the breach of one of the most important norms in Israeli society and reaffirmed the central importance of the ideal. Therefore, in addition to resolving the ambiguity of their own roles, and mediating between competing groups with opposed interests and ideologies, these criticisms orchestrated a commentary on the major contradictions and paradoxes in Israeli society.

In fact the members of the Standing Committee were grappling with universal human dilemmas within the specific context of their party and society. They were dealing with the problem of the meaning of consensus, democracy, equality, socialism, Judaism etc. Their very actions symbolized the juxtaposing of the need for structure, order, and control in the face of the threat of uncertainty, chaos, and anarchy. For the party, and even more so for the society, the overriding need for unity was constantly subjected to the strains of the demands of conflicting groups, interests and ideologies to be heard, to assert themselves, and to gain greater representation in the centers of power. The dangerous situation of the society makes the price of sacrificing unity so terrifying that extraordinary measures are required to maintain unity in spite of all the objective difficulties.

It was as if at some level, consciousnessly or subconsciously, the performers were aware that the party, while still dominant politically, had gradually lost its moral ideological dominance in Israeli society. It was probably beyond their conscious level of perception to analyse the failure of the party and the political structure to adapt adequately to the forces of social change, yet, through their ritual performance they generated, or at least reaffirmed, the effectiveness, in the face of reality, of a symbolic relationship – a normative code – which they had internalized and which was meaningful to them. Yet this had a conservative, if not a counterrevolutionary, effect in the sense that it helped to keep the system going. Although they constructed a code which helped them cope with a complex and, at times, oppressive situation, they did not generate new ideas, forms, or norms designed to cope with the changed situation. They contented themselves with reaffirming the validity of the old norms without reinterpreting them in the context of new problems.

Given the structural and cultural constraints, and the other choices available, the particular ritual 'solution' to the major problem confronting the actors can be better understood. The character of the structure of the dominant party in the Israeli political system was such that it could allow the controlled expression of dissent and discourse on the social and normative order, because the outcome of consensual unity was predictable – given the nature of dependence of the performers in the ritual and their internalization of party norms, and the overriding necessity of unity imposed by external threats. The normative imperative dictated the need for a semblance of democratic procedure and participation in the process of making decisions. The problem of the discrepancy between ideology and reality could be resolved through a logically limited number of solutions. Reality could be ignored, denied, or in the long run changed. Ideology could be reinterpreted, or affirmed, or rejected with a new ideology more meaningfully related to reality offered in its place. There is evidence that for several years various aspects of changing social reality have been 'ignored' by the decision-makers who successfully prevented a confrontation with the problems created by these changed social realities. The 'suppression' of two crucial and highly important issues from the arena of the party Conference, illustrates one of the means by which this has been done. It becomes increasingly more difficult, if not impossible to ignore, dismiss or deny a social reality which manifests itself in problems which greatly trouble the public, and indeed the professional politicians themselves. For example, the problem of the increasing gap between the 'haves' and the 'have nots', a gap which in Israel is intimately related to the problem of ethnic relationships, was given forceful expression by the demonstrations of the 'Black Panthers' and other protesting groups, and received wide coverage by the mass media. It intrudes in many ways into the life of the party as shown by the 'Oriental caucus' in the Conference, and is deeply felt even by some of the most loyal and trusted members of the Standing Committee. Thus it is an issue so troublesome that it can neither be denied nor ignored. Problems of this kind emerging from a changing social reality, are so complicated that their solution can only be achieved through long-range programs requiring considerable imagination and resources, which are not always available, particularly given the high priority of heavy expenditures for defense and absorption of immigrants (particularly the immediate problems of housing and employment). Other problems, e.g. the inherent contradictions between the values of religiously orthodox and secularly liberal ideologies about the very nature of the society and the State are even less amenable to 'solution', even by any expenditure. If they are to be resolved at all, they will require a great deal of mutual goodwill and an extremely imaginative synthesis of symbolic and legitimating ideas. This leads us from the possibility of coping with reality to the choice of ways of coping with ideology.

The outright rejection of party ideology would have been unthinkable, given the character of the carefully selected actors in the ritual of the Standing Committee. Not only would this have been political suicide, but it would have represented a traumatic challenge to the actors' own perceptions of their roles and very selves. The extremely complicated problems posed by changing social reality rendered them not easily amenable to resolution through a reinterpretation of traditional ideology, particularly in the context of a political forum, the major function of which was to maintain the political status quo, in which the actors themselves had considerable vested interests. They were not chosen to produce nor did they produce, imaginative new solutions to the problems of social reality or to make these problems meaningful either through a reinterpretation of their ideology or through its replacement with a new ideology. Lacking either the freedom, or the resources, including imagination, to opt for other possible solutions for the problem of the conflict between ideology and reality, they asserted the former in the face of the latter.

The successful ritual performance in the Standing Committee allowed for a successful pageant of unity in the national party Conference. The 3,000 assembled delegates of the Conference more accurately reflected the composition of the general membership of 300,000 than did any other party institution. The ceremonial gathering of these delegates symbolized the unity and strength of the Israel Labor Party, and affirmed their support of their leadership and its policies to their fellow members and countrymen. It also symbolized the unity and strength of the Israeli people in full view of friend and foe alike. The necessity of presenting this united front to all the different audiences made particularly crucial the successful ritual of consensual relationships of power in the Standing Committee; and the success of this ritual made possible the ceremonial demonstration of unity and strength of the Conference.

But, as I indicated previously, there is widespread discontent among party activists who complain that they are not able to influence decisions on policy, particularly on issues which appear to the general public to be the most pressing domestic problems. These significantly were the very issues which were most carefully controlled, or even suppressed, in the Conference. I stress that the 'solutions' of consensual formulation within the context of carefully bracketed rituals and the suppression of issues through ritual procedures are *temporary*. Vital issues such as the relationships between ethnic groups, problems of poverty which are tied to the former issue and also to wage policies and labor relations, the question of what should be the proper role of religion in the state, and so forth, are questions which demand policies aimed at their solution in spite of the inherent difficulties involved.

The general public has increasingly stated its demands that solutions to these problems be found. The procedures which the top leaders have used successfully to postpone decisions on these issues have given them a temporary respite in which they have consolidated their control of the party. They have thus far refrained from proposing controversial policies which they feared might antagonize important sectors within the party and the public. But their successful use of these procedures of control was most effective with that supporting category closest to them and most dependent on the elite. The sanctions, both normative and otherwise, which enforced loyalty of the members of the Standing Committee to the top leaders were becoming increasingly less effective as against the third level of local leadership, the general party membership, and the electorate.

In fact the last general election which took place in the cataclysmic aftermath of the war of October 1973, appears to represent a new threshold in the development of the Israeli political system. The leadership of the Labor

Party bore the brunt of severe criticism for what was perceived as near-fatal errors in the preparation for, and handling of, the war – particularly in its earliest stages.

Although it lost substantial electoral support, the Labor Party managed to stay in power with a coalition which gave it, for some time, only a narrow single vote majority in the Knesset. Internal party criticism and mass public criticism, including new protest groups and demonstrations, eventually forced the resignation of the Prime Minister and Minister of Defence. The party and the political system are presently in a state of flux and transition, but it would appear that because of these changed conditions it will be increasingly difficult to manage a carefully controlled ritual such as that of the Standing Committee in the future.

In conclusion, I would like to draw from this particular case-study some points which I think may have general application. First of all I would expect this kind of political ritual to be more common in a certain kind of structural and cultural environment than in others. I would expect that dominant party systems would be more conducive to the creation of this type of political ritual for several reasons. In the first place, such systems by definition have limited possibilities that the control of major political resources and office may be altered. They offer various categories of political actors much more limited options for other socio-political roles by making such choices prohibitively costly. Obviously different degrees of dependence or autonomy between various categories of leadership, e.g. top leaders, secondary echelon, and grassroots leaders, would affect the types of performances that are possible. The type of ritual I have described is dependent upon a fairly rigid structure in which control can guarantee eventual outcomes. Therefore the actors' freedom or choice must be limited.

Another important factor in the rituals which are characteristic of many societies in which there are dominant party systems, is that the dominant party is a mass party encompassing and attempting to conciliate a wide range of conflicting groups and interests. This is particularly true in socially and culturally heterogenious societies where the dominant party has been the vanguard of a successful revolution and/or the party which led the country in its drive for independence (e.g. the P.R.I. of Mexico, the Congress Party of India, and many of the dominant parties in Africa). In such cases there is usually an attempt to conciliate social and ideological differences within the context of the need for national unity to face the struggle which is legitimated within values of the revolutionary ideology. In such contexts there is usually a period after the goal has been achieved, i.e. independence, when the revolutionary or nationalistic fervor cools down, the party becomes institutionalized, and the contrast between the normative goals of the ideology and situational reality become more visible. This tendency has been observed by Brezesinski (1962: 115) who states: 'One could almost say that there is a kind of 'dialectical' relationship between an ideologically oriented party and reality. The ideological party attempts to change reality and, in this way, is a revolutionary force: the new changed reality for a while corresponds to the ideology even while changing itself; in time the ideology may become a conservative force; a new adjustment is eventually forced, and the ideology may then again become a revolutionary force'. (cf. Seliger, 1970 for a discussion of the inherent asymmetry of ideologies). But, particularly in the cases (for which there are ample examples) in which new ideological adjustment has not been made, or in the interim before this has been accomplished, the dominant elites are generally very anxious to maintain the semblance of democratic participation while at the same time controlling outcomes. This kind of situation is ripe for the ritualization of political activities. But because of the everpresent danger that ritual rebellion and/or assertion may break out into a real political revolt, such rituals are only likely to be held when there is virtual certainty that the ritual performance can be successfully bracketed and controlled.

Given the changes now taking place in the Israeli political system, it would appear that the previous certainty of predictable outcomes is becoming increasingly more doubtful. It is not clear whether or not the political actors themselves perceive the implications, and the new possibilities arising from the new situation. Early indications are that they do not yet do so. For example, in the aftermath of the last war and national election there was a widespread feeling, expressed by large numbers of party activists and leaders, who reflected an equally widespread public sentiment, that the top leaders, such as the Prime Minister, Minister of Defence, and other key Ministers, as well as party policy, should be changed. The first meeting of the party's Central Committee after the war which was to discuss these issues was postponed for several hours while the top leaders met to thrash out a compromise among themselves and thereby to avoid an open confrontation in the Central Committee.

While the top leaders sat one floor below, I sat with a group of the secondary leaders in a room at party headquarters. They seriously discussed the need to change the top party and Government leadership and to drastically revise party policy. As if the reality of what was taking place below radiated upwards to the floor above, the tone of the discussion between the secondary leaders began to change markedly. They gradually began to turn their previously serious discussion into a farcical mocking of what they thought was going on below. They satirically nominated the most unqualified party functionaries for the key cabinet posts. Their conduct reminded me of a scene in the film 'M.A.S.H.' where a team of army doctors joked as they operated in a field hospital on men whom they knew were likely to go back into combat and get killed after they recuperated from their operations. Both the doctors and the functionaries of the Labor Party resorted to satire and paradox to express their feelings of helplessness in the absurdity of their situations. The functionaries of the Labor Party expressed symbolically through their behavior their perception of their own dependence on the top leaders and their own inability to change the order of things in spite of their sincerely felt need to do so. This is the stuff of which the type of political ritual I have described is made. It remains to be seen whether the perception of the political actors concerned will be altered by the increasingly changed political reality, or whether this will produce new ritual forms or lead to the dropping of such ritual. It is also uncertain whether new programs designed to change social reality in order to bring it into line with ideology or new sets of symbols will be produced, that are more meaningfully related to this reality.

Acknowledgements

My field-work on the Israel Labor Party was conducted in two main stages, September 1969-July 1971 and November 1973-April 1974 (although I was in residence in Israel during the interum period and continued research at a less intense level). The first stage was sponsored by the Social Science Research Council of the United Kingdom, SSRC grant HR/779/1, Socio-Cultural Patterns of Adjustment and Conflict Among Israel's Veterans and Immigrants. The second stage was sponsored by the Ford Foundation through the Israel Foundation for Research Grants, grant 8613, The Internal Dynamics of the Israel Labor Party in the 1973 Elections. I also wish to express my gratitude to the sponsoring institutions for their generosity and the complete freedom they gave me to pursue my research interests. I also wish to express my sincere thanks to the Wenner-Gren Foundation For Anthropological Research which made it possible for me to attend the Burg Wartenstein Symposium No. 64, and to the co-organizers, the late Max Gluckman, Sally Moore, and Victor Turner for having invited me to participate in it. I am grateful to N.I.A.S. for having provided a most congenial environment in which I revised this article.

Numerous people have given generously of their time and experience in commenting on various drafts of this article, and I wish to express my sincere gratitude to them. Max Gluckman commented on every draft. Asher Arian, F. G. Bailey, Shlomo Deshen, Emanuel Marx, Joel Migdal, David Rapoport, Victor Turner, Harry Scoble, Moshe Shokeid, and Moshe Schwartz commented on the early draft. My fellow participants in Burg Wartenstein Symposium 64 commented on the second draft and I especially acknowledge my debt to them. It is impossible to sufficiently emphasize my intellectual debt to my fellow participants in the symposium, because there was such an unusual meeting of the minds, and genuine intellectual exchange that it is difficult, if not impossible to always differentiate between ones original ideas and those which have been assimilated from intensive discussions with one's colleagues. Where possible I shall credit individuals for their personal contributions, and if no reference is cited the contribution was made in the course of the discussions of the session. I ask the reader to keep in mind that what I write is a personal distillation and interpretation of a most unusual and memorable communal intellectual experience. I would like to express my special gratitude to Terence Turner whose inciteful comments pointed me in the direction of the reanalysis which I have undertaken. Three of my colleagues at N.I.A.S., R. Th. J. Buve, J. M. F. Jaspers, and J. D. Speckman, read and commented on the present draft as did Abner Cohen, Don Handelman and S. N. Eisenstadt. I am grateful to all of these people.

I also thank the many people in the Israel Labor Party whose generous help and cooperation made it possible for me to participate in and observe the internal life of the party.

LITERATURE CITED

ARIAN, ALAN. 1972. Editor, *The Elections in Israel – 1969*. Jerusalem: Jerusalem Academic Press.
–. 1975. Editor, *The Elections in Israel – 1973*. Jerusalem: Jerusalem Academic Press.
ARONOFF, MYRON, J. 1972. Party Center and Local Branch Relationships: The Israel Labor Party, in *The Elections in Israel – 1969*. Edited by Alan Arian, pp. 150-183. Jerusalem: Jerusalem Academic Press.
–. 1973. Ritual in Consensual Power Relationships: The Israel Labor Party. A paper presented to the IXth International Congress of Anthropological and Ethnological Sciences, Chicago, in *Political Anthropology and the State*. Edited by S. Lee Seaton, 70 pages, The Hague: Mouton (forthcoming).
–. 1974. Fission and Fusion: The Politics of Factionalism in the Israel Labor Parties. A paper presented to the 1974 Annual Meeting of the American Political Science Association, Chicago, in *Faction Politics*. Edited by Frank P. Belloni and Dennis C. Beller, 64 pages. Santa Barbara: ABC Clio Press (in press).
–. 1975. The Power of Nominations in the Israel Labor Party, in *The Elections in Israel – 1973*. Edited by Alan Arian, pp. 21-40. Jerusalem: Jerusalem Academic Press.

–. Forthcoming. *Power and Ritual in the Israel Labor Party.* Assen: Royal Van Gorcum.
BAILEY, F. G. 1972. Conceptual Systems in the Study of Politics, in *Rural Politics and Social Change in the Middle East.* Edited by Richard Antoun and Iliya Harik, pp. 21-44. Bloomington: Indiana University Press.
BERGER, PETER. 1969. *A Rumor of Angels.* Garden City: Doubleday.
–. and LUCKMAN, THOMAS. 1966. *The Social Construction of Reality.* Garden City: Doubleday.
BOCOCK, ROBERT. 1974. *Ritual in Industrial Society.* London: George Allen & Unwin.
BREZEZINSKI, A. K. 1962. *Ideology and Power in Soviet Politics.* New York: Frederick A. Praeger.
COHEN, ABNER. 1974. *Two-Dimensional Man.* London: Routledge & Kegan Paul.
DA MATTA, ROBERTO. 1974. Constraint and Licence: A Preliminary Study of Two Brazilian National Rituals. A paper presented to the Burg Wartenstein Symposium No. 64, Austria, in *Secular Ritual: Forms and Meanings.* Edited by Sally F. Moore and Barbara Myerhoff, 29 pages, forthcoming.
DESHEN, SHLOMO. 1970. *Immigrant Voters in Israel: Parties and Congregations in a Local Election Campaign.* Manchester: Manchester University Press.
DOUGLAS, MARY. 1970. *Natural Symbols.* London: Barrie & Rockliff: The Cresset Press.
DUVERGER, MAURICE. 1963. *Political Parties.* New York: Wiley.
EDELMAN, MURRAY. 1964. *The Symbolic Uses of Politics.* Urbana: University of Illinois Press.
–. 1971. *Politics as Symbolic Action: Mass Arousal and Quiescence.* Chicago: Marham Publishing Co.
GLUCKMAN, MAX. 1954. Rituals of Rebellion in South-East Africa (The Frazer Lecture – 1952). Manchester: Manchester University Press.
–. 1955. *Custom and Conflict in Africa.* Oxford: Basil Blackwell.
–. 1962. Les Rites De Passage, in *Essays on The Ritual of Social Relations.* Edited by Max Gluckman, pp. 1-52. Manchester: Manchester University Press.
–. 1963. *Order and Rebellion in Tribal Africa.* New York: The Free Press of Glencoe.
–. 1965. *Politics, Law and Ritual in Tribal Society.* Oxford: Basil Blackwell.
GOFFMAN, ERVING. 1961. *Encounters: Two Studies in the Sociology of Interaction.* Indianapolis: Bobbs-Merril.
GOODY, JACK. 1974. Against 'Ritual': Loosely Structured Thoughts on a Loosely Defined Topic. A Paper presented to the Burg Wartenstein Symposium No. 64, Austria, in *Secular Ritual: Forms and Meanings.* Edited by Sally F. Moore and Barbara Meyerhoff, 20 pages, forthcoming.
HANDELMAN, DON. 1976. Some Contributions of Max Gluckman to Anthropological Thought, *Political Anthropology* Vol. 1 Nr. 3-4; 7-14.
LANGER, SUSANNE K. 1942. (1967 third edition, fourth printing), *Philosophy in a New Key.* Cambridge (Massachusetts): Harvard University Press.
MAIR, LUCY. 1934. *An African People in the Twentieth Century (Baganda).* London: Routledge.
MEDDING, PETER. 1972. *Mapai in Israel: Political Organization and Government in a New Society.* Cambridge (Massachusetts): Harvard University Press.
SELIGER, MARTIN. 1970. Fundamental and Operative Ideology: The Two Principal Dimensions of Political Argumentation, *Policy Sciences* 1: 325-38.

TURNER, TERENCE. 1974. Groping for the Elephant: Ritual as Process, as Model, and as Hierarchical System. A paper presented to the Burg Wartenstein Symposium No. 64, Austria, in *Secular Ritual: Forms and Meanings*. Edited by Sally F. Moore and Barbara Myerhoff, 41 pages, forthcoming.

TURNER, VICTOR. 1968. Mukanda: The Politics of a Non-Political Ritual, *in Local-Level Politics*. Edited by Marc J. Swartz, pp. 135-50. Chicago: Aldine.

–. 1969. *The Ritual Process*. Chicago: Aldine.

WOLF, ERIC R. 1969 (1974 edition). American Anthropologists and American Society, in *Reinventing Anthropology*. Edited by Dell Hymes, pp. 251-63. New York: Vintage Books (Random House).

ZASHIN, ELLIOT and CHAPMAN, PHILLIP C. 1974. The Uses of Metaphor and Analogy: Toward a Renewal of Political Language, *The Journal of Politics* 36: 290-326.

Max Gluckman
Summarised Curriculum Vitae (30-9-1974)

Born:
January 26, 1911 at Johannesburg, Union of South Africa.

Status:
British subject and citizen of the United Kingdom.

Degrees:
B.A. Hons. (Witwatersrand), M.A., D.Phil. (Oxon), M.A. (Manchester), D.H.C.Soc.Sc. (Bruxelles).

Honours:
1934   Transvaal Rhodes Scholar.
1961   President, Section N (Sociology and Social Anthropology), British Association for the Advancement of Science.
1965   Doctor Sciences Sociales Honoris Causa, Université Libre de Bruxelles.
1968   Fellow of the British Academy.
1970   Honorary Foreign Member of the American Academy of Arts and Sciences, 1970.

Appointments:
1939/41 Assistent Anthropologist, Rhodes-Livingstone Institute of Social Studies in British Central Africa.
1941/47 Director of Rhodes-Livingstone Institute.
1947/49 University Lecturer in Social Anthropology in the University of Oxford.
1949/71 Professor (first) of Social Anthropology in the University of Manchester, and Head of the Department of Social Anthropology and Sociology 1949-1965.
1971   Research Professor in Social Anthropology in the University of Manchester and holder of a Special Fellowship from the Nuffield Foundation.
1957   Center for Advanced Study in the Behavioral Sciences. Visiting appointments taken up from many invitations in Holland, Norway, Australia, United States (notably three times at Yale Law School) and Israel.

Distinctions:
1947   Wellcome Medal of the Royal Anthropological Institute.
1952   Rivers Memorial Medal of the Royal Anthropological Institute.
1952   Fraser Lecture, University of Glasgow.

1954 Six 50-minute Third Programme Lectures, BBC.
1955 Josiah Mason Lectures, University of Birmingham.
1958, 1960 Two sets of Munro Lectures, University of Edinburgh.
1959 Special Lecture, Sorbonne, Université de Paris.
1962 Principal's Lecture, University of Aberdeen.
1963 Stores Lectures in Jurisprudence, Yale Law School.
1964, 1965 Two Marett Lectures, Exeter College, Oxford.
1966 Lecture to Plenary Session of the American Anthropological Association.
1970 One of five lectures to celebrate United Nations Human Rights Year, UNESCO, Paris.
1971 First Maxwell Cummings Lecturer in the Humanities and Social Sciences, McGill University, 1971.
1972 Invited Lecture to Plenary Session of Scientific Congress for the Study of Sport, XXth Olympiad, Munich.
1973 J. B. Willens Lecture, University College of Wales at Aberystwyth.
1973 Wilson Memorial Lecture, School of Scots Law, University of Edinburgh.
1974 Radcliffe-Brown Lecture in Social Anthropology. The British Academy and the Association of Social Anthropologists of the Commonwealth.

Fieldwork:
1936/1938 Zululand, South Africa.
1939/1940, 1941/1942, 1945, 1947, 1965, Barotseland, Northern Rhodesia.
1944 Tongaland, Northern Rhodesia.
1946 Lambaland, Northern Rhodesia.
1951 Football players and crowds, England, especially Manchester.
1963 onwards Israel.

Major Publications:
1941 *Economy of the Central Barotse Plain*, Rhodes-Livingstone Paper No. 7.
1943 *Essays on Lozi land and royal property*, Rhodes-Livingstone Paper No. 11.
1943 *Administrative organisation of the Barotse Native Authorities*, Communications from the Rhodes-Livingstone Institute No. 1.
1948 *Malinowski's Sociological Theories*, Rhodes-Livingstone Paper No. 16 (reprinted essays).
1948 (with W. Allen and others) *Land-holding and land usage among the Plateau Tonga of Mazebuka District, Northern Rhodesia*, Rhodes-Livingstone Paper No. 14.
1954 *Rituals of rebellion in South-East Africa, Fraser Lecture 1952*, Manchester: Manchester University Press.
1955 *Custom and conflict in Africa*, Oxford: Blackwell; Glencoe, Ill.: Free Press; New York: Barnes and Noble (in 8th. impression).
1955 *The judicial process among the Barotse of Northern Rhodesia* (Zambia), Manchester: Manchester University Press for the Rhodes-Livingstone Institute; 2nd. edition, 1967, with two additional chapters; 3rd. edition, 1973, with new 'Preface'.
1958 *Analysis of a social situation in modern Zululand*, Rhodes-Livingstone Paper No. 28 (reprinted articles, with introduction by J. Clyde Mitchell).
1963 *Order and rebellion in Tribal Africa: Collected essays with an autobiographical*

introduction, London: Cohen and West; Glencoe, Ill.: Free Press (now in 4th. impression).

1965 *The ideas in Barotse jurisprudence: Stores Lecture in Jurisprudence, Yale School of Law, 1963*, New Haven: Yale University Press: 2nd. edition, 1972, with new 'Preface'. Manchester: Manchester University Press for the Institute of African Studies, Zambia.

1965 *Politics, law and ritual in tribal society*, Oxford: Blackwell; Chicago, Aldine; New York; Mentor Books.

1974 *African traditional law in historical perspective (Radcliffe-Brown Lecture in Social Anthropology, separate from Proceedings of the British Academy, 1974.*

in press *The Rise of the Zulu Empire*, London: International African Institute.

Editor of and contributor to:

1951 (with E. Colson) *Seven tribes of Central Africa*, London: Oxford University Press for the Rhodes-Livingstone Institute.

1962 *Essays on the ritual of social relations*, Manchester: Manchester University Press.

1964 *Closed systems and open minds: the limits of naiveté in social anthropology*, Edinburgh: Oliver and Boyd; Chicago: Aldine (in 2nd. impression).

1969 *Ideas and procedures in African customary law* (8th. seminar of the International African Institute), London: Oxford University Press for the International African Institute.

1972 *The allocation of responsibility; essays presented to E. E. Evans-Pritchard*, Manchester: Manchester University Press.

Other publications:

Essays in 30 important symposia; 55 articles in various journals and other symposia; and 17 substantial and theoretical forewords to books by others.

Offices:

Many held in national and international academic organisations.

H. M. Gluckman
Biography and Publications Education and Posts

Compiled by Mary Gluckman

BORN 26/1/1911 in Johannesburg, South Africa.
       British subject: citizen of the United Kingdom and Colonies.
1918-27 King Edward VII School, Johannesburg.
1928-34 University of the Witwatersrand.
1930 Bachelor of Arts (Social Anthropology First Class, Logic First Class).
1934 Bachelor of Arts with Honours in Social Anthropology First Class.
1931 Passed Preliminary Examination for Bachelor of Laws.
1932 Passed Intermediate Examination for Bachelor of Laws.
       (Did not study for Final Examination of LL.B as concentrating on Honours in Social Anthropology, which involved two theses).
1934 Selected Transvaal Rhodes Scholar.
1934-36 Exeter College, Oxford.
1936 D. Phil. (Oxon) for thesis on 'The Realm of the Supernatural among the South-Eastern Bantu'.
1936-39 Field work in Zululand, South Africa, on a grant from the National Bureau of Educational and Social Research (Carnegie Fund) of the Union of South Africa Department of Education.
1938-39 Returned to Oxford on Rhodes Scholarship 3rd year: tutored in Institute of Social Anthropology.
1939-47 Rhodes-Livingstone Institute of Social Studies in British Central Africa: Assistant Anthropologist (1939-41); Acting Director (1941-42) Director (1942-47).
1947-49 University Lecturer in Social Anthropology in the University of Oxford.
1949-71 Professor (first) of Social Anthropology in the Victoria University of Manchester, and Head of the Department of Social Anthropology and Sociology (1949-65).
1958 Volunteered grant for personal research, Ford Foundation.
1963 Grant for travel in U.S.A. – Rockefeller Foundation.
1970 Grant for personal research, Nuffield Foundation.
1971 Research Professor in Social Anthropology in the University of Manchester and holder of a Special Fellowship from the Nuffield Foundation.
1975 April 13th. Died in Jerusalem.

ACADEMIC DISTINCTIONS

D.Soc.Sc., Honoris Causa, Université Libre de Bruxelles, 1965.
Fellow of the British Academy, 1968.

Foreign Honorary Member of the American Academy of Arts and Sciences, 1970.
Philosophical Essay Prize, U. of the Witwatersrand, 1932.
Wellcome Medal of the Royal Anthropological Institute, 1947.
Rivers Memorial Medal of the Royal Anthropological Institute, 1954.
Frazer Lecture, U. of Glasgow, 1952.
Mason Lectures, U. of Birmingham, 1955.
Munro Lectures, U. of Edinburgh, 1958 and 1960.
Storrs Lectures in Jurisprudence, Yale School of Law, 1963.
Marett Lectures, Exeter College, Oxford, 1964 and 1965 (delivered 1965).
Plenary Address to the American Anthropological Association meeting, 1966.
Maxwell Cummings Lecture in the Humanities and Social Sciences, McGill U., 1971.
Wilson Memorial Lecture, School of Scots Law, U. of Edinburgh, 1973.
J.B. Williams Lecture, University College of Wales at Aberystwyth, 1973.
Radcliffe-Brown Lecture in Social Anthropology, The British Academy and the Association of Social Anthropologists of the Commonwealth, 1974.

VISITING APPOINTMENTS (taken up)

Visiting Lecturer, U. of Utrecht, Leyden and Amsterdam, 1952; Visiting Lecturer, Sorbonne, 1959; Visiting Lecturer, Hebrew U., 1959; Visiting Fellow, Australian National University, 1960; Visiting Professor, U. of Delhi, 1960; Visiting Professor, M.S. University of Baroda, 1960; Visiting Professor, Norway, 1966; Visiting Lecturer, McGill U., 1971; Visiting Professor, Nijmegen, 1973; Visiting Lecturer in Law and Anthropology, Yale U., 1966, 1968 and 1974.
Fellow-select of the Center for Advanced Study in the Behavioral Sciences, 1957; taken up, 1967 and 1971-72.
Lady Davis Distinguished Visiting Scholar, Hebrew University, Jerusalem, 1974-75.

OFFICES

President of Section N (Sociology) of the British Association for the Advancement of Science, 1961;
Member of the UNESCO Tensions Project, 1948;
Member of the Inter-Professional Advisory Committee of the World Federation of Mental Health, 1951-5;
Executive Council of International African Institute, 1956-65, Consultative Director, 1966-1974; Vice-Chairman, 1974.
Council of the Royal Anthropological Institute (various years);
Member of the Human Sciences Committee of Her Majesty's Department of Scientific and Industrial Research, 1957-1962;
Honorary Secretary of the Association of Social Anthropologists of the British Commonwealth, 1951-57, and Chairman, 1962-66;
Chairman (with Prof. Georges Balandier) of the Social Anthropology Section of the Third International Congess of Sociology, Stresa, 1959;
Social Anthropology Committee of the Social Science Research Council, 1967-70;
Social Studies Sub-Committee of the University Grants Committee, 1966-71;
Member of the new Advisory Committee to Her Majesty's Sports Council, 1974.

FIELDWORK (on which published)

Natal   Zululand 1936-38 (14 months).
N.Rhodesia (Zambia) Barotseland 1940-47 (30 months), 1965 (3 weeks); Tonga 1945 (1 month); Lamba 1946 (3 weeks).
Israel   1963-71 (9 months).
Sundry visits (no publications) to other parts of Africa.

PUBLICATIONS (arranged by fields)

Library Research for D.Phil. on South-Eastern Bantu.
1935   'Zulu Women in Hoeculture Ritual', *Bantu Studies*, ix, 3, pp. 255-272.
1937   'Mortuary Customs and the Belief in Survival After Death among the South-Eastern Bantu', *Bantu Studies*, xi, 2, pp. 117-136.
1938   'Social Aspects of First Fruits Ceremonies among the South-Eastern Bantu', *Africa*, xi, 1, pp. 25-41.

Field Research on Zulu

1940   'The Zulu of South Africa' in *African Political Systems*, edited by M. Fortes and E. E. Evans-Pritchard, London: Oxford University Press for the International African Institute, pp. 25-55.
1940   'Analysis of a Social Situation in Modern Zululand', *Bantu Studies*, xiv, 1, pp. 1-30; 2, pp. 147-174.
1942   'Some Processes of Social Change, illustrated with Zululand Data', *African Studies*, i, 4, pp. 243-260.
1945   'Chief, Commissioner and People', *Trek* (Johannesburg), X, 8 October 19.
1950   'Kinship and Marriage among the Lozi of Northern Rhodesia and the Zulu of Natal', in *African Systems of Kinship and Marriage*, edited by A. R. Radcliffe-Brown and C. D. Forde, London: Oxford University Press for the International African Institute, pp. 166-206.
1958   *Analysis of a Social Situation in Modern Zululand*, with a Foreword by J. C. Mitchell, Rhodes-Livingstone Paper No. 28: 17 pp. (reprinted articles from *Bantu Studies*, 1940, and *African Studies*, 1942).
1960   'The Rise of a Zulu Empire', *Scientific American*, cc ii, 4 (April) pp. 157-168.
Going to Press: *The Rise of the Zulu Empire*, London: International African Institute.

Field Research on Barotse

1941   Economy of the Central Barotse Plain, Rhodes-Livingstone Paper No. 7, pp. 134.
1942   'Prefix Concordance in Lozi, Lingua Franca of Barotseland', *African Studies*, i, 2, pp. 105-114.
1943   *Essays on Lozi Land and Royal Property*, Rhodes-Livingstone Paper No. 10, pp. 96.
1943   *Administration Organization of the Barotse Native Authorities*, Communications from the Rhodes-Livingstone Institute No. 1, pp. 96.
1943   'The Social Background of Barotse Music', in A. M. Jones, *African Music*, Rhodes-Livingstone Museum Collections No. 1.
1949   'The Role of the Sexes in Wiko Circumcision Ceremonies', in *Social Structure:*

Essays Presented to A. R. Radcliffe-Brown, edited by M. Fortes, Cambridge: University Press: 145-167.

1950 'Kinship and Marriage among the Lozi of Northern Rhodesia and the Zulu of Natal' (see under Zulu).

1951 'The Lozi of Barotseland in North-Western Rhodesia', in *Seven Tribes of British Central Africa*, edited by E. Colson and M. Gluckman, London: Oxford University Press: for the Rhodes-Livingstone Institute (2nd impression Manchester University Press and New York Humanities Press, 1959): 1-93.

1954 *The Judicial Process among the Barotse of Northern Rhodesia,* with a Foreword by Sir Arthur Goodheart, Manchester University Press; Glencoe, Illinois, Free Press, pp. 386; 2nd impression, with new introduction, 1966.

(a) Commented on by James G. March in 'Sociological Jurisprudence Revisited, A Review (more or less) of Max Gluckman', *Stanford Law Review*, viii, 3 (May 1956), pp. 499-534, which replied to by M. Gluckman in same journal viii, with reply by J. G. March, ix, 1 (December 1956).

(b) Reviewed at length (with two other books) by E. A. Hoebel in 'Three Studies of African Law', *Stanford Law Review*, xiii, 3 (March 1961), pp. 418-442, and reply on factual point by M. Gluckman, 'Comment: The Role of the Barotse King in the Judicial Process', same journal, xiv, 1 (December 1961), pp. 110-119.

(c) Review articles on this book by T. H. Marshall, 'Gluckman on the Judicial Process of the Barotse', *British Journal of Sociology*, vi, 4 (December 1955), pp. 369-373 by M. Douglas, 'L'homme primitif et la Loi', *Zaire*, No. 4 (April 1956), pp. 367-374; by S. E. Stumf, *Harvard Law Review*, ixix, 4 (February 1956); (with two other books) by S. F. Nadal, 'Reason and Unreason in African Law', *Africa*, xxxi, 2 (April 1956), pp. 160-173; (with one other book) by V. Ayoub, 'Review: The Judicial Process in Two African Tribes' in *Community Political Systems*, Edited by M. Janowitz, International Yearbook of Political Behaviour Research, Glencoe, Illinois, Free Press (1961), pp. 237-250.

(d) Republished in precis in *Judicial Behavior: A Reader in Theory and Research,* G. Schubert, ed., Chicago: McNulty (1964), which precis republished, in *Law and Warfare: Studies in the Anthropology of Conflict*. P. J. Bohannan, ed., American Musem Sourcebooks in Anthropology, 1976, pp. 59-92.

(e) Sections republished in D. Lloyd, *Jurisprudence: With Selected Texts*, London: Stevens, V. Aubert, ed., *Sociology of Law*; Hamondsworth: Penguin; N. Rubin and E. Contran, *Readings in African Law*, London: Frank Cass, 1955-56. 'The Reasonable Man in Barotse Law' (BBC Third Programme Broadcasts), *Journal of African Administration*, vii, 2: 5155; vii, 3: 126-131; viii, 2: 101-105; viii, 3: 151-156; reprinted in A. Dundes, ed., *Every Man His Way.* Englewood Cliffs: Prentice-Hall (1968).

1959 'The Technical Vocabulary of Barotse Jurisprudence', *American Anthropology*, lxi, 5 (1): 743-759.

1963 'Civil War and Theories of Power in Barotseland. African and Medieval Analogies', *Yale Law Journal*, vol. 72, no. 8, 1515-46.

1964 'Natural Justice in Africa', *Natural Law Forum* IX, 25-44.

1965 *The Ideas in Barotse Jurisprudence*: The Storrs Lectures in Jurisprudence, Yale Law School, April 1963, with a Foreword by Professor Charles Black, Jr., New Haven and London: Yale University Press, pp. 299.

1967 2nd edition, enlarged, of *The Judicial Process among the Barotse of Northern*

Rhodesia, Manchester: Manchester University Press for the Institute of African Research, Zambia.
1971 'Introduction' to Francois Coillard, *On the Threshold of Central Africa*, Third Edition, London: Frank Cass; originally published in 1897, London: Hodder and Stoughton.
1972 *The Ideas in Barotse Jurisprudence*: 2nd edition, with new preface, Manchester: Manchester University Press, for the Institute of African Studies, Zambia.
1972 *The Allocation of Responsibility*: essays presented to E. E. Evans-Pritchard, Manchester University Press ('Introduction' and essay on 'Moral crises: magical and secular solutions, Marett Lectures', 1964 and 1965).

Field Research on Tonga and Lamba

1948 *Land-holding and Land-usage among the Plateau Tonga of Northern Rhodesia* (with W. Allan and others), Rhodes-Livingstone Paper No. 14: pp. 192.
1950 'Introduction' to *The Lamba Village*, by J. A. Barnes and J. C. Mitchell, Communications from the School of African Studies in the University of Cape Town, xxiv: (my own field research is embodied in the main text).
1954 (With W. Allan, C. G. Trapnell and D. U. Peters) 'Rejoinder to (E. Colson's) 'The Tonga and the Shortage of Implements', *Rhodes-Livingstone Journal*, XIV, pp. 39-41.

Africa in General

1944 'Studies in African Land Tenure', *African Studies,* iii, 1: 1-8.
1945 'African Land Tenure', *Rhodes-Livingstone Journal*, 111, pp. 1-12 (republished in *Readings in Anthropology* by Bobbs-Merrill in 1963).
1945 'How the Bemba Make Their Living: An Appreciation of Richards' *Land, Labour and Diet in Northern Rhodesia', Rhodes-Livingstone Journal* 111, pp. 55-75 (republished in Hoebel, E. A. and others, *Readings in Anthropology* (1945) and republished in another *Reader* by Bobbs-Merrill (1963).
1949 'The Village Headman in British Central Africa' (with J. A. Barnes and J. C. Mitchell), *Africa*, xix, 2: pp. 89-106.
1954 Contributor to discussion in A. Leslie Banks, editor, *The Development of Tropical and Sub-Tropical Countries*, London: Arnold.
1955 'Anthropology in Central Africa', *Royal Society of Arts Journal* RL15, 20.
1960 'Tribalism in Modern British Central Africa', *Cahiers D'Etudes Africaines* 1 (January): pp. 55-72, republished in Vandenburg, R. L., ed., *Africa: Social Problems of Change and Conflict*, San Francisco: Chandler (1965); in I. Markovitz, *African Politics and Society*, New York: Free Press (1970): 81-95.
1960 'From Tribe to Town', *Nation* (Sydney, Australia), No. 53 (September 24): 7-12 (similar to previous article).
1961 'Anthropological Problems Arising from the African Industrial Revolution', in *Social Change in Africa*, edited by A. W. Southall, London: Oxford University Press for the International African Institute: 67-82 (similar to previous articles).
1965 'Reasonableness and Responsibility in the Law of Segmentary Societies', in L. and H. Kuper, *African Law: Adaption and Development*, Berkley: University of California Press.

1966 'Problems and Research Arising from the Study of Traditional Systems of Law', in A. Tunc, ed., *Legal Aspects of Development in Africa*, Paris: UNESCO.
1969 'Interhierarchical Roles: Professional and Party Ethics in the Tribal Areas of South and Central Africa', in M. Swartz, ed., *Local-level Politics*, Chicago: Aldine.
1969 'Property Rights and Status in African Traditional Law' and (with A. N. Allott and A. L. Epstein) 'Introduction' in M. Gluckman, ed., *Ideas and Procedures in African Customary Law*, London: Oxford University Press for the International African Institute.
1969 'The Tribal Areas of South and Central Africa', in L. Kuper and M. G. Smith, ed., *Pluralism in Africa*. Berkeley: University of California Press.
1970 'Tribalism, Ruralism and Urbanism in South and Central Africa', in V. W. Turner, ed., *Profiles of Change: The Impact of Colonialism on Africa*, Cambridge: Cambridge University Press.
1971 'Postscript' to reprinted section of 'Kinship and Marriage among the Zulu of Natal and the Lozi of Northern Rhodesia' (above under Zulu), in J. Goody, ed., *Readings on Kinship and Marriage*, Hamondsworth: Pelican.
1973 'Conflict et règlement: dimensions nouvelles in *Le racisme* devant la science, Paris: UNESCO.
1973 'Sport and Conflict' in *Sport in the Modern World – chances and problems:* Scientific Congress, Munich, 1972, O. Grupe, editor, Berlin: Springer-Verlag for the Organizing Committee for the Games of the XXth Olympiade Munich 1972.
1973 'Limitations of the case-method in the study of tribal law' in *Special Issue of Law and Society review: essays in honour of E. Adamson Hoebel*.
1974 'Spouse, child, parent or sibling? – who shall be saved? (The disputed passage in Sophocles' *Antigone* in B. A. Chapman & A. Potter, editors *W.J.M.M.: political questions* (essays presented to W. J. M. Mackenzie), Manchester, Manchester University Press.
1974 'The Makishi masked dancers of Barotseland', in M. Dias, editor, *Essays in memoriam Jorge Dias*, Lisbon, 1975.

Theoretical

1944 'The Difficulties, Achievements and Limitations of Social Anthropology', *Rhodes-Livingstone Journal*, 1, 22-44. Republished in R. A. Manners and D. Kaplan, eds., *Theory in Anthropology, A Source Book*, Chicago: Aldine (1968), pp. 31-46.
1944 'The Logic of African Science and Witchcraft: An appreciation of Evans-Pritchard's *Witchcraft, Oracles and Magic among the Azande*', *Rhodes-Livingstone Journal*, 1, 22-44 (republished in Hoebel, E. A. and others, *Readings in Anthropology*, New York: McGraw-Hill (1958), and republished in a *Reader* by Bobbs-Merrill (1963); and in P. J. M. McEwan and R. B. Sutcliffe, *The Study of Africa*, London: Methuen (1965).
1947 'Malinowski's "Functional" Analysis of Social Change', *Africa*, xvii, 4: 103-121, republished in I. Wallerstein, ed., *Social Change: The Colonial Situation*, New York: John Wiley (1966).
1947 'Malinowski's Contribution to Social Anthropology', *African Studies*, vi, 1: 41-46.

1949 *The Sociological Theories of Bronislaw Malinowski* (essays reprinted from 1947), Rhodes-Livingstone Paper No. 16: pp. 28.

1950 'Social Beliefs and Individual Thinking in Primitive Society', *Memoirs and Proceedings of the Manchester Literary and Philosophical Society,* xci: pp. 1-26.

1953-4 'The Stability of Marriage', Correspondence with D. M. Schneider and E. R. Leach in *Man*: own letters, liii (September, 1953) No. 223, pp. 141-2; liv (April, 1954) No. 96, p. 67.

1954 *Rituals of Rebellion in South-East Africa*: The Frazer Lecture 1952, Manchester: University Press: 36 pp.

1954 'Succession and Civil War among the Bemba: An Exercise in Anthropological Theory', *Rhodes-Livingstone Journal*, XVI, pp. 6-26.

1954 'The Magic of Despair' (on Mau Mau), *The Listener*, li, No. 1313 (29th April 1954).

1955 *Custom and Conflict in Africa*. Oxford: Blackwell, Glencoe, Illinois: Free Press (in 2nd impression): pp. 173 (section republished in Coser, L. A., *Readings in Sociology* (1959). Later published by Barnes and Noble, New York, in paperback.

1956 'The Peace in the Feud', *Past and Present*, pp. 1-14 (reprint of one chapter from 1955 book above).

1961 'Ethnographic Data in British Social Anthropology', *The Sociological Review*, ix, 1: 5-17 (published in summary form in *Transactions of the Third International Congress of Sociology, Stresa, 1959*).

1962 'African Jurisprudence: Presidential Address to the Sociology Section of the British Association for the Advancement of Science', *The Advancement of Science*, No. 75 (November).

1962 'The Crises in the Folk Societies' in *The Ethic of Power,* edited by H. D. Lasswell and H. Cleveland, New York: Harper for Conference on Science, Philosophy and Religion, pp. 323-342.

1962 'Les Rites de Passage' in *Essays on the Ritual of Social Relations*, edited by M. Gluckman, Manchester: University Press: pp. 1-50.

1962 *Order and Rebellion in Tribal Africa*: Collected Essays with an Autobiographical Introduction. London: Cohen and West; Glencoe, Illinois: The Free Press: pp. 240.

1963 'Gossip and Scandal: Papers in Honour of Melville J. Herskovitz', *Current Anthropology* IV, 3, 307-16, to be reprinted in *Readings in Anthropology*, ed. by E. A. Hoebell and S. Jennings.

1965 'Introduction' and 'Conclusions'; 'Procedures for Demarcating a Field of Study' (both with E. Devons) in *Closed Systems and Open Minds: The Limits of Naivety in Social Anthropology*, edited by M. Gluckman, Edinburgh: Oliver and Boyd; Chicago: Aldine.

1965 *Politics, Law and Ritual in Tribal Society*, Oxford, Blackwell; Chicago, Aldine, pp. 339. New York: Mentor Books.

1965 (with F. Eggan) 'Introduction' to Association of Social Anthropologists Monographs I-IV, ix-xl.

1967 'Introduction' to *The Craft of Social Anthropology*, edited by A. L. Epstein, London: Tavistock.

1968 'Judicial Process: Comparative Aspects' in *International Encyclopedia of the Social Sciences*, vol. 8, 291-7.

1968 'The Utility of the Equilibrium Model in the Study of Social Change', *American Anthropologist*, vol. 70, No. 2, 219-37.
1968 'Psychological, Sociological and Anthropological Explanations of Witchcraft and Gossip: a clarification', *Man*, vol. 3, No. 1, 20-34.
1969 'Concepts in the Comparative Study of Tribal Law', in L. Nader, ed., *Law in Culture and Society*, Chicago: Aldine.
1971 'New dimensions of change, conflict and settlement', *International Social Science Journal*, vol. XXIII, No. 4, 548-63: one of five lectures delivered at UNESCO, Paris, March 1971, for UN Year Against Racial Discrimination.
1972 'Moral crises: magical and secular solutions', in M. Gluckman, ed., *The Allocation of Responsibility*, Manchester: Manchester University Press.
1974 African traditional Law in historical perspective (Radcliffe-Brown Lecture in Social Anthropology), separate from *Proceedings of the British Academy*, 1974.
In Press 'Limitations of the Case-method in the Study of Tribal Law', *Law and Society Review: Essays Presented to E. Adamson Hoebel*.
Prepared for Press 'Honest Men Fear Burglar-Alarms: The Effects of Ritual Crisis and Trials on Ideals', (written) in S. F. Moore, B. Myerhoff and J. Abarbanel, editors, *Communal Ideologies and the Management of Disputes*.
In Press 'A Bandwagonload of Monkeys: Review of L. Tiger and R. Fox, *The Imperial Animal*', *The New York Review of Books*.
Prepared for Press 'Theory and Comparison in Legal Anthropology', Yale Law School, Program for Modernization and Development, Conference November 1971.
— Paper on 'Sport and Conflict', multilithed, for Congress on Sociology of Sport, Olympic Games, Munich, August 1972.
— 'A Social-anthropological Approach to Aggression', for *Symposium on Rage, Aggression and Violence,* organized by Dr. Larry Z. Freedman.
— 'Community Ideals and Individual Interests in Israel', The first Maxwell Cummings Lecture in the Humanities and Social Sciences, McGill University, 1971', submitted for publication.

At work on (basic research done)

'Introduction' to Pelican edition of Henry S. Maine's *Ancient Law* (general editor: J. H. Plumb).
'Introduction' to A. van Gennep's (translated) *Rites of Passage* (Pelican) (general editor: I. Schapiro).
'Primitive Contract' in *International Encyclopedia of Comparative Law*.
(with Mary Gluckman) 'Hypotheses about Factors Determining the Stability and Instability of Marriage in Tribal Societies', for *Essays Presented to Meyer Fortes* (ed. J. Goody).

Various other Topics

1945 'The Use of Sociological Research in Museum Display', *Rhodes-Livingstone Journal*, IV, pp. 66-73.
1959 'Football Players and the Crowd', *The Listener,* February 1959.

1960 'The Scandalmongers', *The Observer* (fortnightly, Sydney, Australia), iii, 20 (1st October 1960): pp. 5-7.

'Popular' Writing

1945 'Zambesi River Kingdom', *Libertas* (Johannesburg), v, 8: 20-39.
1945 'African Land Tenure', *Rhodes-Livingstone Journal*, III, pp. 1-13 (to be reprinted in *Reader in Anthropology*, Bobbs-Merrill Co., 1963).
1946 'Human Laboratory across the Zambesi', *Libertas* (Johannesburg), vi, 4: 38-49.
1951 'The Origins of Social Organization', *Rhodes-Livingstone Journal*, XII, pp. 1-12. Republished in M. Fried, *Readings in Anthropology*, New York: Crowell (1959), ii, 246-249, and republished in another *Reader*, Bobbs-Merrill Co. in 1963.
1954 'Political Institutions' in *The Institutions of Primitive Society*, edited by E. E. Evans-Pritchard, Oxford: Blackwell: 66-80.
1955 'Social Anthropology in Central Africa', *Journal of the Royal Society of Arts*, ciii, No. 4957, August: 645-665 (reprinted in *Rhodes-Livingstone Journal*, XX (1956): 1-27.
1957 'As Men are Everywhere Else' (on David Livingstone), *Rhodes-Livingstone Journal*, XX (1956): 68-73 (reprinted from *The Listener*, 3rd September 1955).
1959 'Man, the Social Animal' in series of broadcasts on 'Man's Knowledge of Man', *The Listener*, 22nd October 1959; reprinted in *The Journal of Education of New Africa*, I, 9 (1964), pp. 8-10.
1959 'How Foreign are You', *The Listener*, 15th January 1959 (reprinted in Journal of the Institute of Race Relations, London, IV, i (1962), 12-21).
1962 'The Study of Society' in N. Mitchison, ed., *What the Human Race is Up To*, London: Gollanz.

Administrative

1944 'Director's Report to the Trustees of the Rhodes-Livingstone Institute on the Work of the Years 1941-2-3'; Livingstone: 1-18.
1945 'The Seven-Year Research Plan of the Rhodes-Livingstone Institute', *Rhodes-Livingstone Journal*, IV, pp. 1-32 (awarded Wellcome Medal).
1948 'Director's Report to the Trustees of the Rhodes-Livingstone Institute on the Work of the Years 1944-5-6'; *Rhodes-Livingstone Journal*, VI: pp. 64-79.

Forewords which contain Theoretical Analyses

1957 'Foreword' to V. W. Turner, *Schism and Continuity in an African Society*, Manchester University Press for the Rhodes-Livingstone Institute, ix-xiii.
1957 'Foreword' to R. J. Frankenberg, *Village on the Border*, London: Cohen and West: 1-8.
1958 'Foreword' to W. Watson, *Tribal Cohesion in a Money Economy*, Manchester: University Press for the Rhodes-Livingstone Institute: v-xvi.
1958 'Foreword' to L. H. Gann, *The Birth of a Plural Society*, Manchester: University Press for the Rhodes-Livingstone Institute: vii-xiv.
1960 (with W. Allan), 'Preface' to the late D. U. Peters, *Land Usage in Barotseland*, Rhodes-Levingstone Communication No. 19, pp. ii-xiv.

1962 'Foreword' to E. Colson, *The Plateau Tonga of Northern Rhodesia: Social and Religious Studies*, Manchester: University Press for the Rhodes-Livingstone Institute: v-xii.
1962 'Foreword' (with I. G. Cunnison) to J. P. Singh-Uberoi, *Politics of the Kula Ring*, Manchester: University Press: v-viii.
1965 'Foreword' to M. Meggitt, *The Lineage System of the Mae Enga of the New Guinea Highlands*, Edinburgh: Oliver and Boyd; v, xiii.
1965 'Foreword' to W. Allan, *The African Husbandman*, Edinburgh: Oliver and Boyd, v-vii.
1965 'Foreword' to M. G. Marwick, *Sorcery in its Social Setting: a Study of the Northern Rhodesia Cêwa*, Manchester University Press, v-viii.
1966 'Foreword' to N. Sheth, *Social Relations in an Indian Factory*, Manchester: Manchester University Press.
1967 'Foreword' to English edition of Sol Tax, ed., *Horizons in Anthropology*, London: Allen and Unwin.
1970 'Foreword' to S. A. Deshen, *Immigrant Voters in Israel: Parties and Congregations in a Local Election*, Manchester: Manchester University Press, xi-xxxiii.
1971 'Foreword' to M. Shokeid, *The Dual Heritage: Immigrants from the Atlas Mountains in an Israeli Village*, Manchester: Manchester University Press, xiii-xxix.
1972 'Foreword' to E. Baldwin, *Cooperation and Competition in an Israeli Veteran Moshav*, Manchester: Manchester University Press, x-xi.
1974 'Foreword' to J. Abarbanel, *Individual Enterprise and Collective Restraint in an Israeli Village*.
(going to press) 'Foreword' to E. Marx, *Patterns of Violence to Bureaucratic Situations in an Israeli Town*.
1971 'Preface' to second edition of Elizabeth Bott, *Family and Social Network*, London: Tavistock; New York: Macmillan - Free Press, pp. xiii-xxx.

EDITED THE FOLLOWING BOOKS

1951 (with E. Colson) *Seven Tribes of British Central Africa*, Cape Town: Oxford University Press.
1962 *Essays on the Ritual of Social Relations*, Manchester: Manchester University Press.
1964 *Closed Systems and Open Minds: The Limits of Naivety in Social Anthropology*, Edinburgh: Oliver and Boyd; Chicago: Aldine (reprinted with brief 'postscript' by Aldine).
1969 *Ideas and Procedures in African Customary Law*, London: Oxford University Press for the International African Institute.
1972 *The Allocation of Responsibility*, Manchester: Manchester University Press.

OTHER EDITORIAL WORK

(i) Founder and Chief Editor of *Rhodes-Livingstone Journal: Human Problems in British Central Africa*, from 1944-1947, thereafter to date on Editorial Board.
(ii) Edited *Rhodes-Livingstone Papers* from 1942-1947, and thereafter on Editorial Board until 1958.

(iii) Founded and edited *Rhodes-Livingstone Communications* from 1943 to 1947.
(iv) On Editorial Board of *African Studies* from 1942 to 1947.
(v) From 1949 onwards, edited some 35 books of Manchester University Press in social anthropology and sociology.
(vi) In 1963 to 1964 edited three books for new series by Oliver and Boyd, but series discontinued when firm taken over by another publisher.